3703114822

Citizenship through Secondary Geography

D0347636

FRANCIS CLOSE HALL
LEARNING CENTRE
Swindon Road Cheltenham
Gloucestershire GL50 4AZ
Telephone: 01242 714600

UNIVERSITY OF
GLOUCESTERSHIRE
at Cheltenham and Gloucester

All secondary schools are now obliged to teach citizenship, and geography has been pinpointed as one of the key subjects through which citizenship can be taught. This book will lead teachers of geography through this new and challenging development in the curriculum.

Citizenship through Secondary Geography reveals the potential of geography to engage with citizenship. It provides:

- theoretical signposts in the form of short, digestible explanations for key ideas such as racism, values, identity, community and social exclusion
- a number of inset activities 'For Further Thinking'
- a critique of the discipline and the pitfalls to avoid in teaching citizenship through geography
- practical teaching suggestions

All the contributions to this valuable book point to the capacity of geography to engage with citizenship, values education and people-environment decision-making, on scales that range from the local to the global. It offers positive and direct ways to become involved in the thinking that must underpin any worthwhile citizenship education, for all experienced teachers, student teachers, heads of department, curriculum managers, and principals.

David Lambert is Reader in Education, University of London Institute of Education. He is the co-author of several books including *Learning to Teach Geography in the Secondary School* and *Understanding Assessment* (also published by RoutledgeFalmer). **Paul Machon** is Senior Director of Studies at Wyggeston and Queen Elizabeth I College, Leicester.

Citizenship Education in Secondary Schools Series
Series Editor: John Moss
Canterbury Christ Church University College

Citizenship through Secondary Geography
Edited by David Lambert and Paul Machon

Citizenship through Secondary History
James Arthur, Ian Davies, Andrew Wrenn and David Kerr

Citizenship through Secondary English
John Moss

Citizenship through Secondary Geography

Edited by David Lambert
and Paul Machon

FRANCIS CLOSE HALL
LEARNING CENTRE
UNIVERSITY OF GLOUCESTERSHIRE
Swindon Road, Cheltenham, GL50 4AZ
Tel: (01242) 532913

London and New York

First published 2001
by RoutledgeFalmer
11 New Fetter Lane, London EC4P 4EE

Simultaneously published in the USA and Canada
by RoutledgeFalmer
29 West 35th Street, New York, NY 10001

RoutledgeFalmer is an imprint of the Taylor & Francis Group

© 2001 David Lambert and Paul Machon for selection and
editorial material; individual chapters the contributors

Typeset in Baskerville by
Keystroke, Jacaranda Lodge, Wolverhampton
Printed and bound in Great Britain by
TJ International Ltd, Padstow, Cornwall

All rights reserved. No part of this book may be reprinted or
reproduced or utilised in any form or by any electronic,
mechanical, or other means, now known or hereafter invented,
including photocopying and recording, or in any information
storage or retrieval system, without permission in writing from
the publishers.

British Library Cataloguing in Publication Data
A catalogue record for this book is available from the British
Library

Library of Congress Cataloging in Publication Data
A catalog record for this book has been requested

ISBN 0–415–23160–4

To Angela Genn-Bash
1951–2000
a good citizen

Contents

Figures

Tables

Boxes

Contributors

Mary Biddulph is Lecturer in Education at the University of Nottingham where she is course tutor for the Post Graduate Certification of Education (PGCE) geography course. Before joining the School of Education she taught in a comprehensive school in Derby where she was in charge of the World Studies curriculum. Mary is currently undertaking research into pupils' perceptions and subject choices at 14+ between history and geography. She is also joint series editor of *Theory into Practice* published by the Geographical Association, and is developing a research interest in the changing values of early-career geography teachers.

Dr Graham Butt is a Senior Lecturer in Geography Education and Senior Tutor for PGCE courses at the University of Birmingham. He is a member of the Geographical Association (GA) and of the British Sub-Committee of the International Geographical Union (IGU). Graham's research interests have predominantly focused on the establishment of the geography national curriculum, assessment in geography education, language in the geography classroom and aspects of initial teacher training.

Gwyn Edwards was a Lecturer in Geographical Education and Curriculum Studies at Goldsmiths College, University of London, before being appointed in January 2000 to his present post of Associate Professor in the Department of Curriculum Studies at the University of Hong Kong. His research interests come from working in the field of curriculum organisation and change. Previously, he spent twelve years teaching geography and integrated humanities in secondary schools in Leicestershire and Kent.

John Huckle is a Visiting Lecturer at South Bank University where he teaches on the M.Sc. in Environmental and Development Education. He was previously Principal Lecturer in Geographical and Environmental Education at De Monfort University, Bedford. John is a consultant to the World Wide Fund of Nature (WWF), and the main author of Reaching Out, WWF-UK's programme of professional development for teachers. His most recent book *Environments in a Changing World* was written with former colleague Adrian Martin.

Crispin Jones is Reader in Education at the Institute of Education, University of London, where he works in the International Centre for Intercultural Studies. He has written numerous books and articles on urban education and has taught geography in urban comprehensive schools. His main research interests are intercultural education within urban contexts and education and warfare. A book on the latter topic, written with David Coulby, is shortly to be published by Ashgate.

Dr David Lambert is Reader in Education at the Institute of Education, University of London. After teaching in comprehensive schools for twelve years he became a teacher educator, developing special interests in the concept of prejudice in geography education, the role of assessment in geography education and, more recently, the part textbooks play in teaching and learning. He has published, with David Balderstone, *Learning to Teach Geography in the Secondary School* (RoutledgeFalmer, 2000).

Paul Machon is Senior Director of Studies at Wyggeston and Queen Elizabeth I College in Leicester. He has been teaching geography in schools and colleges for over thirty years. His main research interests concern geography's relationship with other disciplines, particularly politics and social theory and the analysis of education policy. He was Ordnance Survey Award winner in 1999 for his contribution to the teaching of geography in secondary schools.

Professor Bill Marsden is Emeritus Professor of Education in the University of Liverpool. His books include *Evaluating the Geography Curriculum* (1976); *Primary School Geography* (1994) (coedited with J. Hughes); *Geography 11–16: Rekindling Good Practice* (1995); *Unequal Educational Provision in England and Wales* (1987); *Educating the Respectable* (1991); *The City and Education in Four Nations* (1992) (coedited with R. K. Goodenow); and *An Anglo-Welsh Teaching Dynasty* (1997). He has also edited publications for the International Geographical Union Commission on Geographical Education.

Dr John Morgan is Lecturer in Geography Education at the University of Bristol. He previously worked at the Institute of Education, University of London, and as a geography teacher in schools and colleges. He completed his Ph.D. on postmodernism and school geography in 1998, and his current research interests include the cultural politics of school geography and the geography of education.

Dr Frances Slater is Emeritus Reader in the University of London. She taught at the Institute of Education for twenty-three years and for other periods in schools and universities in New Zealand, Australia, Canada and the USA. Her special interests growing out of her work in teaching and teacher education are those reflected in *Language and Learning in the Teaching of Geography* (Routledge, 1989), values in geography and environmental education and research in geography education. She is currently co-operating with the Department of Education in the University of Zambia on redeveloping the school geography curriculum.

Ros Wade taught in London schools for ten years and is now joint course director of the M.Sc. in Environmental and Development Education at South Bank University. She is co-author of the unit Change Processes and the Management of Change. For the past ten years, she has worked for Oxfam Education as a Curriculum Adviser and she has worked closely with many ITE geography departments to promote development education. She contributed to Oxfam's Curriculum for Global Citizenship and a number of its teaching resources, including The Big City Pack and Developing Rights.

Professor Michael Williams is an Emeritus Professor of the University of Wales Swansea and a Visiting Professorial Fellow at the Institute of Education, University of London. In 1999 and 2000 he was a consultant to two projects in the What Works in Innovation in Education series of the Centre for Educational Research and Innovation of the OECD (Paris). His recent publications include *Understanding Geographical and Environmental Education: the Role of Research* (Cassell, 1996) and (coedited with D. Tilbury) *Teaching and Learning Geography* (Routledge, 1997).

Series editor's preface

The editors and authors of the books in this series share the conviction that all teachers who are concerned with the integrity of the education they provide need to take an interest in the relationships between citizenship education and the rest of the school curriculum. Citizenship and citizenship education are highly contested concepts. Historically, they have been appropriated by politicians and educators at every point in the political spectrum, to promote local, regional, national, international or global agendas, and social, cultural, political or commercial interests. The extent to which the citizen's role is constructed as active or passive, radical or conservative, communitarian or individualistic varies in every definition. Correspondingly, different versions of citizenship education place varying degrees of emphasis on civil rights and responsibilities, on compliance with and challenges to authority, and on participation in and critique of dominant practices in society. All citizenship education teachers need to consider where the curriculum and pedagogy they adopt places their teaching and their pupils' learning in this contested field. One aim of this series is to contribute to the development of teachers' awareness of how their citizenship education teaching is positioned.

In addition, the series is concerned with the fact that the version or versions of citizenship education taught in particular classrooms, schools, regions and nations will inevitably present pupils with messages which are held in tension with those they learn from other curriculum subjects, from the hidden curriculum, and from their broader social and cultural education in and beyond school. Where citizenship education is taught entirely as a discrete subject, unless (and perhaps even if) it is completely trivialised, its explicit presence in the curriculum will still influence pupils' perceptions of subjects which purport to explore any aspect of the social contexts of the knowledge, understandings, skills and experience with which they are concerned. Moreover, what is taught and learned in these subjects, and indeed what is not taught and learned, will influence pupils' experience of citizenship education. The books in this series consequently invite an assessment of the tensions that will exist in the curriculum in schools which choose to teach citizenship education discretely. However, they are also concerned, more ambitiously, to encourage schools, departments and individual teachers to seek out the ways in which citizenship education can be productively integrated with other parts of the curriculum, to redefine and enrich pupils' experience of both citizenship education and those other subjects.

The immediate context of the series is the statutory introduction of citizenship education into the National Curriculum in England, which makes it necessary for schools to make decisions about how and where to place it in the curriculum. The series is intended to help teachers and schools to inform these practical decisions with an understanding of the issues outlined above. Most of the individual books in the series focus on the relationship between citizenship education and one other subject in the secondary curriculum, because the authors and editors believe that secondary teachers will want and need to focus on the implications and possibilities of citizenship education for the subject they teach most. Because primary teachers tend to teach across the curriculum, a single book will be included in the series with a whole school primary perspective.

In this volume, the contributors make a case for dialogue between the traditional school subject disciplines and citizenship education as a means of avoiding the pitfalls of both the false certainties which some dogmatic forms of citizenship education have promoted in the past and the stultifying uncertainties of postmodern relativism. Because other subjects, including geography, have their own criteria for truth, such dialogue can prevent the citizenship education agenda from becoming dangerously narrow or overdetermined by short-term political goals, and, instead, encourage critical thinking by teachers and their pupils.

The contributors also insist that all geography teachers should pay attention to citizenship education because, if nothing else, the way in which they teach geography inevitably contributes to the way in which pupils construct the world and perceive their citizenship in it. They show that the geography curriculum may distort these perceptions, firstly, if it delineates local, regional, national and global topics in simplistic ways which do not account for the problematic definition and reciprocal constitution of many geographical features, secondly, if it isolates its descriptions of geographical features from discussion of their historical, political, social and cultural contexts, or thirdly, if its accounts of geographical matters do not take note of the perspectives of all those affected by them.

Different contributors then emphasise to different extents the need for geography: to develop and use the methods of critical literacy in the analysis of geographical texts; to generate empathetic experiences giving different perspectives on geographical situations using drama or simulations; to use social theories, such as dialectical materialism, to interrogate geographical features and effects which might otherwise be thought to be natural, 'given' or capable of only one interpretation; to enable pupils to construct their own geographical identities, or to take social action as a consequence of their reading of geographical situations. Some contributors contend that a radical vision of the possibilities of citizenship education could become a means for rendering geography more radical: for example, both citizenship education and geography could promote inclusion both through the curriculum and pedagogy.

The book also provides some practical examples of how the conversation between geography and citizenship education could be developed: for example, Butt suggests how it might work in a scheme of work on the Longbridge car plant; Machon and Lambert critically examine the contribution geography could make to teaching of the Holocaust; Wade discusses the geographical and citizenship education issues involved in Western tourism to Maasai country. Some contributors also recognise that for the conversation to be effective, it will be dependent on whole school culture, or even the development of what Wade calls schools for global citizenship.

Above all, the book's editors insist that the conversation must allow for interpenetration of the aims and objectives of citizenship education and geography: it is not enough for geography to use citizenship to serve its own ends, or to try to justify its existence by claiming superficially that it can address the citizenship education agenda. They believe that this interpenetration should contribute to the deepening of the moral character of education: the capacity of the curriculum to describe, account for and critique the world. As they put it quite bluntly, one of the challenges of this book to the geography teachers who read it is to become less precious about the boundaries of geography. They see dialogue with citizenship education as a means by which geography could free itself from the fixed and already outdated curriculum set in stone by the National Curriculum and redefine itself in ways which would confirm its relevance and even contribute to its survival.

John Moss
Head of Secondary Education
Canterbury Christ Church University College

Foreword

The biographical snapshots of the authors of this book reveal a diverse group of people. True, they are dominated by geographers, as this is after all a book concerned with the study of geography in schools, but they have other things in common. Most significantly, although most of the authors would not want to describe themselves simply as *geographers* (indeed one or two would struggle to describe themselves in such terms without heavily qualifying what they meant by it), all of them would want to confirm, because they have all taught 'geography', their belief in its potential as a school subject.

The authorial group (it is in no sense a *team* because of this diversity) was chosen in a spirit of openness and another shared belief, namely that a worthwhile and sustainable treatment of citizenship through geography education can emerge because of the discipline's historic willingness to look beyond its traditional subject boundaries, to adopt a critical approach to the subject – and to accept the challenges this creates. We wanted this to be a dynamic book and to convey a dynamic impression of the discipline. We anticipated that the main readership would be geography teachers, but also expected this book to be read more widely, by teachers and educationalists from outside the subject and the school realm. We wanted the book's content to help stimulate conversation among all those who have a curriculum role to play in extending knowledge and under-standing of citizenship in secondary schools. It is for this reason that the authors were asked to provide full bibliographic references for their chapters. The intention was that these would more properly support those wishing to engage in further thought and reflection. This sets aside the approach of producing brief lists of annotated further readings or useful addresses, looking instead to support a more thorough grounding for these fascinating debates.

We would like to declare our great thanks to the authors, in particular for their forbearance – for this has not been an easy book to put together. It took longer than we thought and for that we apologise! We would also like to acknowledge many colleagues, and even more students, who over recent years have been instrumental (though perhaps unwittingly) in helping our cloudy thoughts to settle on the kind of book this ought to be. Such professional contacts have been invaluable, though whether we got it in the least bit right was in the end down to us.

DL/PMn
August 2000

Acknowledgements

We are grateful to the following:

The Guardian for permission to reprint the headline of 6 July 1995 in Figure 4.1; Pearson Education for permission to reprint the columns, 'Values education approach', from John Huckle, 'Geography and values education', in R. Walford (ed.) *Signposts for Geography Teaching* (London: Longman, 1981), given here as Table 4.1; the Geographical Association for permission to reprint the article 'Mission blessed by Foreign Office' (*The Guardian*, 18 November 1992), from Frances Slater, 'Education through geography, knowledge, understanding, values and culture', *Geography* 79(2) (1994): 147–63, given here as Box 4.3; the table from E. Rawling, 'Geography and cross curricular themes', *Teaching Geography* 16(4) (1991): 147–54, given here as Table 5.2; and the table from H. Walkington, *Theory into Practice: Global Citizenship Education* (Sheffield: GA, 1999), given here as Table 5.3; Continuum International Publishing Ltd for permission to reprint the extract from Graham Haydon, *Teaching about Values: a New Approach* (London: Continuum, 1997), given here as Box 4.2; and the table from P. Broadfoot, M. Osborn, C. Planel and K. Sharpe, *Promoting Quality in Learning: Does England Have the Answer?* (London: Cassell, 2000), given here as Table 5.1; Routledge/Taylor & Francis for permission to reprint the figures 'Hungarian Jewry's journey to Auschwitz', 'Deportations from Budapest's outlying districts into the city' and 'Deportations from Budapest's suburbs into the city' from Martin Gilbert, *Atlas of the Holocaust* (London: Michael Joseph/Routledge, 1982), given here as Figures 9.4–6.

The publishers have made every effort to contact authors/copyright holders of works reprinted in *Citizenship through Secondary Geography*. This has not been possible in every case, however, and we would welcome correspondence from individuals or companies we have been unable to trace.

Chapter 1

Introduction

Setting the scene for geography and citizenship education

David Lambert and Paul Machon

Introduction

From 2002 'citizenship' will be a statutory part of the curriculum experienced by secondary pupils in England and Wales. Most geography teachers can expect to have some kind of role in fulfilling this duty. In some schools, the geography department will seize the chance to play a leading part in the school's delivery of citizenship by creating a meaningful, relevant and worthwhile (and enjoyable) citizenship education through the content and design of geography lessons. This book has been produced to encourage and help inform such a process.

Throughout the editorial work on this book we often reflected upon its audience and their needs. We considered *why* geography teachers, those responsible for the training of geography teachers and those geography teachers now in training would find themselves looking for books with titles such as this. What would they expect from a book such as this? What would they need? What could we deliver? After all, it was only in March 1998 that Bernard Crick's Citizenship Advisory Group (accounts of its work are contextualised throughout this book) produced its *Initial Report* that was intended to inform the consultation that would follow. In that *Report* only one subject, history, was associated with citizenship as having 'obvious educational merit' (Citizenship Advisory Group, 1998: 7). No other subjects were acknowledged in the 'Essential recommendations' section, although elsewhere the capacity of other subjects to deal with 'controversial issues' did refer to both 'geography . . . [and] . . . English' (ibid.: 5). However, the *Final Report*, published in September 1998, did acknowledge that there are 'advantageous overlaps with elements and approach of other subjects, most notably of History, Geography and English' (ibid.: Section 7.3, 52); the *Report* also provided extensive details of precisely why geography is so placed (ibid. Section 7.5, 53).

This is not the place to consider the details of what occurred between March and September 1998, except to note that the Advisory Group took the consultation seriously and that there were other significant shifts of emphasis between the two *Reports* apart from geography's inclusion. Notably the Group's brief was extended by the Secretary of State during the consultative period following a direct intervention from Crick, to include post-16 education and training (Section 4.8, 27–8). But from September 1998 onwards geography, as a discipline taught in schools, found itself at the centre of the continuing citizenship debate. Hence this book and our concern with its audience.

In the book's final chapter these concerns are expressed in terms of the discipline's preparedness to deal with citizenship (a certain hesitancy may also be perceived in some of the other chapters). We argue that this hesitancy is an appropriate stance, given both the nature of citizenship and its novelty in Britain's schools. We have faith in the geography education community, born of many years' witness to its adaptability and the resilience of its teachers. Consequently, as the chapters unfold, we believe that the discipline's practitioners will be able to see that what is here is the start of a mapping process, showing where we are and where are we going. This mapping clearly indicates that **what** we already do is directly relevant to the issue at hand and, as important, **how** geography is being taught in our classrooms offers the chance to exploit the opportunities that the citizenship imperative offers. The hesitancy, therefore, is only the hesitancy at the start of all journeys, providing a chance to check what we've come with, that nothing's been forgotten, to reflect upon the distance that has already been covered and, as best we're able, to check the routes ahead.

We also argue that the hesitant tone of this book has other origins, associated, as we have already noted, with the 'nature of citizenship', and we turn briefly to these later in this chapter. First, however, we provide an overview of the structure of the book.

The structure of this book

We believe that the structure that we have imposed upon the order of the book's chapters will help readers in the inquiry process. The book is divided into two main parts, 'Contexts' and 'Curriculum issues', but we want to emphasise that readers will be able to find – and should look for – themes in many of these chapters that point towards different structures and linkages. If they do, the book will be achieving some of the aims we have for it – to promote and support dialogue, debate and discussion. To assist in these aims many of the chapters contain asides, pauses for further thought and examples. These are intended to support those further discussions without risking the thrust of the argument in the chapter itself.

In 'Contexts' four authors reflect upon citizenship's place in education – or perhaps that order should be reversed! In Chapter 2 Bill Marsden traces the evolution of citizenship education, establishing a clear link between the specificities of earlier initiatives and their particular social setting. In this important observation there is an implicit call for us to consider what is now so special about our 'social setting' that we find ourselves, once again, with citizenship on the agenda. A curt answer to this is the rate of contemporary social change and this observation is developed towards the end of the chapter.

Change stalks this book. In schools change has come to the curriculum, to the relationship of schools to both central and local government and to the regulatory processes to which we are all subject. It seems significant to us that during our time with this book the two co-editors were both inspected! Change is also present in how nation-states 'construct' their notions of citizenship: in Chapter 3 Michael Williams makes this point clearly with examples drawn from three continents. Education's role in this 'construction' is paramount and echoes of this are found throughout the book (for example, in Gwyn Edwards's references to changes in the British state and John Huckle's and Ros Wade's reflections upon a citizenry that is not merely national but international and global).

In Frances Slater's and Graham Butt's chapters the geography curriculum is the focus of attention. In the former the place of values is central; the author particularly emphasises the implicit values content of the school curriculum before proceeding to exemplify how making those values explicit can promote change among students. In the second of the two chapters a path is traced through various government initiatives to our present position and then the connections between citizenship and geography at Key Stage 3 are mapped. How these connections can be realised practically is then shown in a brief scheme of work.

In 'Curriculum issues' eight authors consider some of the 'routes ahead' and the implications of these for the geography classroom. In the first three of these chapters, those by John Morgan, Crispin Jones and Gwyn Edwards, the issues of how one 'belongs' (that is, how one is included and so becomes a citizen), or fails to belong (that is, how some people are excluded and so fail to become citizens), are examined. The 'citizen idea' is a social act and not merely the product of some natural, biological imperative, and so how citizenship is defined societally is critical. All three authors see this process as a discourse to which different actors having unequal access. As a consequence of this who is included and who excluded will reflect the prevailing structures of socio-economic power and authority. The powerful derive their strength from many sources but among them, and this is particularly significant for academic disciplines like geography, are those that attach intellectual credence to one viewpoint over others. All three chapters direct attention to the location of the *status quo* and to challenges to that hegemony. It thereby begins to be possible to establish exactly why it is so dangerous to perceive citizenship education as being wholly product-led, a series of 'objectives' to be 'delivered'. To be on guard here, it is necessary to ask *whose* product it is that is being advocated, and whose interests it serves (and whose it denies), and to recognise that such judgements are made on a moral basis.

Chapter 9, by the editors, exemplifies these points by reference to a very specific example of citizenship being *denied*, an event normally 'covered' by history but which can also be understood through its geography. The chapter also emphasises geography's place in that denial, invites further discussion about the teaching of political geography in our schools and colleges, and draws attention to the importance of interdisciplinary approaches to such events. We note with dismay that the recent publication *Teaching the Holocaust* (Davies, 2000) makes no reference at all to geography, rather as though it all took place on the head of a pin and not, as we assert, where space itself is directly implicated. Finally the difficulty with such subject matter is underlined by an encounter with the geography of the Holocaust by teachers in training.

The chapters by John Huckle and Ros Wade have already been referred to because of their location of citizenship outside the narrow borders of the nation-state. In the first of the two chapters John Huckle grounds his persuasive argument for ecological citizenship in constructs drawn from social and political theory. In doing so, he establishes the essential unity of this inquiry, now including the natural world. Readers should also take note of the special place accorded to teachers when a choice is made to further 'democratise' civil society, an observation also made by John Morgan. In Ros Wade's chapter global citizenship is located in the geography classroom with, again, the teacher centre stage. This chapter's authority derives from the extensive support provided for its central argument. This should help teachers embarking on their own journeys and the examples of successful practice should be encouraging. A practical approach, this time to pedagogical issues, concludes the chapter. Finally Mary Biddulph reminds us all of the relationship between subject matter and pedagogy, as well as cautioning geography teachers about the risks of failing to reflect upon the task at hand. The price of an inadequately informed or an apathetic citizenry is very great.

The 'nature of citizenship'

Earlier, it was indicated that one of the challenges facing subject-specialist teachers of citizenship lies in the rather slippery nature of the concept of citizenship itself. Clearly there is not the space here for a fully developed treatise, but there are some starting points in this interesting argument that are worth briefly sketching out.

We begin by repeating that citizenship is not a fixed concept. However, for argument's sake the concept can be reduced to the dialectical relationship between a state, the protection it offers to its citizens as rights, and the duties to the state that those citizens are expected to offer in return. In short, this is a political concept. Unfortunately the simplicity of this 'definition' conceals more than it reveals. We find, for example, the structure of this basic iterative relationship between individuals and state in many different guises, in varied places and over a long historical period. The differences between the many examples we could choose can usefully be pinned down by examining who counts, or was counted, as a citizen and the basis upon which that inclusivity was made. It is worth recalling that in Britain political citizenship was not extended to women until 1919 and 1929, and the basis of that exclusion is instructive.

So, where does the 'hesitancy' we have described in this book come from? If citizenship is primarily concerned with the individual and the state we might usefully start by noting that both concepts are currently contested. Concern with the **individual** draws our attention to issues of identity that are addressed in the book. What does it mean to be British? What will it mean to be English, as Welsh and Scottish nationalities are consolidated? What is education's role in the formation of such categories? Contemporary concern with the **state** shows that this idea is in flux, and many of the questions being raised here are familiar to geographers. For example, what is the impact upon states, particularly the smaller states, of multinationals and their ability to form new hegemonies that pay no attention to state borders during a period of intense global-isation? Equally, why is the marked resurgence in regional political assemblies (Scotland, Wales) matched by increasingly powerful supra-national bodies (the European Union)? Conventional political science would argue that states create a citizenry in their own image or 'state form', but that becomes harder to achieve when other influences, the emotional attachment to places for example, are so persuasive and pervasive (Leyshon and Thrift, 1997). In this book the message is that politics is not everything and that other social sciences, including geography, can begin to account for these complexities.

But if politics is not all, we nevertheless assert that geography, particularly the geography taught in our schools and colleges, needs to reflect upon matters political, much as it has done in the past with other disciplines. Such work would need to make it clear that the model of citizenship to which we in Britain have become accustomed derives from a state form that is liberal and representative. The idea of a **liberal** state starts with the notion of individual ownership and rights to property, with most social acts echoing this relationship. This view elevates self-interest and so shapes decisions about collective issues, especially those that won't stay within spatially defined boundaries; pollution is an example of this. Geography has much to say that can inform these hard-to-make decisions that are so full of contradictory tensions. **Representativeness** describes the mode of the political machinery the state employs. In essence this means irregular and uninvolved voting for members of political parties who have other imperatives – like getting re-elected. There is conflicting evidence about public support for this form of democratic participation, with low turnouts in many elections. Clarke (1996) suggests that such a model of citizenship is shallow and calls for more involvement, a 'deep' citizenship that looks for an alignment between personal and particular interests and those that are more universal. If this sounds fanciful it is matched by notions of 'deep ecology' (Devall and Sessions, 1985), and touches on what Bill Marsden in Chapter 2 calls 'eco-citizens'.

Change

Earlier in this chapter it was stated that 'change stalks this book' and no chapter fails to contemplate change of one sort or another. It is tempting to connect the present rate of social (and other) change with a contemporary urge to reconsider citizenship. It is almost as if, in times of upheaval, the tensions affecting our place as individuals in the societies within which we exist become explicit, leading to a need to state (or is that restate?) our place once more. It is also tempting to look at other periods (or other places) when debates about a citizen's place take on real urgency. It is anecdotal, but in the late 1980s serious discussions about 'being a citizen' were easier to find in Warsaw, Prague or Budapest than in Britain's staffrooms.

The changes that we seem to be witnessing today in Britain are so all-enveloping that some have attached the term 'postmodernism' to them. Intriguingly, several contributors checked with us that this 'wouldn't be a postmodern book, would it?' Well, that was certainly never our intention, but because we wanted to give contributors room to write their own accounts it was not a forbidden term either. In the end the phrase turned up so rarely that postmodernism seemed almost to have become a concept without meaning or significance. However, change *was* signalled, and with it came some of the assumptions associated with postmodernism, leading us to conclude that the term could not be ignored. So, as with other important ideas or influences relating to discussions opened up in this book that have been tackled in 'boxes' designed to spell out their provenance or origin, we felt the need to address 'postmodernism' head on. After all, 'postmodernism' is part of the *Zeitgeist*, the spirit of the times, in which this book has been created. Thus, in the closing part of this chapter we try and rescue at least something of that term's original power.

Postmodernism

Talk of the postmodern presupposes the existence of 'the modern'. But in the intractability of finding definitions there are also the roots of postmodernism's definitional troubles. These are seriously slippery terms. It is possible, however, to claim modernity's time, place and social specificity in some West European cockpit of economic, social and scientific change. Such changes combined together to produce 'disembedding mech-anisms' (Giddens, 1999: 53) that stretched and then broke prevailing social relations, provided new tools and concepts in the pursuit of understanding – the Enlightenment. These changes set in train widely different processes, on the one hand, for example, extracting dyes from coal and, on the other, underpinning imperialism on 'racial' grounds. The pace and the effects of these changes, although there were always untouched peripheries, prompted commentators of all persuasions to try to describe and account for what was being experienced. Towering above them Karl Marx portrayed a world of constant tension, specifically promoted by the needs of capitalism, to the extent that modernity *was* change and not some 'alien rhythm within capital' (Jameson, 1986: xxx). And these changes were understood to be complete, constant and a call to action, caught in that well-known sentence that describes the world we still see and calls upon us to remember childhood's lost sites:

> *All that is solid melts into air, all that is holy is profaned, and man is at last compelled to face, with sober senses, his real conditions of life, and his relations with his kind.*
>
> (Marx, 1986: 37)

But if modernity is built on material tension it is, profoundly, a productive tension. As significantly, we should not overlook the aside that *progress* also has bleak, dark, nihilistic and irrational friends; the state protects *and* makes Auschwitz-Birkenau, science cures *and* kills, the philosophers of hope are joined by Nietzsche and at a personal level we have the pursuit of happiness *and* blatant displays of our 'dark side' (Giddens, 1989: 405).

How history is constructed is changed by the experience of modernity. Nineteenth-century commentators saw these changes in terms of bivalent ideologies, socialism *versus* capitalism, democracy *versus* authoritarianism (and in all of these the citizen's place is critical). History was also not blind and did not lack direction and so these 'big ideologies' became 'meta-narratives' – complete and inclusive accounts of everything. The end of modernity was first signalled in the aesthetic realm, and it was architectural critics who first wrote of postmodernism as single, definitive and modern answers began to be rejected in favour of choice and playfulness. The certainty of the skyscraper as the modern form (Landau and Condit, 1996) was replaced by the symbolism of Las Vegas (Venturi *et al.*, 1977) and Philip Johnson's historical references in the A.T. & T. Building in New York built between 1978 and 1982.

Other changes were attached to the emerging postmodern venture. In the political realm the collapse of Soviet centralism was joined to arguments that emphasised capitalism's triumph and announced a single winner in America's hegemony and the 'end of history' (Fukuyama, 1989, 1992). Now it seemed, in former President George Bush's terms, that there was a 'new world order' that would insist upon liberal and representative democracy alongside open and free markets. This 'new' internation-alisation of capitalism relaunched a new geopolitics referred to as globalisation, and with a seeming inevitability rippling changes ran through everything – home, work and leisure. People everywhere were urged to consider themselves, and particularly their market position, as producers and consumers in a world setting: do *your* skills allow *you* to compete on world markets? This was not, of course, the *post*-industrial society that had been prophesied but rather its convulsive relocation. The geographies of this changing world are profound. We were now in a postmodern world.

Used loosely in this way, 'postmodernism' implies the end of the belief in single answers and, instead, the celebration of choice. This choice is often expressed as though it were a huge form of shopping, what we choose to eat and wear, where we choose to go on holiday and the geographies we therefore come to 'know'. Undoubtedly this is a period of enormous change, although its temporal scale is not yet clear – nor its outcome, but we know it won't be final. For the reflective geographer postmodernism poses interesting questions, the first of which must be whether sophisticated models of modernity widely, if implicitly, taught at all levels of secondary school and college geography, really have (or ought) to be replaced.

Maybe periods of very rapid change always feel like this for those close to them. If that is the case, then postmodernism sinks back to being an interesting didactic tool – but not much more – and modernity still rules with its many faces, and the geographer's task remains to describe, account for and critique these.

Reading this book

This chapter started by noting that in the first few years of the twenty-first century geography teachers will need to engage with the citizenship idea in their classrooms. It is our strong belief that they are equipped to do so, and this belief is founded on at least two central arguments. The first is that much of the material that the discipline already deals with – and as importantly how it is dealt with – is already bound up with the 'citizenship idea'. Secondly, we know that geography teachers are used to dealing with change and particularly the creative change that comes from dialogue with other disciplines, as the last thirty years show.

We consciously endeavoured to put together chapters by authors able to address both these arguments, and this offers a way to approach the book. Some chapters map out the subject terrain that will be affected by building citizenship into what we do, and it would be an instructive exercise to consider existing syllabuses and specifications in light of those. This exercise could be done departmentally, using the expertise of the geography team and other staff, and would also be a powerful theme for schools of education and local branches of the Geographical Association to support teachers at a local level. The 'For further thinking' boxes are intended to support such activities, as are the references that indicate where further support for a developing idea may be found.

Other chapters pay particular attention to the classroom itself and again invite geography teachers to reflect upon their existing practice, adjusting what they do to incorporate new material into the curriculum and approaches to their pedagogy. The teacher will be at the heart of these changes. But we think it is also very important to be clear that teaching citizenship will be challenging and at times problematic. The root of this can be captured in the obvious tension in teaching for an active, critical and assertive citizenry in a classroom, school or college that is likely to be organised as an authoritarian hierarchy. This difficulty has echoes in the subject matter: Whose geography are we teaching? Does it encourage acquiescence or promote activity? Does it underpin some *status quo* or encourage personal involvement? Does it leave alone or have the potential to change lives? We think that this book is hugely reassuring about the rewards for letting go of restrictive practices in our classrooms and for evolving our subject matter. Geography teachers have the ability to do both those things and we hope this book supports such a venture.

References

Citizenship Advisory Group (1998) *Education for Citizenship and the Teaching of Democracy in Schools, Part One: Initial Report.* London, QCA.

—— (1998) *Education for Citizenship and the Teaching of Democracy in Schools, Final Report.* London, QCA.

Clarke P.B. (1996) *Deep Citizenship.* London, Pluto.

Davies I. (ed.) (2000) *Teaching the Holocaust.* London, Continuum.

Devall B. and Sessions G. (1985) *Deep Ecology: Living as if Nature Really Mattered.* Salt Lake City, Utah, Peregrine Smith.

Fukuyama F. (1989) 'The End of History?' *The National Interest* No. 18 (Winter), pp. 21–8.

—— (1992) *The End of History and the Last Man.* London, Hamish Hamilton.

Giddens A. (1989) *Sociology.* Cambridge, Polity Press.

—— (1999) The Reith Lectures. London, BBC.

Jameson F. (1986) Introduction to J.-F. Lyotard, *The Postmodern Condition: A Report on Knowledge.* Manchester, Manchester University Press. Originally published as *Postmoderne: Rapport sur le Savoir.* Paris, Les Editions de Minuit (1979).

Landau S.B. and Condit C.W. (1996) *The Rise of the New York Skyscraper, 1865–1913.* New Haven, Conn., Yale University Press.

Leyshon A. and Thrift N. (1997) *Money/Space.* London, Routledge.

Marx K. (1986) *Manifesto of the Communist Party.* Moscow, Progress Press. Originally published in 1848.

Venturi R., Scott Brown D. and Izenour S. (1977) *Learning from Las Vegas: the Forgotten Symbolism of Architectural Form.* Cambridge, Mass., MIT Press.

Part I

Contexts

Chapter 2

Citizenship education: permeation or pervasion?

Some historical pointers

Bill Marsden

If you educate for citizenship, you educate for the State, and for good membership of the State. That . . . is a terrifying idea.

(Barker, 1937: 154)

In short, what we are considering is not the teaching *of* international understanding but teaching *for* international understanding, a very different thing.

(Paul, 1952: 699)

In the course of over 200 years of citizenship education, the same concerns have constantly resurfaced, and corresponding remedies have with a degree of inevitability been recycled. Its proponents have habitually claimed that the underlying task of education is to produce good citizens. Many school subjects, in particular geography, history and social studies, have all laid claims to having crucial contributions to make to this end (see Batho, 1990). Citizenship education lobbies have in turn argued that citizenship education is too important to leave to individual subjects. They have therefore advocated a more pervasive curriculum framing as a more effective solution than the mere permeation of citizenship issues into separate subject areas.

Though the labels have changed, there has been a long-standing acceptance of three basic elements in citizenship education. With the terminology used by environmental educationalists since the 1970s adapted, these may be defined as education *about* citizenship (i.e. the matter); education *in* or *through* citizenship (i.e. the method); and education *for* citizenship (i.e. the mission). The voluminous historiography of citizenship education makes clear that of these the main priority has normally been education *for* citizenship. The Association for Education in Citizenship's (AEC) well-known handbooks of the 1930s, for example, were so entitled. (See, for example, Simon, 1935: 2, and Hutchinson, 1939: 2.) Additionally, there has generally been, and still remains, agreement that, however delivered, citizenship education must be part of a broader moral and spiritual educational provision (see Lambert, 1997: 11). An argument presented here, however, will be that citizenship education has *de facto* normally been a cloak for a narrower, what could more appropriately be termed civic, instruction.

Within the limited space available, the main focus of this chapter will be on uncovering and probing relevant documentation on citizenship education from three periods: first, on conceptions of Christian citizenship education; then later, on the more nationalistic and imperialist priorities for citizen making, counterpointed with the broader view of fostering world citizenship; and, finally, on just one element in the broader field of more recent citizenship education, namely the formation of good eco-citizens. Concluding sections will consider the perennial over-expectation of what education can achieve, tensions between education and indoctrination, and the potential contribution of geography to citizenship education in the light of what history has, or has not, to tell the present generation.

Good Christian citizens

In the early nineteenth century there was a clear-cut sense of what was required in the transformation of children of different social classes into good citizens. The lower orders were unlikely to escape from their misery in their earthly existence, but by labouring diligently, obeying their superiors, and repenting of their sins, they could be assured of rewards in the after-life. For the upper classes, a more formal civic instruction was necessary. Approved precepts of good citizenship could be acquired both from biblical study and through acquaintance with the ancient civilisations, covered in classical studies.

In the rapidly expanding early nineteenth-century elementary sector, controlled by the various denominations, there could be no questioning the centrality of religious instruction in the curriculum. This should 'pervade its beginning, its progress and its end' (quoted in Chancellor, 1970: 91). A core text was available for the training of good Christian citizens: 'What a wonderful book the Bible is . . . I am sure there is not another like it in the world. It teaches persons in all stations what they ought to do at all times' (quoted in Goldstrom, 1972: 19).

Biblical injunction had obviously to be translated into behaviour. Many examples of the process to be followed were offered in all the relevant journals and in the methodological texts of the different denominations. In the domestic sphere, for example, the women of the nation's working classes were regarded as a critical improving influence on future citizens. The activity of the prudent housewife was a model for the running of the nation. So training in domestic economy was a key element in citizenship education: 'Economy means the wise management of labour, whether shown in the administration of a house or a kingdom, or of God's beautiful world' (Anon., 1858: 117).

Even as education became more secularised, the Protestant Christian view remained as an essential element in citizenship education.

> All will agree with the main aim of these lessons – the inculcation of respect for the law, a reasoned obedience, the conception of social duty, and a noble patriotism, is worthy, and even lofty; but . . . the foundations of civic virtue will be stronger if the intellectual appreciation of civic duty is supplemented by religious sanction – if these lessons in civics are also made 'Bible-lessons'.
>
> (Bavin, 1912: 60)

Christianity continued to provide the moral basis for the many textbooks entitled *Good Citizenship* or *The Good Citizen* (see, for example, Higham, 1932). Leeson, Headmaster of Winchester College, author of a textbook of this type, affirmed that he was in the temper of those for whom Christ's command was everything. Minds should dwell on one thought, that 'the horizons of our citizenship enlarge beyond the bounds of one country and one commonwealth. Our citizenship is in Heaven' (1935: 11).

Good national citizens

Not all agreed, however, that citizenship instruction should have a religious basis. The Moral Instruction League, formed in 1897, advocated a secular approach to morality, in which history, literature and life itself provided an alternative training basis to the Bible (Hilliard, 1961: 53, 62). The shift in emphasis was from a 'religion-sanctioned personal morality' to the fostering of a 'common civic morality' (Berard, 1987: 242–4). Graded courses in citizenship were issued by local authorities, closely reflecting the model of the Moral Instruction League. The West-Riding approved syllabus of 1905 for elementary schools was typical. Its first stage topics included cleanliness, tidiness, manners (such as punctuality), fairness, truthfulness and courage. Year by year further elements were introduced, in turn kindness (e.g. to animals), honesty, humanity, obedience, order, work, zeal, thrift and so on. The syllabus for Standard VII included also patriotism, peace and war, ownership, co-operation, the will, self-respect and ideals (Brown, 1905: 142–3).

The humanist movement supported the concept of non-doctrinaire morality, evident in Hughes's *Citizens to Be*, in which the significance of geography and history as 'humanities' was highlighted. The current reforms in geography teaching were approved as 'the best possible augury for Humanism' (Hughes, 1915: 151). Hughes's call, unusual in the historiography of citizenship education, was for a liberal education.

> Humanism stands for the full and free development of the individual. . . . Humanism must war eternally upon all systems, political, social, or educational, which either suppress individuality by a one-sided or mutilated development, kill it by excess of routine, or distort it by the omission of social obligation and privilege. . . . Upon a Humanist foundation of social individuality and freedom no educational system can be maintained that stops short of international fellowship. The main value of each stage of widening interest is as a passport to the next.
>
> (1915: 281–2)

The citizenship lobby was closely allied with those of health education and eugenics. The thrift ideology included the 'conservation' of human resources, seen as necessary for improving national economic efficiency (see Marsden, 1998). In line with eugenics thinking, Swann placed citizenship training in the context of a population divided into 'efficients' and 'non-efficients', the latter including the idle, the vicious, the intemperate, the shiftless, the spendthrift and the uncleanly. To combat these evils, training involved the formation of character, with 'virtue' the 'bed-rock' of all 'citizenship' (Swann, 1918: 238–9).

The British Association (BA) set up a committee on 'Training in Citizenship' at its Cardiff meeting in December 1919. Its advice conformed with the dominant thinking of its time, namely that citizenship education comprised two parts, the first being character training, building up a sense of civic duty, and the second being the education of the individual in the history of civilisation (BA, 1920: 281). Its preoccupations were with education as a curative for social ills, instancing as major sources of concern the perils of the public house, problems of idleness and luxury, the evils of gambling, and the preference for passive sports (1920: 295–7). Baden-Powell was a member of the Committee, and one of the *Report*'s appendices was the scheme of citizenship training used by the scouts (1920: 298–9), a widely approved organisation. 'The daily good deed of the scout was the harbinger of a considerable social revolution' (Paul, 1946: 394).

Good imperial citizens

Central to the thinking of British promoters of citizenship education was the premise that good national citizens would by definition also be good empire citizens. The doctrine was only too evident in late nineteenth- and early twentieth-century textbooks. Geography was presented as a subject heaven-sent for promoting imperial interests on the great world stage (see, for example, Freshfield, 1886, and Mackinder, 1911), and so too was history. Some of the more rampant examples in geography are to be found in Yoxall's text (*c.* 1870) for pupil teachers, used from about 1870 and into the early years of the twentieth century. It extolled among other things the general character of the British, the 'valour and enterprise' of Britain's colonisers in winning an 'Empire on which the sun never set', and London as 'the mightiest camp of men the world has seen' (*c.* 1870: 31–2). In history, the militarist 'drum and trumpet' text found its apogee in the beguiling jingoism of Fletcher and Kipling's school history (1911), which recycled all the old stereotypes: Turks as barbarians and Russia as a 'half-barbarous state', among others. The great poet wrote racy patriotic ditties as conclusions to chapters (1911: 245).

There was at the same time an emerging backlash against late nineteenth-century militant imperialism; this was in part intellectual and in part reflective of a less xeno-phobic patriotism. A new proposition emerged, that of the ungrasping colonist who, while still wishing to spread abroad the benefits of British values and liberties and of a democratic constitution, would at the same time admire the heritage of other races, and offer them the prospect of education, economic advancement and self-determination (Bowtell, 1920: 227). But the traditional lobbies remained strong. One historian described the animus he perceived against matters imperial as a 'silly prejudice', against which the Great War was providing a 'wholesome corrective' (Lucas, 1916: 5).

Many of the old geography and history textbooks remained in use after the First World War, though these gradually faded out as the demand for more academically respectable approaches was translated into a new generation of texts. Social and environmental determinism remained, but explicit racism was often, though far from always, toned down or simply omitted.

The same was less the case with the 'new' civics/citizenship texts of this period, how-ever, which, if anything, took over the traditional geography/history patriotic mantle: the self-congratulatory tone of the old hard-core imperialism. Wilson, for example, described the British realm as a greater empire 'not even than any that have existed in the world before, but greater than has ever been dreamt of in the world before' (Wilson, 1920: 215). To Worts equally, our state, with its constitution, was 'nearly as good as it can be' (1919: 2, 277). As in the religious readers of the nineteenth century, homilies and/or panegyrics concluded the justification:

The people of England today are strongly anti-militarist, Liberal, Democratic, seeking no quarrel, jealous of none, hoping for world peace and determined to make great sacrifices if necessary to secure it. . . . It is necessary to live among the people to realize how great they are. The whole country is now seething with new mental life.

(Quoted in Houseley, 1921: 204–5)

In civics textbooks also allusion was made to promoting citizenship through extension of the public school spirit, bringing into the peace what had been demonstrated in the trenches during the previous war (Blakiston, 1920: v–vi). One public school teacher indeed suggested that on the whole his schoolboys were more prepared to die for their country than to live for it. His evidence was that while his pupils would cheerfully fight at battles such as Passchendaele, they would shy away from attending a town council meeting. Another averred that the English public school system, through instilling a spirit of sinking differences, facing discomfort and making sacrifices, was that best geared to producing 'the very perfect citizen', though he accepted that this did not always transpire in practice (Hankin, 1909: 2–3).

Good world citizens

Another mission of citizenship education, fervently argued following the First World War, was that of making good world citizens. The concept had already been evident in the pre-war campaigning of bodies such as the Friends' Guild of Teachers and the School Peace League, representatives of a peace movement that could be traced back to the early years of the nineteenth century (Beales, 1931). Pollard looked to geography to awaken minds to the idea that other countries had great literary figures, military leaders, missionaries and explorers, and so on: 'a host of fertile topics await the broadminded geographer' (1910: 19). Rowntree at the same time reflected on the aims of the School Peace League, namely to foster the work of the international peace movement (1911: 2).

After the war the Civic Education League was formed, which published the *Civic Education Chronicle*. In the 1930s the Association for Education in Citizenship (AEC) was established. This took a more international line, and also published a journal, *The Citizen*. While imperial pride continued to characterise the work of many geographers and geographical educationalists in the inter-war years, there were many cross-currents. Some writers were, for example, more attuned to the moral ramifications of the concept of geography for international understanding. Welpton urged using the subject to promote 'sympathetic understanding' (1923: 7). Unstead similarly recommended that children should be 'taught to try and imagine themselves in the place of other people, to think how they would act and live if they were in that environment, to see things with their eyes, to look at the world from their point of view' (1928: 131).

Dempster (1939) regarded geography's greatest value and essential contribution to citizenship education as 'the possibilities it offers for developing a sympathy for the lives and problems of other peoples'. This meant, for the primary school, pruning the physical and regional sides, so beloved of academic geographers, and focusing not only on local geography but also on case studies of small areas overseas, essentially the idea of bringing local worlds overseas into the home classroom (1939: 81).

The general tenor of the time was that a good national citizen *per se* would have acquired the qualities of a good world citizen. Most parties subscribed to the view that true patriotism was a benign force but needed to start with the local, spreading out to the regional, the national, the imperial, and then extending into true world brotherhood. Dempster defined the starting point, local study, as 'the teaching of citizenship through geography' (1939: 84). The recommended extension was known as the 'concentric' approach in geography, and in social studies as 'widening circles' or 'the widening vision', as in Jones and Sherman's *League of Nations Schoolbook* of 1928 (see Figure 2.1).

Figure 2.1 The widening vision. Home-school-city-country-world

Source: R. Jones and S.S. Sherman, *The League of Nations Schoolbook* (London: Union of the League of Nations, 1928).

A.J. Herbertson was an early example of an academic geographer and textbook writer promoting the concentric approach.

> Geography is essential for the proper understanding of the problems of the different parts of the Empire, and for the promotion of a sympathetic attitude towards the other nations, great and small, with whom our contact becomes closer every year. Its study should thus be utilised to give a true appreciation of the conditions and needs of the home region, and of its relations to the great world outside, and thus to develop first a local patriotism, then the larger patriotism of country and Empire, and, finally, as knowledge widens, and imagination and sympathy become more acute, the largest patriotism of all – that of a citizen of the World.
>
> (1907: 147)

Another ardent inter-war supporter of geography's role in improving world understanding was Celia Evans, who wished to eliminate the temptations of previous subject writers to overstate the achievements of the British Empire. The war had 'redirected the conscience and the consciousness of the world towards the problems of conciliation and co-operation'. Geography must be at the forefront of the new mission: 'the fact of world interdependence and the actuality of modern economic co-operation, which is essential to modern civilisation, must be the basis of geography teaching' (1933: 16–20).

Among non-subject specialists, Hayward advised the use of a sequence of five 'celebrations': Home; City or Region; Country or Nation, Empire or Commonwealth; and the League of Nations (1935: 438). Similarly, starting on the community level, the Geddes-inspired Le Play Society, viewing civics as 'applied sociology' (Geddes, 1905), regarded the regional survey, combining geography, history, biology and sociology, as the key to citizenship education. It was regarded as high on 'civic sense and initiative'. Mastery over local issues was 'a necessary preliminary to effective political democracy' (see Adkins, 1933: 7). The *Civic Education Chronicle* also viewed civics as based on 'common sense sociology' (Farquharson, 1921: 6). A *Times Educational Supplement* columnist suggested that education in citizenship for younger children should not just be conducted in the classroom but should involve cultivating a sense of fair play in the playground, 'rehearsing the practice of good citizenship'. The school should be 'a practising ground for civic virtues in miniature' (Anon., 1934: 270).

The rise of Fascism confounded the case of educators for peace and world citizenship. League of Nations supporters, for example, found themselves charged with whitewashing aggression. Already by the 1930s the credibility of the Union of the League of Nations had been significantly undermined by the opposition of members of the inspectorate, the Historical Association, and elements in the Conservative Party. League of Nations teaching was accused of bringing bias, sentimentalism and sheer propaganda into state schools. At ill-attended conferences, teachers informed the peace campaigners that parents disliked the Union and thought it was anti-government (see Elliott, 1977: 137–40). The onset of the Second World War confirmed the suspicions of sceptics who had argued that the unremitting inculcation of hard-line nationalistic and racist ideas by the Fascist powers had succeeded (see Figure 2.2) while the liberal approaches of the inter-war peace education movement had failed. One such sceptic was the editor of the *Times Educational Supplement*, who questioned whether the idea of 'world citizenship'

Figure 2.2 Education and dictatorships. 'Fichte and the powerful men who have inherited his ideals, when they see children, think: Here is material that I can manipulate, that I can teach to behave like a machine in furtherance of my purposes.' (Bertrand Russell, at the annual meeting of the Union of Educational Institutions)

Source: *Schoolmaster and Woman Teacher's Chronicle*, 22 October 1936, p. 603.

was anything more than a slogan 'awakening satisfying emotions in the hearts of the believers'. He concluded

> To encourage the illusion that all have a part to play on the world stage is to divert the minds of teacher and pupil from the urgent and limited tasks which await them in private, working and public life. The international idea is very young, and no good can come from teaching a loyalty that is too wide to be effective.
>
> (Anon., 1940: 135)

Nonetheless, the flag of world citizenship education was kept alive during the war by, for example, the Council for Education in World Citizenship. A rekindled line of argument was that the only solution to the world's problems lay in a fresh religious underpinning of civic education. Before the war in fact, a former President of the Headmistresses' Association had strongly complained that the statements of the AEC had contained one grave omission, namely the importance of religious knowledge in education for citizenship (Addison-Phillips, 1937: 5). Such feelings were to appeal to a number of commentators during the Second World War. In building a new 'Commonwealth of United Nations', the individual had 'to win the internal holy war between good and evil', and spread the gospel of personal sacrifice in building a better world, renouncing preoccupation with himself alone, and centring his interest on service 'to God and all mankind'. An education that makes good citizens, including world citizens, 'will have to be religious' (Garnett 1943: 63, 70, 230).

Extravagant optimism for the future was expressed, however dispiriting the situation was in reality. In 1944, for example, Nordon foresaw that technical and scientific advances, combined with an education for world citizenship, would prevent future wars. These would enable mankind to 'cast the Evil Spirit of Aggression into the bottomless pit for the 1000 years so prophetically and graphically described in the Revelation of St. John the Divine', and usher in a 'new era of happiness, based on ethical, and therefore enduring, foundations' (1944: 3). Other writers such as Lauwerys (in Anon., 1946: 6) also urged that world citizenship education must have the Christian ethic as its basis, providing 'the ultimate doctrine of human brotherhood'. The twin objectives were the achievement of 'a way of thought and a moral outlook' (Paul, 1952: 699).

A fresh drive to promote citizenship education through social studies was evident after the Second World War, renewing the contest between those arguing for permeation through subjects, and those seeking a more pervasive and 'holistic' solution. Burston's (1948) claims for history as the key subject in teaching citizenship, rather than some civics amalgam, were subtly, even slyly, articulated. Hemming's (1949) counter-arguments for a more 'daring' social studies approach were more grandiose. Teachers of social studies, in involving pupils in the subject matter of human experience and struggle, were 'right in the front line in the battle for civilization' (1949: 172).

Textbooks arranged on concentric lines again appeared. In Strong's text, the framework was based on 'Citizens and their Neighbourhood', 'Citizens and their Country', and 'The Citizen and the British Commonwealth of Nations' (1944). Dray and Jordan made much of their 'widening circles' framework (1950). Bunting and Perkins (1967) started with home, school and community, the latter represented by three citizens, Mr. Active, Mr. Passive and Mr. Bad. These illustrated the various aspects of the moral spectrum, as exemplified in conduct and in health, in capacity and willingness to participate in local and national elections, and finally in demonstrating the potential or lack of it for becoming a true 'Citizen of the World'.

The social studies movement, after initial successes in some secondary modern schools, flickered and for a time died. In part this was the result of derogatory campaigns of subject specialists, playing on its derivation from the United States and associated lack of academic respectability (see Scarfe, 1950). The fact that it was argued to be particularly suited to less well-motivated pupils also reinforced the soft-option stereotype. During the late 1960s a renewed bid was made for a more social scientific approach in 'the new social studies'. Integrated curriculum frameworks were again presented as a way of improving the motivation of less academic pupils of the new comprehensive school system, but this time preserving a strong academic input from the social sciences.

Good eco-citizens

A novel element since the 1970s has been the emergence of a new cause: 'eco-citizenship', one of many contemporary 'ecological buzzwords'. As Haubrich has indicated, the debate has been marked by polarisation, eco-optimism or, even more, eco-pessimism rather than by a more centre-of-the-road eco-realism (1999: 1). The case of eco-citizenship is introduced here for two reasons. First, the notion of citizenship has in recent years been extended from its former concentration on the social world to the natural environment (Machon, 1998: 117). Second, it has become a crusading arena, redolent of past zealotries which have been demonstrated in the chronicling of key elements of Christian citizenship, national and imperial citizenship and, on the other side, the peace movement. The strictures here relate to the radical and evangelical manifestations of the environmental movement, and not to the notion of environmental education in general.

The concept of the eco-citizen can, at least to an extent, be dated back to Earth Day, 1970. To implement the reforms of the 'environmental revolution' it was necessary for every teacher to become 'a paradigm of environmentally responsible behaviour' (Wallace, 1971: 38). Earth Day's 'loudest if not clearest note was of righting wrongs, desisting from evil, walking the path to virtue'. One parade banner read: 'Pollution, Gateway to Hell; Ecology, Gateway to Paradise . . .'. President Nixon offered 'quasi-biblical assurances' at a Billy Graham rally: 'I want the air to be clean and it will be clean: I want the water to be pure and it will be pure'. Equally angry opposing responses came from the political extremes. The event was roundly condemned as a communist plot by right-wing bodies such as the Daughters of the American Revolution, and by the radical left as merely diverting attention from racism, the Vietnam War and urban poverty (Lowenthal, 1970: 5–7).

The evangelical movement in environmental education has spawned a number of sub-sects, variously tinged by 'deep ecology', Gaian philosophy, bio-ethics and new age thinking (see Pepper, 1996: 17ff). Among the most influential voices in this sphere has been D.W. Orr, whose book is riddled with the polarities of right and wrong, of virtue and evil, linking ideas rooted in religion and eco-mysticism (1992: 182–3). Even before his book appeared, Bramwell had questioned not only the fundamentalist spirit of the more fervid ecological invective, but also the 'fantasy solutions' offered (1989: 246–8). Grün in turn drew attention to the 'language of terror' deployed in the literature of the eco-catastrophists, which he criticised as a danger to democracy and personal freedoms (1996: 345–6).

Education and indoctrination

A common thread in the more radical political, social and educational thinking from the late 1960s has been that education *about* and *in* the environment is not enough and that education *for* the environment must be prioritised as a means of promoting action. A similar purpose is evident in citizenship education. While such a proposition is, as we have seen, by no means novel, the nature of the action has in recent times been made politically more overt, the intention being to reconstruct a sustainable socialist alternative to a corrupt and inevitably transient multinational capitalism (Hatcher, 1983: 27; also Huckle, 1983: 151–2; Fien, 1993: 12; and Pepper, 1996: 301–5).

Tensions are inevitably posed where so strong and proactive a mission is entailed, between libertarian views of what education is about, and the more interventionist intent to instruct and control the individual. How politicised should the school curriculum be allowed to become? The issues were much discussed in the inter-war years, and we can infer from the historical evidence that upholders of any 'good cause' have found indoctrination more effective where schooling *for* some extrinsic end is envisaged. As Ernest Simon of the AEC expressed it at the time, a striking feature of the Fascist states was 'the complete confidence of their adherents in the justice and rightness of their cause', legitimating the deployment of the full power of the authoritarian state to inculcate its political values. Their rulers had been successful in instilling 'a high degree of enthusiastic and self-sacrificing devotion' among their citizens, which democracies could not match and should not imitate, for cultivating reason and tolerance was their goal (1935: 4, 7).

There were clearly different points of view within the AEC. Supporting Simon, one contributor to *The Citizen* described the use of indoctrination of dogma of whatever form as 'offensive to the spirit of free enquiry and rational discussion on which both education and democracy finally rest' (Teale, 1937: 5). Dodds stated the grave danger of education for citizenship as that of 'treating the young as a means – means to a greater and finer England: chosen instruments for the setting of Jerusalem in this land'. It was reasonable to hope for them to work for that consummation, 'but the fact remains, the ultimate fact, that they are ends – ends in themselves' (1941: 161).

He scornfully dismissed as an 'infection' the totalitarian production of political 'yes men'. 'The democratic answer to Education as Propaganda is not education as Counter-propaganda but Education as prophylaxis against Propaganda – the cultivation of that invaluable quality known to Americans as "sales-resistance"' (1941: 30–2).

Countering this was the question of whether or not in a democratic state, facing serious external threat, it was vital to contemplate indoctrination. Eva Hubback of the AEC was much less sure of the validity of arguments dismissing this idea. There were in her view social as well as personal values which the vast majority of citizens in a democratic state would not wish to question, as well as a political faith, which must justify an element of 'specific and definite' indoctrination, more fine-grained, however, than that in totalitarian states, and so different in degree as to constitute a difference in kind (Hubback, 1935: 29–30). Similarly, Michael Stewart (1938) differentiated 'non-rational' and 'rational' propaganda, citing *Mein Kampf* as a high point of the 'art' of the former. Rational propaganda meant marshalling evidence to support a cause to which was added an emotional appeal to rouse enthusiasm. No one could object to such campaigning to promote, for example, cleanliness and honesty (and, presumably, democracy) (1938: 10–12). The British politician Eleanor Rathbone (1938) was even less inhibited in arguing the case, stating forcefully that the success of Fascist and Nazi propaganda relied on the way in which it seized upon the very young. Democracy had to be defended in similar ways, not least through making 'our propaganda as all-pervasive and effective as that of those who hold opposite beliefs. There is current today an absurd prejudice against the very word propaganda – as though propaganda must necessarily be unfair and exaggerated if not mendacious' (1938: 2).

Jumping ahead into the era of the eco-citizen, the Australian environmental scientist R.D. Linke reintroduced the notion that indoctrination might be both desirable and necessary. If education *for* the environment was to achieve its objectives, and if these were shown not to be achievable through intrinsic interest or the provision of experience, 'then we must consider more seriously the possibility of compulsory conditioning' (1976: 129). Jickling and Spork, however, more recently have attacked the ideology of radical environmentalism, objecting to the use of the language of activism and not of education (1998: 315). Education *for* something

> implies that education should aim for something external to itself and that educators are invited to prescribe a preferred end. It follows then that the slogan 'education for the environment' provides a linguistic invitation for co-option by those who feel they have the best answer.
>
> (Jickling and Spork, 1998: 322)

There exists, in their view, a deep-seated problem in that the rhetoric stresses the need for students to be 'critical' – to 'deconstruct' conventional wisdom. But in so doing, 'then we must accept that they may well reject the externally imposed aim that has been pre-selected for them' (Jickling and Spork, 1998: 323–4), reiterating Dodds (1941) and also Postman and Weingartner's risky maxim: 'one of the tenets of a democratic society is that men be allowed to think and express themselves freely on any subject, even to the point of speaking out against a democratic society' (1969: 1).

Conclusion: some pointers from history

Schools have perennially been charged with the task, 'usually thankless', of promoting the citizenship ideal (Gilbert, 1995: 110). Yet one of the first lessons of history is surely that in any direct or verifiable sense education for citizenship has not obviously succeeded. The possible exception is where it has been based on inculcation and backed by later coercion, whether physical, political, social or moral. The procedures of all authoritarian states and fundamentalist and radical groups have been frighteningly similar, and indeed successful in the short and medium term. The Church and imperialist and totalitarian states of whatever political hue all turned out active and committed 'patriots' for their cause.

In the situation of the democratic state, however, Findlay was sceptical of the 'naïve faith in schooling as a grand panacea for human ills'. Can we in any case, he argued, 'trust one generation to settle the destiny of the next'? (1920: 285). He observed: 'It needs only a moment's reflection to see that the appeal [to education] merely shifts the solution of political difficulties from the shoulders of the present generation [of politicians] to the next' (1920: 161).

Another serious concern is over the sort of citizens governments and other bodies over time have expected that the schools should produce. An 'authorised version' has erstwhile been the basis of civic education. The inter-war teachers' journals and method-ological civics texts in their guidance invariably prioritised the generation of dutiful, loyal and socially well-behaved subjects (Figure 2.3). Among the variety of activities they proposed in working towards these ends were school plays, often in verse, simulating approved civic duties, such as one entitled 'Our town: a play for junior citizens'. At its conclusion, an alderman rose to propose a vote of thanks to his fellow aldermen and councillors.

Figure 2.3 Are these boys and girls good citizens?

Source: *Teacher's World*, 1920.

No wages do they seek for all their toil:
Their true reward is having served their Town.
That they have acted wisely and with skill
Is plain to see for all who look around
With careful gaze upon th' improvements made.
Let those who think that they could better do,
Cease grumbling, forward step, and take their place.
(Tuckett, 1926: 1046)

There is not space in this chapter to explore the comparative dimension, but the United States offers strikingly interesting historical similarities to those described in Britain, as reflected in Figure 2.4. Taken from a textbook *The Good Citizen* (Hepner and Hepner, 1924: 318), it depicts the behavioural criteria required for entry into this responsibility, based on commandments almost like those required at the gateway to eternal life. While some are eminently supportable, there are clearly significant omissions to do with basic freedoms, the pursuit of happiness, the development of critical thinking and so on, all of which would loom large in a liberal statement.

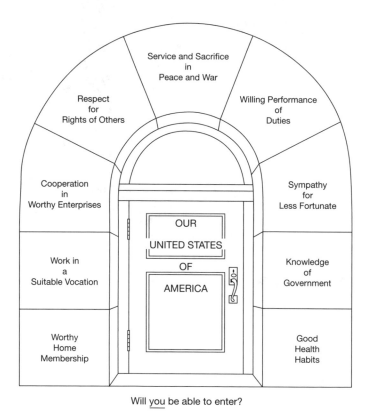

Will you be able to enter?

Figure 2.4 The door to good citizenship

Source: W.R. Hepner and F.K. Hepner, *A Good Citizen: a Textbook in Social and Vocational Civics* (Boston: Houghton Mifflin, 1924). © 1924 Houghton Mifflin Company. Used by permission.

Such recommendations encapsulate a far from liberal ideology that has been passed down through the corridors of time, chiming harmoniously with latter-day government thinking, from both major political parties, exemplified by Waddington, Home Secretary at the time of the National Curriculum Council, who, it was said, 'took the view that it was up to the [National Curriculum] Council to tell teachers in school what they should teach. Specifically, teachers should concentrate on the evils of car thefts, and the need to co-operate with the police' (Graham and Tytler, 1993: 105).

The suspicion must remain that the official conceptualisations of the purposes of citizenship education are those of old-time civics instruction, rather than the liberal education of active and questioning citizens who hopefully would turn out to be socially equally decent, but also more than that (Heater, 1990: 175). Guidance in the National Curriculum Council's *Education for Citizenship* (1990) was inveterately inward-looking, 'as English as a house in the suburbs', as Machon observed (1991: 128). And while there was little overtly objectionable in the later Advisory Group on Citizenship's report, produced by the Qualifications and Curriculum Authority (QCA, 1998), there was also much of importance left unsaid. The rhetoric of promoting critical thinking sits uneasily with that element in these official statements with which Pring was particularly concerned, namely the preoccupation with business metaphors, with products and 'tight learning outcomes' (1999: 86). Followers of Postman and Weingartner could legitimately conclude that the main objectives were to create 'eager consumers . . . smoothly functioning bureaucrats', rather than what they hoped for, namely 'crap detectors' (1969: 3, 15), never a popular category with high authority.

What can we learn from history about the place of geography in citizenship education? In his critique of the evangelism of some elements in current environmental education, Grün wrote of their propensity to begin their discourse by appealing to the need for a 'holistic vision' (1996: 344). What Heater and many other proponents of citizenship have demanded is also historically embedded in the notion of an integrated curriculum framework, the process which supposedly sits easily with the elements of both education *through* and education *for* citizenship. It is indeed useful to be on the side of the angels in respect of matter, method and mission. Hubback earlier took a more pragmatic view, suggesting that it was 'a matter of organisation and not of principle' whether a subject-focused or more integrated approach was used, in stating her preference for the eclectic (1937: 25).

While accepting that the case is not clear-cut, and aware of the likely criticism that this will be perceived as a defensive and traditional subject-specialist reaction, my own judgement, based in part on reflection on the long historical experience treated here, is that citizenship education permeated into subjects such as geography and history is, in terms of protecting the cause of education *for* education, a less risky proposition than reverting to the pervasion principle, re-expressed by Heater in stating that citizenship should be 'at the heart of modern education' (1990: 342). Let it be remembered that the 'integrated' and 'project-based' Empire Days, and the many civics textbooks of the first half of this century, were often more xenophobic than what was being transmitted in geography and history materials, culpable though these also were.

There is therefore in the end a profound dilemma over which approach, permeation or pervasion, is more prone to the imposition of indoctrination and propaganda. The fact is, where zealots have hi-jacked the curriculum, under whatever label, whether advocating pervasion or holism and integration, what has followed has often been instruction and inculcation. At least the subjects, which can of course also be taken over for extrinsic ends, have their own criteria for truth, and can offer some resistance. Governments may be uncertain about what should or should not be introduced into geography or science. They are generally crystal clear about what should go into citizenship education. John Stuart Mill famously warned of such interventionism:

> A general State education is a mere contrivance for moulding people to be exactly like one another; and as the mould in which it casts them is that which pleases the predominant power in the government in proportion as it is efficient and successful, it establishes a despotism over the mind.
>
> (1948: 161)

In Mill's time, science (in which geography claimed a part) and the evidence it provided, together with the secularisation and successful colonisation of the curriculum by subjects, was of some influence in gradually overcoming the yoke of a religious indoctrination. And who was it who affirmed that 'the youthful brain must not be burdened with subjects'? Not Froebel, not Dewey, but Adolf Hitler (see Mann, 1939: 40).

Ultimately and more positively, however, it is argued here that the polarisation of choice between curricular pervasion versus permeation through subjects, backed up by the simplistic tendency in educational writing to equate these with stereotypical 'interactionist' versus 'transmission' models of teaching and learning, is not a constructive way of looking at the issues. A potentially productive alternative for citizenship education would be to conceptualise a more varied and eclectic framing, responsive to how teachers function differentially in classrooms, one that does not allow any of matter, method or mission to step out of balance. This would presume that education *about*, *in* and *for* citizenship are all equally important. It would need to be conceived in conjunction with a libertarian – dare one say liberal-humanist? – 'rehearsing the practice of good citizenship', as the taken-for-granted underpinning of the human relationships operating within and without the classroom.

FOR FURTHER THINKING

1   If, as the historical evidence suggests, education *for* citizenship has almost invariably brought in its train instruction, inculcation and indoctrination, under what circumstances is this likely to remain inevitably so, or might contemporary educators be able to resolve the dilemma?

2   Do official statements promote or limit confidence in any optimistic view that a liberal approach to citizenship education is envisaged?

3   Is the permeation approach, through subjects such as geography and history, more likely to offer liberal solutions than the pervasion approach of an all-embracing education for citizenship, as advocated by some proselytes?

4   Is not the elevation of a concept such as education *for* citizenship liable to distort what might arguably be regarded as a desirable balance in education as between matter, method and mission?

5   To what extent does the current preoccupation with citizenship education
     exemplify what Findlay (1920) warned of as the 'naïve faith in schooling as a
     grand panacea for human ills'?

References

Addison-Phillips, E. (1937) 'Training for citizenship through religious instruction', *The Citizen* 5:
    8–9.
Adkins, F.J. (1933) *The Approach to Citizenship through History and through Regional Surveys*, London: The
    Le Play Society.
Anon. (1858) 'The importance of domestic economy', *Educational Record* 4: 117.
Anon. (1934) 'Citizenship as a school subject', *Times Educational Supplement* 11 August: 269–70.
Anon. (1940) 'Too wide a loyalty', *Times Educational Supplement* 13 April: 135.
Anon. (1946) 'World citizenship conference', *Schoolmaster and Woman Teacher's Chronicle* 3 January: 6.
Barker, E. (1937) *The Citizen's Choice*, Cambridge: Cambridge University Press.
Batho, G. (1990) 'The history of the teaching of civics and citizenship in English schools', *Curriculum
    Journal* 1, 1: 91–100.
Bavin, W.D. (1912) *Good Citizenship: a Scheme of Lessons Correlating Civics with Religious Instruction*,
    London: Pilgrim Press.
Beales, A.C.F. (1931) *The History of Peace: a Short Account of the Organised Movements for International Peace*,
    London: G. Bell and Sons.
Berard, R. (1987) 'Frederick James Gould and the transformation of moral education', *British
    Journal of Educational Studies* 35, 3: 233–47.
Blakiston, C.H. (1920) *Elementary Civics*, London: Edward Arnold.
Bowtell, T.H. (1920) 'Training for citizenship', *Teacher's World* 3 November: 227.
Bramwell, A. (1989) *Ecology in the Twentieth Century: a History*, New Haven, Conn.: Yale University
    Press.
British Association (BA) (1920) *Interim Report of the Committee on Training in Citizenship* (Cardiff meeting
    1919), London: J. Murray.
Brown, W.H. (1905) 'Training in citizenship: County Council of the West Riding of Yorkshire
    scheme', *Practical Teacher* 26, 3: 142–3.
Bunting, J.R. and Perkins, W.A. (1967) *Civics: a Guide to Active Citizenship*, London: Evans Brothers.
Burston, W.H. (1948) 'The contribution of history to education in citizenship', *History* 33: 226–40.
Chancellor, V.E. (1970) *History for their Masters: Opinion in the English History Textbook: 1800–1914*,
    New York: Augustus M. Kelley.
Dempster, J.B. (1939) 'Training for citizenship through geography', in Association for Education
    in Citizenship, *Education for Citizenship in Elementary Schools*, London: Humphrey Milford/Oxford
    University Press.
Dodds, E.R. (1941) *Minds in the Making*, London: Macmillan.
Dray, J. and Jordan, D. (1950) *A Handbook of Social Studies for Teachers in Secondary Schools and County
    Colleges*, London: Methuen.
Elliott, B.J. (1977) 'The League of Nations Union and history teaching in England: a study in
    benevolent bias', *History of Education* 6, 2: 131–41.
Evans, C. (1933) 'Geography and world citizenship', in Evans, F. (ed.) *The Teaching of Geography in
    Relation to the World Community*, Cambridge: Cambridge University Press.
Farquharson, A. (1921) 'The scientific basis of civics', *Civic Education Chronicle* 5: 6–8.
Fien, J. (1993) *Education for the Environment: Critical Curriculum Theorising and Environmental Education*,
    Geelong: Deakin University Press.

Findlay, J.J. (1920) *An Introduction to Sociology for Social Workers and General Readers*, Manchester: Manchester University Press.

Fletcher, C.R.L. and Kipling, R. (1911) *A School History of England*, Oxford: Clarendon Press.

Freshfield, D.W. (1886) 'The place of geography in education', *Proceedings of the Royal Geographical Society*, New Series 8, 11: 698–718.

Garnett, M. (1943) *The World We Mean to Make and the Part of Education in Making It*, London: Faber and Faber.

Geddes, P. (1905) 'Civics as applied sociology', in The Sociological Society, *Sociological Papers*, London: Macmillan.

Gilbert, R. (1995) 'Education for citizenship and the problem of identity in post-modern political culture', in Ahier, J. and Ross, A. (eds) *The Social Subjects within the Curriculum: Children's Social Learning in the National Curriculum*, London: Falmer Press.

Goldstrom, J. (1972) *The Social Content of Education 1808–1870*, Newton Abbot: David and Charles.

Graham, D. and Tytler, D. (1993) *A Lesson for Us All: the Making of the National Curriculum*, London: Routledge.

Grün, M. (1996) 'An analysis of the discursive production of environmental education: terrorism, archaism and transcendentalism', *Curriculum Studies* 4, 3: 247–329.

Hankin, G.T. (1909) *The Teaching of Civics in Public Schools*, London: Historical Association Leaflet No. 15.

Hatcher, R. (1983) 'The construction of world studies', *Multi-racial Education* 11, 1: 23–35.

Haubrich, H. (1999) 'The ecocitizen: a challenge to geographical and environmental education', in Kent, W.A. (ed.) *Geography and Environmental Education: International Perspectives*, London: International Geographical Union Commission on Geographical Education/University of London Institute of Education.

Hayward, F.H. (1935) 'Education for citizenship: instruction or inspiration?', *Times Educational Supplement* 14 December: 438.

Heater, D. (1990) *Citizenship: the Civic Ideal in World History, Politics and Education*, London: Longman.

Hemming, J. (1949) *The Teaching of Social Studies in Secondary Schools*, London: Longmans, Green.

Hepner, W.R. and Hepner, F.K. (1924) *The Good Citizen: a Textbook in Social and Vocational Civics*, Boston: Houghton & Mifflin.

Herbertson, A.J. (1907) 'Geography', in Adamson, J.W. (ed.) *The Practice of Instruction* London: National Society's Depository.

Higham, C.S.S. (1932) *The Good Citizen: an Introduction to Civics*, London: Longmans Green.

Hilliard, F.H. (1961) 'The Moral Instruction League 1897–1919', *Durham Research Review* 12: 53–63.

Houseley, E.E. (1921) *An Introductory Reader in Civics*, London: George Harrap.

Hubback, E.M. (1935) 'Bias and dogma', in Association for Education in Citizenship, *Education for Citizenship in Secondary Schools*, London: Humphrey Milford/Oxford University Press.

Hubback, E.M. (1937) 'Education for citizenship in the school', *The Citizen* 4: 24–7.

Huckle, J. (1983) 'The politics of school geography', in Huckle, J. (ed.) *Geographical Education: Reflection and Action*, Oxford: Oxford University Press.

Hughes, M.L.V. (1915) *Citizens to Be: a Social Study of Health, Wisdom and Goodness with Special Reference to Elementary Schools*, London: Constable.

Hutchinson, A.L. (1939) 'The aims of education for citizenship', in Association for Education in Citizenship, *Education for Citizenship in Elementary Schools*, London: Humphrey Milford/Oxford University Press.

Jickling, B. and Spork, H. (1998) 'Education for the environment: a critique', *Environmental Education Research* 4, 3: 309–27.

Jones, R. and Sherman, S.S. (1928) *League of Nations Schoolbook*, London: Union of the League of Nations.

Lambert, D. (1997) 'Geography, education and citizenship: identity and inter-cultural communication', in Slater, F. and Bale, J. (eds) *Reporting Research in Geographical Education: Monograph No.5*, London: University of London Institute of Education.

Leeson, S. (1935) *Education in Citizenship*, London: Association for Education in Citizenship.

Linke, R.D. (1976) 'A case for indoctrination in environmental education', *South Pacific Journal of Teacher Education* 4, 2: 125–9.

Lowenthal, D. (1970) 'Earth Day', *Area* 2, 4: 1–10.

Lucas, C.P. (1916) 'On the teaching of imperial history', *History* 1: 5–11.

Machon, P. (1991) 'Subject or citizen?', *Teaching Geography* 16, 3: 128.

Machon, P. (1998) 'Citizenship and geographical education', *Teaching Geography* 23, 3: 115–17.

Mackinder, H.J. (1911) 'The teaching of geography from the imperial point of view, and the use which could and should be made of visual instruction', *Geographical Teacher* 6, 30: 79–86.

Mann, E. (1939) *School for Barbarians: Education under the Nazis*, London: Lindsay Drummond.

Marsden, W.E. (1998) '"Conservation education" and the foundations of national prosperity: comparative perspectives from early twentieth-century North America and Britain', *History of Education* 27, 3: 345–62.

Mill, J.S. [1859] (1948) 'On liberty', in Mill, J.S., *Utilitarianism, Liberty and Representative Government*, London: J.M. Dent and Sons.

National Curriculum Council (1990) *Curriculum Guidance 8. Education for Citizenship*, York: NCC.

Nordon, C.L. (1944) *World Citizenship Education: a War Preventive Measure*, London: Casual Club.

Orr, D.W. (1992) *Ecological Literacy: Education and the Transition to a Postmodern World*, Albany, NY: State University of New York Press.

Paul, L. (1946) 'Character and citizenship', *Schoolmaster and Woman Teacher's Chronicle* 7 November: 394.

Paul, L. (1952) 'The widening circle of citizenship', *Schoolmaster and Woman Teacher's Chronicle* 9 May: 699, 714.

Pepper, D. (1996) *Modern Environmentalism: an Introduction*, London: Routledge.

Pollard, F.E. (1910) *Education and International Duty*, London: Friends Guild of Teachers.

Postman, N. and Weingartner, C. (1969) *Teaching as a Subversive Activity*, New York: Delacorte Press.

Pring, R. (1999) 'Political education: relevance of the humanities', *Oxford Review of Education* 25, 1: 71–87.

Qualifications and Curriculum Authority (1998) *Education for Citizenship and the Teaching of Democracy in Schools: Final Report of the Advisory Group on Citizenship*, London: QCA.

Rathbone, E. (1938) 'On the necessity for propaganda', *New Ploughshare* 1: 2.

Rowntree, A. (1911) *Education in Relation to Internationalism*, London: School Peace League.

Scarfe, N. (1950) 'Geography and social studies in the USA', *Geography* 35, 2: 86–93.

Simon, E. (1935) 'The aims of education for citizenship', in Association for Education in Citizenship, *Education for Citizenship in Secondary Schools*, London: Humphrey Milford/Oxford University Press.

Stewart, M. (1938) *Bias and Education for Democracy*, London: Humphrey Milford/Oxford University Press.

Strong, C.F. (1944) *Today through Yesterday: Book 4: The Young Citizen and the World of Today*, London: University of London Press.

Swann, F. (1918) *English Citizenship*, London: Longmans Green.

Teale, A.E. (1937) 'Propaganda and education', *The Citizen* 5: 4–7.

Tuckett, W.J. (1926) 'The teaching of civics: "Our town": a play for junior citizens', *Teachers World* 3 September: 1024, 1046.

Unstead, J.F. (1928) 'The primary geography schoolteacher – what should he know and be?', *Geography* 14, 4: 315–22.

Wallace, E.S. (1971) 'The individual and the environmental revolution', *Social Education* 35, 10: 38, 43, 52.

Welpton, W.P. (1923) *The Teaching of Geography*, London: University Tutorial Press.

Wilson, R. (1920) *The Complete Citizen: an Introduction to the Study of Civics*, London: J.M. Dent and Sons.

Worts, F.R. (1919) *Citizenship: Its Meaning, Privileges and Duties*, London: Hodder and Stoughton.

Yoxall, J.H. (*c.*1870) *The Pupil Teacher's Geography*, London: Jarrold and Sons.

Chapter 3

Citizenship and democracy education

Geography's place: an international perspective

Michael Williams

> The understanding of the structure and processes of different regions within the global system is the basis for the regional and national identity of people and their international perspectives. . . . Regional studies should encourage consideration of internationalisation and globalisation whilst avoiding the pitfalls of regional separatism.
>
> (Commission on Geographical Education of the
> International Geographical Union, 1992, 8)

> The 'world' in which we now live is in some profound respects thus quite different from that inhabited by human beings in previous periods of history. It is in many ways a single world, having a unitary framework of experience (for instance, in respect of basic axes of time and space), yet at the same time one which creates new forms of fragmentation and dispersal.
>
> (Giddens, 1991, 4)

Geographical curricula are usually defined by national boundaries. The structure, form and pedagogy of geography education vary from nation state to nation state,* reflecting variations in curriculum culture. The place and status accorded to geography in curricula, the way the subject is defined in terms of aims, content, teaching methods and modes of assessment, the resources that are made available for its development, all of these show marked differences from one nation to another. When we look at geography education in other nations we can focus on the obvious differences from or on the similarities with our own national circumstances. We can also decide the level on which to focus: national system, regional system, school sector, individual school or particular classrooms.

In this chapter, I discuss the changing conception of citizenship before reviewing a small number of national systems to illustrate national differences in the ways in which geography education relates to citizenship education.

---

* In using the term nation state I am conscious of the problems surrounding its definition. Connor (1994, 91) has emphasised the 'imprecise, inconsistent, and often totally erroneous usage' of the term.

Citizenship

It is commonplace to consider citizenship narrowly within the context of the nation state: citizenship is commonly conceptualised as the identity of an individual bounded by national frontiers. However, it is extremely important to acknowledge that nation states, as human artefacts, have a remarkably short history. Their frontiers change as a result of alliances, wars and agreements. Changes are made to their names often at times of major ideological and constitutional shifts. Further, the internal authority and power of nation states are being weakened as a consequence of new international trade relationships, ecological trends and the modernisation of telecommunications. These changes are important not only because they alter definitions of citizenship but also because they provide the background against which curriculum changes occur. They impact on both the place of geography education in school curricula and the content and teaching methods of school geography.

T.H. Marshall (1963), a seminal figure in the contemporary field of citizenship studies, distinguished between civil, political and social aspects of citizenship. Civil citizenship emphasised individual freedoms of speech, thought and faith, and included rights to property, contract and justice. Political citizenship was concerned with the right to participate in political activities, and social citizenship highlighted rights to security and welfare. These three aspects focus on citizenship rights. As Isin and Wood (1999) argue, it is important to conceptualise citizenship also in terms of identity – individual and group identity. They acknowledge that 'postmodernism and globalization force us to abandon the unitary, homogeneous concept of citizenship in favour of a multidimensional and plural concept of citizenship' (1999, 22). This pluralism encompasses a range of aspects including the 'political, civil, economic, diasporic, cultural, sexual and ecological', and so citizenship becomes a process of negotiation among all of these. Clearly, this pluralism alters any perception of democracy and citizenship as being based on uniformity and equality.

In Figure 3.1, the forces operating on the contemporary nation state are highlighted. In particular, a distinction is drawn between global and personal forces. Global forces are defined by political, ecological, commercial and telecommunications characteristics. Many descriptors could be used for the personal forces and the ones shown in Figure 3.1 are illustrative rather than comprehensive.

It is important to recognise the location of the tensions implicit in the figure. Thus there is a tension between the sovereignty of the individual, the sovereignty of the state and international forces. Further, at the global level, there are tensions between political, ecological, commercial and telecommunications forces. At the personal level there is the individual acting alone as well as the individual as a member of various groups which may be in harmony or conflict which each other. It is important to acknowledge that some social groups overspill national frontiers; for example, religious faiths are shared by people in many parts of the world as are ethnic/race and gender issues. Further, some social groups, such as nations and language groups, spread across many political boundaries. This bridging of the personal with the international brings into question the sovereignty of the nation state and there is much discussion among theorists about the relative strengths of individual and global identities. For this chapter, it is the way that school curricula, and especially geography within those curricula, take into account these global, national and personal facets of citizenship that is the principal concern.

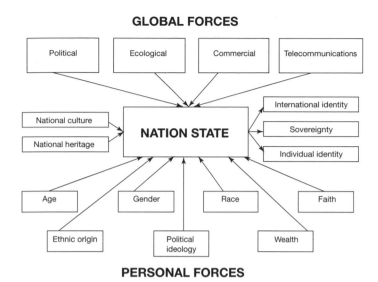

Figure 3.1 Forces operating on the nation state

Citizenship education and geography education

Researchers in geography education have paid remarkably little attention to citizenship education. The comprehensive bibliography of studies of geography education conducted in the English language (Foskett and Marsden, 1998) contains few empirical studies and no comparative studies of the relationship between citizenship and geography education. Much the same is true of the papers presented in recent symposia and conferences organised by the Commission on Geographical Education of the International Geographical Union. To some extent this may be explained by the taken-for-grantedness of citizenship as an aim of school geography. More importantly, school geography in many parts of the world appears to be under pressure for timetable space owing to the increasing priority being given by governments to environmental education, vocational education and information and communication technology. Indeed, the emphasis given in environmental education to experiential learning, critical reflection, active engagement and school–community links strengthens the case for environmental education at the expense of geography. The over-arching concern of governments for lifelong learning as a means of improving their human resources is an essential contextual factor in any explanation of the definition and status of geography in school curricula.

In identifying examples of how governments are seeking to strengthen citizenship education it is tempting, even instructive, to consider those countries that have experienced traumatic constitutional changes in recent times. Such examples can be found in the 'balkanisation' of states in Europe, e.g. the break-up of Yugoslavia, the division of Czechoslovakia and the changes in the former Soviet Union. In the Third World politically inspired violence has been experienced in such states as Burma, Burundi, Chad, Ethiopia, Guyana, India, Indonesia, Iraq, Kenya, Malaysia, Nigeria, Pakistan, the Philippines, Rwanda, the Sudan, Thailand and Uganda. Wars, coups and civil unrest result in governmental changes, leading to curriculum change and the redrawing of atlas maps and the rewriting of geography textbooks.

However, it is just as interesting to consider how more stable states are revising their geography curricula as a result of various pressures. Some helpful insights into the place of citizenship in the curricula of such countries have been provided by Kerr (1999a, 1999b) in his thematic study of citizenship, commissioned as part of the International Review of Curriculum and Assessment Frameworks (IRCAF) project, and by data gathered in the International Association for the Evaluation of Educational Achievement (IEA) study of Civic Education (Torney Purta *et al.*, 1999). Kerr's thematic study drew its evidence from Australia, Canada, England, France, Germany, Hungary, Italy, Japan, Korea, the Netherlands, New Zealand, Singapore, Spain, Sweden, Switzerland and the United States of America. The IEA study is now in its second phase. Initially twenty-four countries participated and qualitative data were gathered, focused on three domains: democracy and governmental institutions, social cohesion and diversity, and national identity. In the second phase these domains were extended to include economics/media and environment. More countries participated and data were gathered from nationally representative samples of 2,000–3,000 students per country.

Kerr (1999a) divided the countries in his project into three categories dependent on the degree of detail in which values were expressed or prescribed in legislation. He emphasised 'one of the major tensions countries face in approaching citizenship education, namely the extent to which it is possible to identify, agree and articulate the values and dispositions which underpin citizenship'. In his conclusion, he drew attention to 'the move in many countries away from a narrow, knowledge-based approach to citizenship education, to a broader approach encompassing knowledge and understanding, active experiences and the development of student values, dispositions, skills and attitudes'.

To illustrate these tensions and trends I have chosen to highlight countries drawn from three continents: Japan, South Africa and Australia. Each is engaged in substantial curriculum revision and the place of geography in curricula is being reconsidered. Each has distinctive social, political, economic and cultural contexts though all are concerned with lifelong learning and the accommodation in curricula of local, regional and global aspects of citizenship.

Japan

Education in Japan is governed by the Fundamental Law of Education promulgated in 1947. This law is set against the backcloth of a nation that is remarkably uniform in its ethnic composition and that has sought to surpass Western countries industrially and commercially. Recent publications from the Japanese Ministry of Education, Science, Sport and Culture (e.g. Ministry of Education, Science, Sport and Culture, 1995 and 1997) have highlighted a number of important pressures on the school curriculum: internationalisation, an information-oriented society, the growing sophistication of science and technology, the changing industrial structure and an ageing population. Within schools there has been serious concern with 'excessive competition in entrance examinations, bullying, refusal to attend school, and insufficient experience of activities in a natural environment and in everyday life' (Ministry of Education, Science,

Sport and Culture, 1995, 3). From these have emerged four principles underpinning curriculum change:

- fostering a richness of spirit;
- an emphasis on the basics and the promotion of education that encourages individuality;
- fostering self-education ability;
- encouraging respect for Japanese culture and traditions while promoting international understanding.

New government-approved courses of study were introduced in kindergartens in 1990, elementary schools in 1992, lower secondary schools in 1993 and upper secondary schools in 1994. With regard to geography education, the importance attributed to the environment by the government (Ministry of Education, Science, Sport and Culture, 1995, 16) can be seen in this quotation:

> The global environment is also a key educational issue. There is a growing need for environmental protection on a global scale, and environmental problems are becoming sufficiently serious to jeopardize the survival of the human race. If we are to preserve the global environment while maintaining and improving living standards, we must all strive to make wise and effective use of our precious heritage of nature and resources. In this sense, the development of people sensitive to and knowledgeable about environmental issues must be regarded as a vital priority. One of the most important tasks facing school education is to foster understanding of the roles and responsibilities of humanity toward the environment, willingness to participate in environment protection activities, and the ability to solve environmental problems.

Note in this quotation the merging of international concerns with national interests, the importance attached to national heritage and resources and the encouragement given to active citizenship in an environmental context.

The place of geography and other social subjects in the Japanese school curriculum has been revised several times since 1947 and reforms were introduced in 1951, 1955, 1958, 1968, 1977 and 1989. If we look at the three most recent reforms we find that, in 1968, a deliberate attempt was made to distinguish the curriculum of the upper secondary school from that of the lower secondary school. While geography, history and civics were taught separately, teachers of these subjects were expected to give attention to political, economic and social issues. The 1960s and 1970s were the period of Japanese rapid economic development. Urbanisation, congestion and pollution were some of the obvious consequences of industrial expansion and concentration. The changing arrangement and content of social studies were responses to them and so a course on modern society was introduced into the upper secondary school curriculum in 1977.

What has emerged in the most recent curriculum reform (Tsukuba Association for International Education, 1998) has been the restructuring of upper secondary school social studies into 'geography and history' and 'civics' and a more flexible approach to the arrangements for teaching history and geography in the lower secondary school.

This flexibility is well illustrated by an innovation in the Hyogo prefecture that owes its origins to two different events. The first was the massive Hanshin-Awaji earthquake that devastated the urban area focused on Kobe in south-west Japan in January 1995. This saw a substantial response from volunteers from all parts of Japan who sought to help survivors of the disaster and contribute to social reconstruction. The second was the shock to the community that resulted from the violent killing of an elementary school student by a teenage boy. The local community organised a meeting to discuss the implications for the community of these events and what resulted was a partnership between schools, families and community organisations that sought to provide lower secondary school students with opportunities to experience community activities at first hand while presenting a positive image of teenagers to community residents. The local partnership principle has been extended to schools throughout the prefecture.

In 1997–8 some 59,000 14-year-olds were released for a week from their lower secondary schools in the Hyogo prefecture to obtain first-hand community experience. Some spent the week in primary production activities (farming, forestry and fisheries), others had work experience in such places as shops, hotels and restaurants, others engaged in cultural and artistic activities, while others were engaged in welfare activities. It is important to note that these activities were not conceptualised as work experience but as community experience. The challenge for the schools has been to incorporate fully students' experience into the conventional subjects on school timetables. For geography teachers familiar with traditional geographical excursions and fieldwork, this Japanese innovation offers an alternative model.

Republic of South Africa

Not surprisingly, the end of apartheid and the introduction of a new political constitution were powerful stimuli for rethinking the nature of education and schooling in the Republic of South Africa. There was a call for the exploration of new ethical, political, economic and educational paradigms (Smit, 1998) in the spirit of national reconciliation. In 1997, the Ministry of Education launched a new national curriculum titled Curriculum 2005. Important features of this curriculum are its emphasis on lifelong learning, its focus on outcomes-based education, a new qualifications framework and a radically designed framework for elementary and secondary school curricula (Grades 1–9). The curriculum framework is currently being introduced in a series of phases ending in 2004.

With regard to outcomes, a distinction has been made between critical outcomes and specific outcomes. Critical outcomes are common to all 'learning areas' while specific outcomes are tied to particular 'learning areas'. Seven 'critical cross-field outcomes' have been specified (Mosidi, 1998):

- identify and solve problems in which responses display that reasonable decisions using critical and creative thinking have been made;
- work effectively with others as a member of a team, group organisation or community;
- organise and manage oneself and one's activities responsibly and effectively;
- collect, analyse, organise and critically evaluate information;

- communicate effectively using visual, mathematical and/or language skills in the modes of oral/written presentation;
- use science and technology effectively and critically, showing responsibility towards the environment and health of others; and
- demonstrate an understanding of the world as a set of related systems by recognising that problem-solving contexts do not exist in isolation.

The term 'learning area' has been introduced to cover eight new groupings of the conventional subjects:

- language, literacy and communication;
- human and social sciences;
- technology;
- mathematical literacy, mathematics and mathematical sciences;
- natural sciences;
- arts and culture;
- economic and management science;
- life orientation.

This list replaces the forty subjects that existed before 1997. For my purposes here, I have focused on the human and social sciences learning area. The human and social sciences are intended to 'contribute to developing responsible citizens in a culturally diverse, democratic society within an interdependent world. They will equip learners to make sound judgments and take appropriate actions that will contribute to sustainable development of human society and the physical environment' (*Education Gazette*, 1997, 49). It is interesting to read, for their geography education relevance and citizenship education relevance, the specific outcomes designated for the human and social sciences learning area:

- demonstrate a critical understanding of how South African society has changed and developed;
- demonstrate a critical understanding of patterns of social development;
- participate actively in promoting a just, democratic and equitable society;
- make sound judgements about the development, utilisation and management of resources;
- critically understand the role of technology in social development;
- demonstrate an understanding of interrelationships between society and the natural environment;
- address social and environmental issues in order to promote development and social justice;
- analyse forms and processes of organisations;
- use a range of skills and techniques in the human and social sciences context.

The organising principles for this learning area were identified as: environment, resources and development; citizenship and civics; and social processes and organisation. Notice the specific references to critical understanding, active participation, the making of judgements and the promotion of development and social justice. These proposals have been much criticised by some geographical educationalists who fear the weakening of geography in school curricula.

Active citizenship in a new democracy is the umbrella over the curriculum. The challenge for syllabus designers is to identify topics and units of study that cluster knowledge, attitudes and skills to meet the specific outcomes. The framework has been designed by the central government as a top-down process heralding a new curriculum for a new society.

Australia

Australia shares with the Republic of South Africa the experience of colonialism although the experience of a civil war between colonisers has not been shared. The division between the aboriginal communities and the colonial settlers has been an ongoing citizenship issue for Australia and this has been rendered more complicated by the multicultural characteristics of recent immigration. With regard to educational policy making, the states and communities are key players since each has its own educational administration.

In 1989 the Ministers of Education in the Australian states and territories met with their Federal counterpart in Hobart to agree to the publication (Australian Education Council, 1989) of ten 'common and agreed goals of schooling' for Australia. While ostensibly this was to facilitate the free movement of people between states, it was seen by many as the first step by the Federal government to introduce a national curriculum. As in South Africa, what emerged was a new foundation for the school curriculum based on a list of what have been termed 'key learning areas':

- the arts;
- health and physical education;
- mathematics;
- studies of society and environment;
- English;
- languages other than English (LOTE);
- science;
- technology.

Interestingly, this list comprises eight areas, the same number as in South Africa though the titles are different, and these have been the basis for curriculum development in each of the Australian states and territories.

Studies of society and environment has proved to be a contentious area dividing those who saw it as a mandate for integration and social activism in the curriculum from those who argued that some subjects crossed over key learning areas and this new arrangement had disadvantages for geography as a distinct subject.

Debate in Australia was sharpened in the 1990s with the publication of reports from two committees both chaired by persons from the world of industry and commerce. The Finn Report (Australian Education Council Review Committee, 1991) reviewed the future of post-compulsory education and training and recommended that education should be based around the acquisition of six employment-related 'key competencies' for all young people. Shortly after, another committee (Mayer Committee, 1992) was established to develop these competencies. What emerged were seven 'key competencies for effective participation in the emerging patterns of work and work organisation'. 'Cultural understanding' was a term used in these reports. Thus, the Finn Report (Australian Education Council Review Committee, 1991, xvii) proposed the following components of cultural understanding as essential elements in employment-related competence:

- understanding and knowledge of Australia's historical, geographical and political context;
- understanding of major global issues, for example competing environmental, technological and social priorities;
- understanding the world of work, its implications and requirements.

Here we see geography education as part of an integrated model for the curriculum serving both citizenship and vocational purposes. Geographical education is located in the search for civic understanding and vocational competencies, a quite different position from that in the other countries I have chosen to highlight.

Responses to these proposals have varied from state to state in Australia. Lidstone (1998, 205) states that 'curriculum committees in New South Wales have apparently rejected both the notion of cultural competencies and Studies of Society and Environment in favour of awarding every student an entitlement to 200 hours of geographical study in their junior secondary years'. In Queensland, a studies of society and environment syllabus has been devised but separate syllabuses for history and geography are also available. The state has required, however, that the 'core learning outcomes' remain the same whichever approach is adopted in the schools.

Australian attempts to revise the curriculum have demonstrated the tensions between those who wish to sustain a conventional subject-based curriculum and those who wish to introduce a more radical integrated curriculum. The injection of pressures to make the curriculum more responsive to civic and vocational interests has further complicated an already complicated situation.

Conclusion

Citizenship education poses a fresh challenge for school geography in many countries. Elsewhere, I have argued that

> Curriculum designers who perceive the nation state as simply one step along a continuum of scale, from the child's experience in a local community via the region, the state, the continent to the world, overlook the power of the state in establishing an individual's identity.
>
> (Williams, 1997, 17)

Individual, group and global identities lie at the heart of the challenge for geographical educators. Political citizenship has to be located within a conceptual framework that incorporates other forms of identity, including employment, race, gender and nationality. As the examples sketched out above show, curriculum policy makers in various parts of the world are engaged in putting into place curricula for their national futures in which citizenship occupies a prominent position. Credentialism, vocationalism, cultural heritage, environmental conservation and improvement will be parts of this jigsaw and geography will have a contribution to make to it. This was recognised in the International Charter on Geographical Education (Commission on Geographical Education of the International Geographical Union, 1992) where: 'ethnic conflict, war, regionalism, nationalism and globalisation on "Spaceship Earth"' were identified in a list of issues as having a strong geographical dimension. Further, 'Appreciation of national identity and international cooperation are important functions of regional studies. Regional studies should encourage consideration of internationalisation and globalisation whilst avoiding pitfalls of regional separatism'. At local, regional, national and international levels there is a need for geographical educators to address these issues directly so that they can contribute to the framing of whole curricula and the design of geography curricula appropriate for active citizens in an increasingly interdependent world.

FOR FURTHER THINKING

1 What, in a nutshell, appears to be the purpose(s) of citizenship education in Japan, Australia and South Africa? Identify the important or interesting contrasts and similarities among these three nation states.
2 Consider another nation state that you know well. How does it contrast with the answers you provided to question 1?
3 What do you understand to be the purpose of citizenship education in England, Northern Ireland, Scotland or Wales? Are these purposes in common with those that you have already identified?

References

Australian Education Council (1989) *Common and Agreed National Goals for Schooling in Australia. An Extract from the Hobart Declaration on Schooling in Australia*, Canberra: AGPS.

Australian Education Council Review Committee (1991) *Young People's Participation in Post-Compulsory Education and Training* (The Finn Report), Canberra: AGPS.

Commission on Geographical Education of the International Geographical Union (1992) *International Charter on Geographical Education*, Freiburg: International Geographical Union.

Connor, W. (1994) *Ethnonationalism*, Princeton, NJ: Princeton University Press.

Education Gazette, Republic of South Africa (1997) Government Notice, Vol. 384, No. 18051, Pretoria: Government of the Republic of South Africa.

Foskett, N. and Marsden, B. (eds) (1998) *A Bibliography of Geographical Education 1970–1997*, Sheffield: The Geographical Association.

Giddens, A. (1991) *The Consequences of Modernity*, Cambridge: Polity Press.

Isin, E.F. and Wood, P.K. (1999) *Citizenship and Identity*, London: Sage Publications.

Kerr, D. (1999a) *Citizenship Education: an International Comparison* (International Review of Curriculum and Assessment Frameworks Paper 4), London: Qualifications and Curriculum Authority.

Kerr, D. (1999b) 'Citizenship education: an international comparison', paper presented at the ECER 99 Conference, Lahti, Finland 24 September.

Klein, J.-L. and Laurin, S. (eds) (1999) *L'Education Géographique: Formation du Citoyen et Conscience Territoriale* (second edition), Sainte-Foy (Québec): Presses de l'Université du Québec.

Lidstone, J. (1998) 'Cultural studies and geographical education: are we losing the way?', in Ferreira, M., Neto, A. and Conceicao, S. (eds) *Culture, Geography and Geographical Education, Proceedings of the Oporto Symposium of the Commission on Geographical Education of the International Geographical Union*, Lisbon: Universidade Aberta.

Marshall, T.H. (1963) *Class, Citizenship and Social Development*, London: Greenwood.

Mayer Committee (1992) *Employment Related Key Competencies: a Proposal for Consultation* (The Mayer Report), Melbourne: Mayer Committee.

Ministry of Education, Science, Sport and Culture (1995) *Japanese Government Policies in Education Science and Culture 1994, New Directions in School Education: Fostering Strength for Life*, Tokyo: Ministry of Education, Science, Sport and Culture.

Ministry of Education, Science, Sport and Culture (1997) *Japanese Government Policies in Education Science and Culture 1996, Priorities and Prospects for a Lifelong Learning Society: Increasing Diversification and Sophistication*, Tokyo: Ministry of Education, Science, Sport and Culture.

Mosidi, S.M. (1998) 'Curriculum confusion? Environmental education or geographical education, a look at the South African outcomes based curriculum development', in Smit, M.J. (ed.) *Geography Education in Multicultural Societies, a Selection of Papers from the IGU/CGE Conference*, Stellenbosch: University Press.

Smit, M. (1998) 'A paradigm shift in geography teaching in South Africa: the outcomes-based approach', in Ferreira, M., Neto, A. and Conceicao, S. (eds) *Culture, Geography and Geographical Education, Proceedings of the Oporto Symposium of the Commission on Geographical Education of the International Geographical Union*, Lisbon: Universidade Aberta.

Torncy-Purta, J., Schwille, J. and Amadeo, J.-A. (eds) (1999) *Civic Education Across Countries: 24 Case Studies from the IEA Civic Education Project*, Amsterdam: Eburon Publishers for the International Association for the Evaluation of Educational Achievement (IEA).

Tsukuba Association for International Education (1998) *Education in Japan: Present System and Tasks/Curriculum and Instruction*, Tokyo: Gakken.

Williams, M. (1997) 'Place and identity: local, national and global', in *Proceedings of the International Geographical Union Commission on Geographical Education Conference*, London: University of London Institute of Education, pp. 15–19.

Chapter 4

Values and values education in the geography curriculum in relation to concepts of citizenship

Frances Slater

Introduction

In this chapter I selectively review developments in the school geography curriculum over a period of thirty years in order to highlight the role of values in geography education and the contribution of geography to the values education of young people. My overall purpose is to provide a values and values education context for understanding the promotion of 'citizenship' through geography education. I describe, therefore, some of the conceptual changes and developments in both geography and citizenship since the 1970s, which, it will be shown, intertwine and enrich each other. It will be suggested that geography provides an education in values and value-laden issues of significance to concepts of citizenship, and that citizens need geographical knowledge and under-standing.

In a recent article on the school journey movement, Marsden (1998) describes the innovatory contribution of G.G. Lewis in the late 1800s and early 1900s. He credits Lewis with introducing a range of creative ideas and a teaching method which he, Lewis, presumably believed to be of value and significant to learning. Within the particular historical setting of colonisation, a geography of new lands and oceans and a geographical imagination informed by imperialism (Morgan, 2000), boys are engaged in an outdoor simulation which requires decisions about priorities and making choices based on those priorities. Fit decisions for citizens of an empire. Some features of the environment and its relationship to people, exploration and settlement are valued more than others. Resources for livelihood and trade are greatly valued and built into the task. Lewis's simulation speaks to any geography teacher, even today.

Here is a scenario laying out the elements of spatial and people/environment approaches to geography, and proceeding as a teacher-structured inquiry (Roberts, 1995). Lewis gave priority to, and placed value upon, a geography lesson set outdoors, using an active inquiry format as a teaching/learning method, and geography as a place-bound people/environment study encompassing spatial relations and contextualised in a particular historical period. Thus, values in geography and in geography teaching are not new. Neither is citizenship education a new demand made of geography education.

Geography's substance as value-laden and its contribution to the development of citizens

The relationship between values and geography, at one level, lies partly in the fact that the substance, or the content making up that broad study we call geography in all its ideological guises, has only developed because people have given that substance a significance and decided it has a value. Its knowledge and understanding are judged to be interesting, important or illuminating by those engaged in the study, and to those gatekeepers over the years who have admitted geography and other subjects into university and school curricula. The development and acceptance of geography as a subject indicate a presupposition of its conceptual value. Subjects are in the curriculum because they are so valued. It can be said that to study geography, or history, or mathematics, is a kind of values education since it is an initiation into knowledge and understanding valued and privileged in those subjects as subjects.

An education in geography is both a cognitive and a value-laden affair through the very selection of what we study and on what we exercise our cognitive faculties. We are engaged in what is fundamentally a value-loaded content and analysis. This is very clear if one thinks of the ideological frameworks for geography. Advocacy of one over another is a debate about values, a debate about means and ends. All geography, and indeed all education, is about values and preferences to do with means and ends. We engage in education either to support the *status quo* or to question it to varying degrees. Within the debate lies a strong moral dimension too: what ought we to be studying, and towards what ends? And so politicians get involved in the debates about educational means and ends as they formulate their views and policies on the goals of education. Education is value-laden, a minefield and always has been. Monica J. Taylor (1998) includes a very useful list (Box 4.1) illustrating a constellation of areas where values enter into, and need to be recognised as entering into, education and schooling (though environmental education does not get included). Within each of the areas specified, geographical matters may be made to count, as other chapters in this book will spell out. It is important to note that no subject is named as 'values education' in the box. The box may be seen as a generalist view of the nature and place of values education. This point will be taken up again later.

Thus, geography in education, like all subjects, is not neutral. Its substance, as one source of its value-ladenness, does not stand apart from our constructions and interpretations of spatial and environmental relations. So geography is shot through with a values bias, linked among other things, to people's experience, perception and conception of their environment, how they evaluate it and seek to live in it as geographically and politically literate citizens.

Geographers as good citizens: examples of bias in substance

A current example of the values bias in the substance of geography is the dominance of the hazard school of geography. The study of floods as hazards of nature, as nuisance, as disaster, as feared and fearful is thought to be important and worthwhile. Undoubtedly, great quantities of excess water unexpectedly flowing over densely

---

> ### Box 4.1 Values, values education and values in education: some definitions
>
> - **What are 'values'?**
> A suggested working definition of 'values' is: 'principles, fundamental convictions, ideals, standards or life stances which act as general guides to behaviour or as reference points in decision-making or the evaluation of beliefs or action . . .' (Halstead, 1996, p. 5). For individuals, including teachers, values are 'closely connected to personal identity and integrity' (p. 5). Schools are also concerned with the values which the school promotes as a learning community.
>
> - **What is 'values education'?**
> This is a relatively new umbrella term for a range of common curriculum experiences: spiritual, moral, social and cultural education; personal and social education; religious education; multicultural/antiracist education; cross-curricular themes, especially citizenship, environment and health; pastoral care; school ethos; extra-curricular activities; wider community links; collective worship/assembly; the life of the school as a learning community.
>
> - **What are 'values in education'?**
> These are the values which a school adopts. Values are conveyed in teaching and learning processes. Values are embedded in school structures, management, policies, language and relationships. Values can be both explicit and implicit. They can be 'substantive values' (such as reflection, caring). Values in school reflect the values and structures of society, of the education system, the National Curriculum, inspection and assessment.
>
> Source: M. Taylor, *Values, Values, Education: a Guide to the Issues*, commissioned by the Association of University Teachers and Lecturers (London: ATL); used with permission.

urbanised areas with underground as well as overground infrastructure is undesirable, a nuisance and a disaster. That is how we see it; it costs money, time and effort to restore the 'normal' environment.

Yet this is not the full story, as Charles Namafe's research has shown (Namafe, 1997). One day, immersed in hazards thinking during a year at McGill University, Charles quite suddenly saw himself walking with an uncle in Bulozi, a region in western Zambia. The land was flooded or about to be flooded. His uncle was happy, happy to welcome the annual flood as it reclaimed its territory. Celebrations would take place. The water would be viewed as a great garment covering the floodplain; it would be seen as a guest in the village space for a period; it would allow the seasonal activities of fishing and canoeing. It was seen to be a friend to be welcomed and enjoyed, a benefactor. His uncle's attitudes to flooding and the values informing those attitudes suddenly made Charles think, and think again, about his academic geography.

The hazard school, Charles suggests, derives from a view of floods as always and implacably enemies (Namafe, 1997). His reading led him to believe that the West since the Middle Ages, and the Dutch culture in particular, have consistently regarded water as a most dangerous and threatening enemy. The Dutch, quite understandably, regard saline floodwaters from the North Sea as their enemy. However, such an 'enemy worldview' is one which has been diffused globally into contexts and cultures very different from their own flood-threatened land. A view which sees all water control as an imperative grew out of the Dutch predicament, he argues. Yet people have fought for their water-based activities against reclamation and drainage projects through the ages.

Through his personal re-evaluation of floods and further research work, involving as it did other people and their thoughts on floods, it could be suggested that Charles Namafe has been what might be called a good citizen and contributed to the concept of an educated citizenry through his contribution to geography education. He has helped from his position in Bulozi culture to expose a values bias. He is not the only person involved in a re-evaluation of floods and their advantages and disadvantages. Other people in higher education institutions are increasingly putting the case for interfering less with nature (see for example Wharton, 2000). Charles's work is cited in this chapter because it lets me make the point of geography's value-ladenness dramatically, even colourfully perhaps, as we think of a regular seasonal flood in Bulozi covering its floodplain like a garment and being welcomed by people in celebration.

Another piece of recent research in geography education similarly exposed a values bias or distortion. Julian Agyeman had long had an interest in plants. He had specialised in his degree work in biogeography. Sensitive, too, to living in a multicultural society, he had been disturbed for quite some time by the ubiquitous references, in the botanical world, to introduced plants as aliens and foreigners. He saw this as having implication, by analogy, for immigrants and the children of immigrants making up the mosaic of multicultural Britain. He worked with some local authorities in London and with botanists personally to try to change the exclusiveness of the language. He noted with concern articles in the quality press which used headlines like those shown in Figure 4.1. He wrote a book about the history and use of some introduced plants and developed the idea of multicultural gardens in school grounds and elsewhere which would include plant species from around the world (Agyeman, 1995). Some schools took up the idea, as did some local authorities. At a basic level, Julian was reacting to a bias he heard in language. Through the work he was able to do, as an education adviser and as a researcher, Julian might also be classified as a good citizen contributing to an educated public. He was re-evaluating an aspect of the culture of botany and acting in geography's world and the wider world of local government and publishing to encourage a change, an essential change for multicultural and good citizenship ends.

The gap between ideals and their execution

The connection between exposing a values bias and making a difference within geography education as to how the world is portrayed and received by its students is not a simple one, however. Rob Gilbert as long ago as 1984 was questioning, in a textbook analysis, the extent to which social science subjects achieved an emancipatory

NATURE

Invaders from the lost world

PAUL EVANS asks how we cope with the beast of Bodmin Moor and other aliens

An alien response

The Guardian
Thursday 6 July 1995

● ● ● ● ● ● ● ● ● ● ● ● ● ● ● ● ● ● ● ●

OFF LINE MAREK KOHN

Ducking the tricky issue of racial purity

17 MAY 1992   ✈ THE INDEPENDENT ON SUNDAY

Ferocious, fast-growing foreign plants and weeds now pose a serious threat to our countryside. **Nicholas Schoon** reports

Encroaching foreigners, the villainous and the benign (left to right): chief villain Japanese knotweed (*Reynoutria japonica*; giant hogweed (*Heracleum mantegazzianum*), bracken (*Pteridium aquilinum*), Himalayan balsam (*Impatiens glandulifera*), acceptable aliens Oxford ragwort (*Senecio squalidus*) and gallant soldier (*Galinsoga parviflora*), rhododendron (*Rhododendron ponticum*) and Japanese seaweed (*Sargassum muticum*)

The barbarians in Britain's back yards

Figure 4.1
Some headlines relating to plants and notions of 'invasion'

Sources: *Guardian*, 6 July 1995; Nicholas Schoon, 'The barbarians in Britain's back yards', *The Independent on Sunday*, 17 May 1992.

understanding of society. He suggested that ideological slants, language and choice of concepts signalled as significant impeded a questioning of the *status quo* and therefore limited the development of a critical citizenship. Others, like Dawn Gill, John Huckle and David Wright, followed the same line of questioning and were in effect, challenging geography's values. More recently, in classroom-based research, Mark Rickinson found evidence of that perennial problem in teaching and learning to do with the congruence between what we set out to achieve and what is actually achieved. The main argument of his thesis (Rickinson, 1999) is that the subject matter tasks of environmental geography lessons are not only carefully constructed and enacted by teachers, *but are also variously experienced and evaluated by students*. Students can misunderstand substantive and procedural matters and/or reject them as appropriate or not to the framework *they* hold of geography and its purposes. At one level, Namafe and Agyeman can shake our cognitive structures, and inform our lesson planning, while at another level the curriculum has to be accepted as 'the events that students and teachers jointly construct in classroom settings' (Doyle, 1992). In other words, there are many intervening variables between the careful working up of lessons and units of work by teachers and student engagement and understanding. Good citizenship, in the sense I have used it above as an expansion and clarification of concepts and values, can be ignored, rejected and questioned by pupils from their own framework of knowledge and expectations.

Concepts of citizenship – or an 'empty concept'?

I need to emphasise that I do not mean that Charles Namafe and Julian Agyeman have been good citizens in what might be labelled as a traditional meaning. Meryl Welsh points out, in her 1978 study 'The contribution of geography to citizenship education', that for more than half of the twentieth century the prevailing concept of a good citizen was held to be one motivated by 'humility, service, restraint, and respect'. This traditional view of citizenship required obedience to rules and respect for authority which encouraged the socialisation of pupils into a passive political role, limiting political activity mainly to voting at elections. Such a consensus view of citizenship, as she pointed out, actually ignores the controversial nature of politics.

Chapter 2 in this collection, by Bill Marsden, has already evaluated geography's contribution to citizenship education and education for democracy. In this chapter, I therefore make only brief references of this kind, in order to set the scene for the most recent periods of recognising values in geography education. For example, from the 1920s:

> Never before was it so necessary that our future citizens should view a world as a whole, that they should see that various lands and peoples have different contributions to make and that all must act and react to each other with ever increasing force. We do not wish to handle in the classroom, political problems as such, but we seek to give the pupils such a training in the geographers' characteristic mode of thought that as citizens they will be better able to find more satisfactory solutions. To no people is a sound knowledge of geography more important than to the British with their far-flung empire and world-wide interests. Many of the home and international problems can be solved only by those who have some training.
>
> (Barker, 1927: 188–9)

Barker's statement gives voice to the prevailing ethos of the period pre-Second World War. Inevitably, there is considerable spillage of such an ethos beyond that time. Today, such statements would omit reference to empire and world-wide interests and speak of the imperatives of the global economy and the need to compete in it. It is a question of 'spin'. The motives, however, may not have changed. Some would want environment and sustainability as the key concepts, others more culturally based postmodern concerns for young citizens. Post-war, the social studies movement initially took up the cause of citizenship but the twin roles of geography and history in the making of a good citizen were acknowledged. At this time the concept suggested an educated person in a democratic society acting autonomously, knowing her/his rights and privileges and acting co-operatively. This concept, an advance on earlier ones, was subsequently to be enlarged too. The changes in the meaning of citizenship which have taken place over the century demonstrate the 'emptiness' of the concept. We load it with meaning, and change those meanings as groups in society put forward their competing beliefs and aspirations. For geography teachers, two developments are particularly significant in this story of change: first, the development and recognition of values in geography teaching since the 1960s and, second, its resulting contribution to concepts of citizenship education. One such concept, which lies outside geography teaching, will be dealt with first. The second, which lies within geography, will be discussed in the following section, 'Changes in geography'.

For those located outside geography and concerned with citizenship education, a distinct shift in emphasis from the 'good citizen' approach to a more sophisticated view of 'politically literate' and 'active citizens' has taken place. As Britain became an increasingly pluralistic society, a reinterpretation of citizenship education was inevitable. The activities of the Politics Association, founded in September 1969 as a pressure group for introducing politics into schools, provided much criticism of past attempts at citizenship education, both in the form of civics, involving the study of the constitution, and also in the form of indirect teaching for citizenship through a study of history and geography. Alternative strategies were put forward for improving political education in schools. In 1975, Crick (who was later to chair the Advisory Group on citizenship – QCA, 1998b) suggested that 'politics is the creative conciliation of different interests, whether interests are seen as primarily material or moral', and that 'the political part of education is primarily, as in any possible moral education, an education in what different viewpoints are held, who holds them, why, in what context and with what restraints'. He believed that an effective citizenry could not be seen in terms of good, dutiful, deferential citizens but in terms of a citizenry which is politically literate in the knowledge, skills and attitudes necessary to understand and influence political decisions. In such a view of citizenship, the necessary ingredients were spelled out as a knowledge of the basic political concepts, a positive attitude towards procedural values, appropriate cognitive skills to critically analyse and evaluate politically sensitive information, and action skills which would provide the capacity to participate in positive action in order to change political situations. This, inevitably, would involve pupils in a study of the main political issues of society, something usually avoided in traditional civics education. Political literacy was, as now, held to be also concerned with the development of moral autonomy. Moral development was considered central to political education, as evidenced in the strong overlap in the vocabularies of morals and politics, e.g. justice, welfare and authority (Entwhistle, 1974).

Entwhistle (1971) also felt that it was necessary to go further and arrange experiences in school for real democratic action by direct involvement with problems and including decision making. 'We have to recognise the limits of mere didactics in political education. In citizenship training, as with teaching any skill, we have to learn to recognise the importance of learning by doing.' This is a point taken up at greater length by Mary Biddulph in Chapter 12 of this book.

Changes in geography

While the concept of citizenship continued to be reconceptualised during the 1960s, this was also a period of conceptual and methodological change in geography which resulted in a more rigorous and scientific, objective 'value-free' approach. By the next decade, however, young geographers working in different frameworks, with different purposes, were more concerned with issues relevant to human welfare, environmental manage- ment and social justice – all matters relevant to good citizenship and political literacy. For example, geography and geographers became concerned with political issues and issues of a social, economic and moral kind which underlie the political. The contro- versial nature of what might be called the 'geographies of relevance' brought geographers into politics, and there is little doubt that an increased political, moral and social consciousness was characteristic of many geographers working in the 1970s. Such a consciousness continues among a number today, and they still argue that geographers should view their role as 'agents or instruments of social change'. Significant to such an attitude and belief was the question 'in what capacity should geographers act as agents of social change?' A number of alternatives, as Welsh (1978) pointed out, suggested themselves:

*   in an advisory or official capacity to those in power;
*   in a more powerful decision-making capacity, whereby the geographer, on account of his/her special knowledge, is directly involved in political decisions;
*   in the capacity of (i) critic, (ii) educator and (iii) autonomous researcher directing knowledge at those in power, at the public and at the younger generation.

Charles Namafe and Julian Agyeman came to their research in the late 1980s, strongly influenced by the geographies of relevance and the view that a university and university study should serve the community and its citizens. Charles's work was closely related to questions of water management and projected water schemes in Zambia. Julian's was within the power structure operating in the botanical community and in education in central London. In their research they can surely be judged to be acting in a citizen-like way as they worked and acted, with their geographical knowledge and understanding, in their professional capacity. They raised questions, re-evaluated understandings and developed fresh concepts such as floods as friends and flora as multicultural. They fit into the third alternative in the above list, if not yet into the first and second, though their professional lives are not yet over.

Though one must expect a certain time lag between geographical knowledge at the research frontier and its modification and use in schools, the controversial and public issues introduced into geography by the social relevance movement found their way into some teachers teaching fairly readily. That content also needed appropriate teaching methods for examining, analysing and debating such issues as planning in cities or social inequalities and deprivation in cities or underdevelopment in the developing world. People in geography education and those in curriculum development projects such as Geography for the Young School Leaver (GYSL) and Geography 16–19 acted as mediators and intermediaries for teachers in schools and their practices. Messages about values education strategies from the US educational literature found their way into geography education writing in Britain. The Institute of Education appointed its first lecturer in politics in 1977 and gradually one became aware of the thinking of Alex Porter and of Bernard Crick. Related closely, at first, to scientific geography and a sense of problem solving, the introduction of games and simulation in all their value-ladenness was another pathway by which values education permeated geography in education. Some wrote on prejudice, others on paternalism, others on bias, race and gender. I give here only the briefest sense of some of the influences and research impinging on the core of geography teaching at that time. A most necessary adjunct to the growing social and environmental consciousness among geography teachers was an identification of strategies which were appropriate to values analysis and debate and, at this time, they were so identified sometimes with worked-through examples (Welsh, 1978; Huckle, 1981; Slater, 1982; Fien and Slater, 1985). Huckle (1981) provided a table based on Superka *et al.* (1976) of values education approaches which is reproduced here to give a sense of the concepts and resources then available and in use (see Table 4.1). Slater (1982) used the same source and classification and then with John Fien (1985) raised concerns about the danger of superficiality in using values education strategies. It is a concern again taken up by Lambert (1999).

Besides developments in academic geography there were trends in environmental and developmental issues which also helped to heighten political and social awareness within geography education. Welsh (1978) suggests that much of the impetus for school pupils' involvement in environmental issues came not from geographers but from planners. The Town and Country Planning Act, 1968, provided a statutory extension of citizens' rights and reflected public demand for participation in planning and provided guidelines for achieving active participation. The Town and Country Planning Association (TCPA) stressed the need to train teachers on how to encourage environmental awareness among pupils. The work of Colin Ward and Tony Fyson appointed by the TCPA in 1971 to initiate a teachers' service and a monthly journal had a marked effect on geography teaching in some schools. The establishment of Urban Studies Centres (USC) brought city environments into focus and a number of influential geography teachers and geography educators strongly backed the TCPA and USC movement.

World environmental issues then, as now, impinged upon and were incorporated into geography teaching by some, and the Belgrade Charter (1975) was a historic landmark and justification for environmental geography on the world scale. The Charter recognised that environmental education had an important part to play in eradicating the basic causes of poverty, the unequal distribution of wealth, hunger, illiteracy, pollution, exploitation and the deterioration of the biosphere. A radical and values-conscious agenda for socially committed geography teachers emerged, and the social relevance research and movements in the wider society nicely reinforced one another.

Table 4.1 Values education approaches

Approach	Purposes	Methods
Analysis	To help students use logical thinking and scientific investigation to decide value issues and questions To help students use rational, analytical processes in interrelating and conceptualising their values	Structured rational discussion that demands application of reasons as well as evidence; testing principles; analysing analogous cases; debate; research
Moral development	To help students develop more complex moral reasoning patterns based on a higher set of values To urge students to discuss the reasons for their value choices and positions, not merely to share with others, but to foster change in their stages of reasoning	Moral dilemma episodes with small-group discussion relatively structured and argumentative
Clarification	To help students become aware of and identify their own values and those of others To help students communicate openly and honestly with others about their values To help students use both rational thinking and emotional awareness to examine their personal feelings, values and behaviour patterns	Role-playing games; simulations; contrived or real value-laden situations; in-depth self-analysis exercises; sensitivity activities out-of-class activities; small-group discussion
Action learning	Those purposes listed for analysis and clarification To provide students with opportunities for personal and social action based on their values To encourage students to view themselves as personal-social interactive beings, not fully autonomous, but members of a community or social system	The methods listed for analysis and clarification as well as action projects within the school and community and skill practice in group organising and interpersonal relations

Source: Huckle (1981).

Local Agenda 21 from the Rio Summit can do the same today and thus contribute to citizenship education.

Alongside increasing environmental awareness went reconceptualisations of development and economy. Radical and conservative explanations conflicted, and without a doubt some geography teachers found ways to include the debate in the curriculum and textbooks. Some felt the debate was unbalanced and that imbalance of views remains today. John Hopkin (1998) recently researched the content of a group of secondary school texts written for the national curriculum. He found that some presented a view of development as modernisation, a Rostovian stages-of-development view, while others promoted alternative and less mainstream ideas. None, however, presented *both* in the form of arguments critiquing the ideas. There has tended to be a bias towards giving either conservative economic explanations or radical historical/economic ones, but not both as alternative understandings of economic development. This is an important realisation, for an under-education in argument and arguments does not help the development of a critical mind and an educated citizenry.

The aid agencies in the 1970s, as now, provided a range of materials which raised political, economic and social questions. A good number of geography teachers used the materials and so introduced controversial questions about development and environment to pupils. The availability of these resources helped to reinforce and diffuse concepts like social justice and spatial inequalities and so raise the level of argument in geography classrooms among young citizens.

Some teachers began to ask questions about the attitudes and values present in geography curricula, particularly in relation to colonisation and views of the Third World, its peoples and cultures. Dawn Gill and David Wright stand out in this respect. They contributed to the explosion of a values awareness of the subject, just as others did in their concern about the invisibility of girls and women in texts and subject content. Others working outside geography like David Hicks and Derek Heater were also influential with some teachers, who incorporated their viewpoints on the importance of such themes as peace and global perspectives into their curriculum.

In the 1970s and 1980s, an explicit recognition of the values dimension in geography developed and was consolidated. The values inquiry, analysis and clarification which formed part of units of work on cities incorporating notions of social justice, on the Amazon Basin incorporating notions of environmentalism, or on trade, aid and development in Africa incorporating notions of human rights and social justice, were generally accepted as lying at the core of geography's educative potential. Crucially there were an increasing number of approaches and strategies available. It is probably true to say that the phrase 'values education', characterised by the use of certain teaching strategies, began to be frequently used in geography in the 1970s, though the phrase itself came from the social studies movement in the USA. Geography teachers – some anyway – had their meaning of 'values education' which can be set alongside that in Box 4.1. It can also be claimed that the strategies were central to citizenship development.

The extent of values work in geography

Today, values education (in the sense of educating pupils to recognise the value-ladenness of issues; to recognise values inherent in viewpoints; to recognise values bias; and to reflect critically upon such matters) has made considerable progress. In the absence of large and detailed surveys one cannot be sure about the full extent of the acceptance of geography as values education or of geography contributing to values education. There is a body of teachers in every decade who, for a number of reasons, do not wish to bring politics into geography, and so do not acknowledge its inevitable presence or deal with controversial issues in the classroom. Some still believe geography to be essentially 'substance', its procedures being values-neutral; they treat it and write it as if it were so. However, it would be reasonable to suppose that geography as a vehicle for an education in values, as well as in concepts and principles, is much more widespread and accepted than at the beginning of the 1970s. At the time of the much publicised excision of statements relating to values from the first national curriculum, a London teacher said, in an unpublished interview, that he judged the view that the national curriculum attainment target of environmental education could carry all of the values dimension in geography as

> a narrow and inadequate view of what attitudes and values are about. We do work in year 9 on India and get our pupils to do a travel brochure for India which says a lot of wonderful things about India. Now that is informing on attitudes and values massively.

Later in the same interview, the teacher indicated that in planning for each year the geography team looked at all the statements of attainments and tried to group them into modules. They then sat down to plan each module and looked at the minimum that they had to do in order to fulfil the national curriculum. In a second stage, they proceeded to include role plays and simulations and other work on values and attitudes because these were considered essential.

But what are the values in geography? In a 1992 workshop, a group of teachers gave the following list of values in geography (Slater, 1994):

- care for the environment;
- human rights;
- justice – social/political/economic;
- appropriateness to a culture/society;
- respect for other cultures;
- preserving landscape quality;
- use/misuse/sustainability;
- absence of exploitation;
- empathy for cultures and environments;
- responsibility towards the environment.

It may be noted here that geography teachers then, and now, claim to promote values of an aesthetic kind, as 'preserving landscape quality' suggests. This value, as much as those to do with social justice and sustainability, is of relevance to citizenship, though less is made of this aspect in official documents.

The contribution of values in geography to an education in values is further strongly signalled in the amount of review and research work which geography teachers and educators have undertaken, often in Master's dissertations. Such work has, for example, illustrated and examined the values:

- presupposed in a study of geography;
- contained in the substance of geography, its ideology and methodology;

- contained in such significant concepts to geography as region, environment, development, sustainability;
- present in teaching approaches and methods;
- present in geography as a function of its embeddedness in particular societies (that is its imperial bias, its bias towards masculinity, for example), in text and textbook approaches and language generally;
- brought into the classroom by children in their attitudes towards environment, development, other peoples, teaching methods and so on (Slater, 1995).

We can illustrate the possibilities of such research through an examination of some work undertaken with sixth-form students. Martin Cox's Master's dissertation is a useful example of values education in the geography curriculum and a good example of a teacher's contribution to an educated public and citizenry. His work touches upon some of the values students bring with them to the geography classrooms, some of the values addressed in the 16–19 curriculum, the teacher's values and the conflict of values at work in the individual students and how this relates to their role in society (Cox, 1993).

Martin had been teaching geography in London schools for a number of years and, as an experienced teacher, he decided to study for a Master's degree which included an extended piece of research. He writes:

> During an 'A' level class one of my students remarked, '. . . not another save the whale lesson!' This was a remark which I felt that I could not ignore. Some twelve months later another student made a similar comment when he said '. . . is this going to be one of those save the gay whale lessons?' Such a sharp quip, although intended to be humorous, did suggest that green issues are part of a broader paradigm of beliefs. As far as my perceptive student was concerned, it was not enough to simply care for endangered species but . . . one has to be liberal and tolerant too.
>
> (Cox, 1993)

These remarks, and a number of lectures addressing concepts of environmentalism within the MA course, influenced the research investigation he decided on. He wanted to come to some understanding of the extent to which environmental concerns influenced the culture and lifestyle of twenty-five 'A' level geography students following the 16–19 'A' level in a boys' comprehensive school in south London. The students were asked 'What do you consider to be the most important issue facing the world today?' Table 4.2 shows the dominance of concern for the environment or a related issue. In informal conversations later many students said they felt that the environment was the issue, the issue of their age.

As a preliminary to the main research question, Cox, during interviews with the students, had them indicate what they considered to be sources of reliable information on the environment. This was followed by a supplementary question on how helpful they found their work in geography in enabling an understanding of environment issues. Zubair, a student in the upper sixth, made the following comment: '*Forty to fifty per cent of my knowledge of environmental issues comes from Geography. I know a heck of a lot more now than before doing Geography.*'

Table 4.2 Students' views on global issues

What do you consider to be the most important issue facing the world today?

The environment	13
Pollution	5
Global warming	2
World hunger	2
War/World peace	3
Total	25 student responses

Source: Cox (1993).

Chris's reply as reported by Cox was even stronger:

> '*I think that Geography is the only real source of information for environmental issues. I think that if I didn't do Geography "A" level there would be a big gap in my knowledge and understanding of the environment. To be honest, I don't think that the work we did in science for GCSE covered anything on environmental issues.*'

Colm, described as an 'able' student, illustrates an appreciation of geography and examining issues in context.

> '*I'm glad that I took Geography. It really has increased my perception of environmental problems and issues. For example, we need to think things through, solving the environmental problems may only cause other more serious problems. I always used to think that H.E.P. was the great saviour, but now I find that it ruins estuaries and things.*'

Jeremy was ambivalent, but on balance appreciative:

> '*Doing Geography enables you to become more aware. Some of the students who come to this school are serious "townies"; and they don't know what it's like to be in the countryside until they go out on fieldtrips and see the ways in which the countryside is being ruined. Also on trips they can see what is available in their own country and feel that it is worth protecting.*'

Quite clearly geography's subject matter is known to be value-laden. As the interviews proceeded, Martin asked questions probing the nature of the students' present and expected adult lifestyle. Many were uneasy about the relationship between their own lifestyle and environmental considerations. Jason said: '*To tell the truth, I haven't made any major changes in my life-style to help the environment, I have made minor ones which include recycling paper and bottles. I don't use anything [with] C.F.C.*'
All of the students in fact felt that their contributions to environmental matters were small and inadequate.

> '*I've tried to persuade my mum to go for greener products and I've gone around turning off the lights and things. Just small changes really.*' (Andrew)

> '*I do things such as take old cans and bottles to the bins provided so that they can be recycled. I try to like never drop litter as I did before I did the "A" level.*' (Matthew)

'I have tried to make changes in my life, for example, I do try to save water but nothing major.' (David)

When asked if they avoided buying certain products because of their contribution to environmental problems, Gavin said:

> *'I make every effort to not buy junk food such as McDonald's. I know that they are very popular among others in my year who often meet in McDonald's when they can. I don't think that people fully realise the damage that is being done to large areas of rainforest. I have managed to persuade some of my friends not to go to McDonald's.'*

Others raised the problem of packaging: *'I think . . . I would be prepared to buy goods that are not overpacked; things like that do bother me. I avoid buying "Duracell" batteries because they seem to be unnecessarily overpackaged.'* (Colm)

There was a certain amount of evidence in replies to suggest the development of responsible eco-friendly consumers and a sensitivity towards the environmental record of companies. One of the least environmentally concerned said: *'If I knew of a particular company that had been having a bad press then, sure, I wouldn't continue to buy goods from them.'* On the other hand, another stated: *'I don't have a preference for any company for its environmental record. I think that it's fair to say that most companies are bad for the environment.'* Overall, a number of large companies were seen negatively in relation to the environment.

Questions of car ownership showed real tension in the students between their environmental understanding and the teenage culture of car ownership and their future lifestyle and social status aspirations. Every student admitted to already owning a car or expecting to own one as an adult:

> *'I am a car user. I think that some times when I'm driving about that I'm wasting valuable energy.'* (Chris)

> *'I've said to my Dad loads of times that it's bad for you to keep driving about. All the gases produced by cars are a serious problem but you have to have a car, it's a materialistic world – you've got to do it, it's part of life!'* (Zubair)

Jeremy wanted technology to solve the problem:

> *'It's inevitable that I'm going to have a car. It's not environmentally friendly but to a certain extent you have to leave it up to the manufacturers to put in all the environmental features like a "cat" [catalytic converter] or a lean burn engine that uses hardly any fuel at all. I think that we should all use hydrogen powered cars because all you would get is water coming out of the exhaust.'*

Drawing from his reading of the evidence gathered, Martin Cox concluded that

> the data contained in this case study indicates that 'A' level geography students often do have a very good technical understanding of environmental issues and in many cases are able to empathise with the natural world. However, among this small group of students the most significant conclusion is that many young people are not able to translate their concern for the environment into significant social action.

Most geography teachers in England and Wales would recognise the teaching and learning going on in Cox's classroom as central to the aims of geography teaching today. Those concerned with promoting citizenship would see the topic as significant too. Geography's particular environmental, as well as spatial, cultural and place, concerns are part of its intrinsic interest and achievements. The development of such concepts and their significance are among its contribution to the mind of an educated person and the understanding needed of well-informed citizens able to appreciate the dilemmas in decision making.

The tension between generalists and specialists in political education

An educational system needs both the concepts developed through subject knowledge (including skills and values) *and* those informed by broad educational aims. The terms in which the latter are expressed multiply, as people try to convey their importance in all subjects and so across the curriculum. Areas of experience, cross-curriculum themes, permeation, common curriculum experiences are some of the terms used (see Box 4.1 again). It is easy to present the curriculum in a conflictual sense when the broad aims of education are juxtaposed with subject-tied aims and objectives. It is easy, for example, for people outside subjects to feel they are saying something entirely new, or that they are bringing something into existence, when they suggest that environmental education or cultural education – or indeed citizenship education – should be common curriculum experiences or whole school policies.

Generalist views and specialist views of education are for ever views from different locations. It behoves the generalists to have a detailed and up-to-date knowledge of what subjects offer, just as it behoves the specialists to be sensitive to the broader possibilities of education relating to society's aims and needs. The metaphor of a *conversation* is useful as a way of bringing together general and particular aims, and the thinking of people in different locations. The emphasis on citizenship in this book, as an important general outcome of a largely subject-structured curriculum, encourages such a conversation between the particularities of learning offered by studying geography and the desired goal of active citizenship as presently defined. The 'conversation' should help to achieve congruence between specific subjects and general aims.

With this metaphor in mind we can now go on to examine in some detail political education and political literacy and their impact on geography teachers. *Political Education and Political Literacy*, edited by Crick and Porter in 1978 (with echoes in Huckle's (1981) early work), engages with the 'conversation' between school subjects (including geography) and general educational aims, including political and citizenship ideas. This dialogue played an important part in the growing understanding of citizenship that was held by geography teachers as they openly tackled the value-ladenness of geography. Crick and Porter (1978: 96) gave a new definition of political literacy that went beyond earlier concepts of political education and citizenship to include the knowledge, skills and attitudes necessary to make people able to apply their political literacy effectively in political settings:

A politically literate person would not only have a high level of understanding of a given context and situation, but would be able to operate efficiently within that context and situation. This would involve having notions of policy, of policy objectives, and an ability to recognise how well policy objectives had been achieved as well as being able to comprehend those of others. Political literacy is not simply an ability to pursue even an enlightened self-interest: it must comprehend the effects on others and their viewpoints, and respond to them morally.

A study of basic concepts like power, force, authority, natural rights, freedom and welfare, to mention a few, were laid out as necessary for the development of a politically literate person. Crick argued that with a sketch map of such basic concepts a pupil would be better able to order and relate the disparate problems and issues of the real political world. In addition, the means to achieving an understanding of such concepts within particular issues and contexts were spelled out in a set of *procedural values*. Along with the importance of a sense of freedom, a tolerance for other views, a concept of fairness, respect for truth and respect for reasoning were all emphasised. These latter two procedural values particularly played their part in 'inquiry learning' procedures which in some geography classrooms involved decision-making exercises and debates.

The prospect of bringing politics into the classroom made some teachers worry a great deal about accusations of indoctrination, and it seemed to be very difficult to remove this fear. Proceeding rationally, for example using Snook's (1972) *Indoctrination and Education* in MA seminars as a basis for weighing up notions of indoctrination, had little effect on teachers not already committed to teaching controversial issues. And yet, 'a person indoctrinates P (a proposition or set of propositions) if he teaches with the intention that the pupil or pupils believe P regardless of the evidence' (Snook, 1972). Perhaps the idea of intending or not intending was too abstract for teachers to feel happy about as a defence.

Stradling *et al.*'s (1984) four teaching approaches to controversial issues were usually received with more sympathy (Figure 4.2). Teachers not convinced that indoctrination could turn on a question of intention in practice, or that this could be a defence against a hostile headteacher or parent, found Stradling's four positions more concrete and practical in view and explanation, and closer to familiar ideas (sometimes already part of their practice). Stradling's four alternatives, therefore, became important stances for teachers exploring attitudes and values. Their acceptance by some geography teachers helped the conversation between geography teaching and citizenship, and it is very likely that they will continue to do so in this present era of citizenship education.

Another strategy incorporated into geography was Alex Porter's strategy of 'detecting', 'correcting' and 'creating' *bias*. Subsequently, Peter Fry (1987) developed an exercise for geography students under these categories and took students through a values recognition inquiry, using accounts of acid rain put out by different authorities. Recently, Lester (1995) has called into question the ability to write bias out of texts and has suggested that teaching students to read and critique argument is a sounder pedagogy.

Values and contemporary curriculum debates

In the late 1990s Bernard Crick chaired the Advisory Group on Citizenship (QCA, 1998b). Its report, while holding to the concept of political literacy developed earlier, added two other strands, one to do with socially and morally responsible behaviour, and

Potential strengths		Potential weaknesses
• Minimizes undue influence of teacher's own bias. • Gives everyone a chance to take part in free discussion. • Scope for open-ended discussion, i.e. the class may move on to consider issues and questions which the teacher hasn't thought of • Presents a good opportunity for students to exercise communication skills. • Works well if you have a lot of background material	*Procedural Neutrality* *In which the teacher adopts the role of an Impartial chairperson of a discussion group.*	• Students find it artificial. • Can damage the rapport between teacher and class if it doesn't work. • Depends on students being familiar with the method elsewhere in the school or it will take a long time to acclimatize them. • May only reinforce students' existing attitudes and prejudices. • Very difficult with the less able. • *Neutral* chair doesn't suit my personality.
• Students will try to guess what the teacher thinks anyway. Stating your own position makes everything above board. • If students know where the teacher stands on the issue they can discount his or her prejudices and biases. • It's better to state your preferences after discussion rather than before. • It should only be used if students' dissenting opinions are treated with respect. • It can be an excellent way of maintaining credibility with students since they do not expect us to be neutral.	*Stated Commitment* *In which the teacher always makes known his/her views during discussion.*	• It can stifle classroom discussion, inhibiting students from arguing a line against that of the teacher's. • It may encourage some students to argue strongly for something they don't believe in simply because it's different from the teacher. • Students often find it difficult to distinguish facts from values. It's even more difficult if the purveyor of facts and values is the same person, i.e. the teacher.
• Essential: I think one of the main functions of a humanities or social studies teacher is to show that issues are hardly ever black and white. • Necessary when the class is polarized on an issue. • Most useful when dealing with issues about which there is a great deal of conflicting information	*A Balaced Approach* *In which the teacher presents pupils with a wide range of alternative views.*	• Is there such a thing as a balnced range of opinions? • As a strategy it has limited use. it avoids the main point by conveying the impression that 'truth' is a grey area that exists between two alternative sets of opinions. • Balance means very different things to different people. The media's view of balnce is not mine. Teaching is rarely value-free. • This approach can lead to very teacher-directed lessons. Like media interviews you are always interrupting to maintain the so-called balance.
• Frequently used by me. Great fun, and can be very effective in stimulating the pupils to contribute to discussion. • Essential when faced by a group who all seem to share the same opinion. • Most classes which I have taught seem to have a majority line. Then I use this strategy and parody, exaggeration, and role reversal. • I often use this as a device to liven things up when the discussion is beginning to dry up.	*The Devil's Advocate Strategy* *In which the teacher conciously takes up the opposite position to the one expressed by pupils or in teaching materials.*	• I have run into all sorts of problems with this approach. Kids identifying me with the views I was putting forward as devil's advocate; parents worried about my alleged views, etc. • It may reinforce students' prejudices. • Only to be used when discussion dries up and there are still 25 minutes left.

Figure 4.2 Four teaching approaches to controversial issues

Source: R. Stradling, M. Noctor and B. Baines, *Teaching Controversial Issues* (London: Arnold, 1984). Reprinted by permission of Hodder & Stoughton Ltd.

the second to do with involvement in and service to the community. Geography's interest in local studies and global studies makes links to both these new strands possible.

Earlier documents (NCC, 1990) on citizenship were strongly attacked by Porter (1993) for their impoverished concepts and a sense of values inculcation, if not indoctrination, lurking beneath the surface. Yet it seems that the substantive and procedural values contained within the document and its *legitimation* of such values in the curriculum could do much to give confidence to and strengthen the beliefs of those teachers who accept geography as an exploration of values in controversial waters. Geography's conversation with citizenship education can be renewed and perhaps proceed and develop as fears of indoctrination recede. Statutory permission is in place for practices that many a liberal and radical geography teacher dreamed of and some practised.

The so-called 'Great Debate' in education started with the Prime Minister James Callaghan's speech of 1976. It has become a continuous debate marked by an increasing number of documents including national curriculum statutory documents in individual subjects issued by government. The continuing questioning and setting out of educational frameworks and goals in England and Wales at least constitute a debate about values and which ones education should support and realise. It is also a debate set among a variety of ideological positions. It was suggested earlier in this chapter that in the 1970s geography gained a great deal by explicitly recognising its values, both substantive and procedural, as a result of both developments within the discipline and influences from outside. The *Citizenship* document (QCA, 1998b), and alongside it the reports from the National Forum for Values and the earlier report *Spiritual, Moral, Social and Cultural Guidelines* (QCA, 1998a), provide support for those geography teachers who acknowledge the value-ladenness of, and potential for, values recognition, exploration, discussion and understanding in their subject. QCA (1998a) is clearly located in a generalist tradition, sketching out a framework using the concept of a whole school policy. It is more of a liberal document than a conservative or radical one, in my opinion. Crucially, it provides considerable scope for geography teachers to deal with controversial and public issues and, like the *Citizenship* document, legitimates the treatment of such issues. The National Forum on Values, in its identification of environment as one of just four groupings of values (with self, relationships and society), can also be read like a set of modules appropriate to a geography curriculum, where that curriculum is wittingly or unwittingly endorsed. Environmental geographers, including those of a radical persuasion, may see their position vindicated by these documents.

It is beyond the brief of this chapter to pick out in excessive detail the linkages between the geography curriculum and the sketches defining and describing spiritual, moral, social and cultural development, though I discuss moral factors on p. 61. The topics that find their place in a geography curriculum can reinforce and enhance SMSC concerns. Geographers as specialists can confidently converse with the generalists and demonstrate their particular contribution. Values education is in the geography curriculum in a very public and explicit way. The awe and wonder which can be promoted by experiences in the geography curriculum speak to the spiritual and the aesthetic, the multicultural and gender equity concerns relate to the cultural, and fieldwork and research projects may be related to concerns about the two former and about the social (Harvey, 1991). All meet each other in overlapping circles. A holistic view would not separate them out for long.

A detailed consideration of the geography curriculum specifications (dealt with more fully by Graham Butt in Chapter 5 of this volume) would find that values and attitudes are prominent. First, from the opening statement in the national curriculum document: 'Geography promotes the exploration of issues about the environment, development and society, and understanding of how these are affected by people's values and attitudes'. It is worthwhile to note the 'about'. The well-known phrases 'educating in the environment', 'for the environment', 'through the environment' or even 'with the environment' are not there. Ideologically, the use of 'about' could be interpreted as indicating a conservative view of geography's potential.

This may not necessarily be so, however. The latter part of the sentence, again conservative in tone as I hear it, widens the scope to allow all the concepts in the documents discussed above to be brought in. While heard as conservative, the statements, if interpreted in the interests of citizenship and spiritual, moral, social and cultural development, can be liberal and, indeed, radical. As a key element within skills, knowledge and understanding in each programme of study, values and attitudes are one of four key elements. This is a great advance on the first national curriculum for geography. Within the sections 'Geographical skills and enquiry' for Key Stages 2 and 3, decision making and problem solving are included as geographical inquiry skills. It is a taste of the developments of the 1970s and 1980s. Geography is ready to meet citizenship as political literacy and community involvement again. Indeed, the language and tone is of the 1970s and 1980s. No account has been taken of the postmodern turn and how subjects themselves may have changed, bringing new insights about culture and society. The potential for good environmental and development geography is there, however. The new can gradually be added in.

Within the strategies for values education (which came out of the USA in the 1970s) was one developed by Kohlberg (1984) and known as 'the moral dilemma'. The dilemma was easy to construct and I well remember persuading PGCE students to try Kohlberg's strategies as homework exercises if they hesitated to raise controversial matters in class. Developing moral understanding, that is being concerned with what is good or bad, right or wrong, has a dimension of the subjective about it. That is, our moral understanding is underpinned by our feelings of rightness or wrongness in conjunction with our cognitive knowledge and understanding. Reid (1986) believed that 'moral knowledge' was centred on people's holistic experiences of real situations and contexts which shaped to some extent their judgement of good and evil.

Graham Haydon has provided a list of the likely features that mark out moral values from other values. Geography teachers could well find his list reproduced in Box 4.2 useful for clarifying moral from other values.

There are many topics studied in geography which bring up the need to debate rightness and wrongness. People, migration and refugees was one such topic I elaborated on some time ago (Slater, 1994; see also Chapter 7 by Crispin Jones in this volume). We can deal with such topics in relation to the facts and figures, as statistics and flow diagrams, or we can add the human dimension, the dimension which brings our understanding and feelings together and asks 'Is it good/right, bad/wrong?' The activity sketched out at that time and reproduced in Box 4.3 may still be helpful as an example of a values inquiry incorporating the moral dimension. In having students work through it and others like it, geography can make a convincing claim to contribute to moral understanding as a dimension of citizenship.

Box 4.2 The likely features of moral values

- Some of your values have to do with the way people behave; not all of them do. What kinds of music you appreciate, for instance, will have a lot to do with your aesthetic values, but these will not necessarily say anything about how people are to behave. It won't necessarily follow, for instance, that your preference for one kind of music over another means that you think that everyone producing or listening to music *ought* to produce or listen to music only of that kind, or that they are doing something wrong if they don't.

- Following on from that, some of your values (unlike aesthetic ones, perhaps) may be ones you're inclined to express by using words such as 'ought' and 'ought not', 'right' and 'wrong'. Of course, this only begins to narrow down the field a bit; using these words doesn't necessarily mean you're expressing anything moral ('you ought not to do that calculation that way; you've got it wrong').

- Some of your values may be ones you consider to be particularly important, ones that in the end you would have to stand by, even if you were to give up on or compromise on all sorts of other things. . . .

- Some of your values you may think make claims on you, as it were, 'from outside', independently of how you happen to feel or what is convenient for you at a certain time. You might realize on a particular occasion, for instance, that it will smooth over a difficulty if you tell a lie; but the idea that you ought not to tell a lie may still be there, and you may feel that you can't just decide to ignore it.

- Some of your values you may think apply not just to you but to everyone (that is, they are 'universal'). Perhaps this will be the case just because you do feel that these values make some sort of claim 'from outside' (and so they can't be making that claim just on you). That one kind of music is better than another, you might think is a matter of preference – if not just you personal preference, then a cultural preference. After all, we're well aware that there are different musical traditions, and some of us acknowledge our ignorance about most of them. But some values – say, the wrongness of torture – you may think everyone *ought* to recognize, even if not everyone does.

- Some of your values may be ones which you don't think are just a matter of what you happen to prefer or choose. Suppose you do feel, as a general rule, that you ought not to tell lies (I won't get into the question now of whether there can or can't be exceptions). Still, you might say to yourself that this value is one you choose to acknowledge. When trying to think in general terms, people will often say that ultimately moral values are all a matter of choice or personal preference. Yet most people, at least, will not think that all of their preferences are on the same level

Source: Haydon (1998: 32).

Box 4.3 A dilemma concerning refugees

Mission blessed by Foreign Office then held at border by newly-imposed visa rule

Maggie O'Kane on the day-by-day saga of Alert's rescue convoy

October 30: Stephen Beesley, director of Alert, visits the Foreign Office and gives details of the trip

He says he is told that the Foreign Office admires the organisation's work and wishes him well on his trip.

November 3: Mr Beesley leaves for Slovenia to prepare for the fifth refugee convoy. Since September, the organisation has brought 472 refugees to Britain.

November 5: Home Secretary Kenneth Clark announces visas are necessary for all Bosnian passport holders.

November 8: Mr Beesley, alarmed by the visa requirement, contacts the Home Office and David Harrison of the Asylum Liaison Unit.

Mr Harrison suggests the buses are not sent out because of the new visa requirement. Mr Beesley replied that he would go ahead on the expectation Alert would get a letter of approval from the Red Cross that would qualify the refugees for admission.

Mr Beesley says that in the course of his phone call Mr Harrison said Alert was one of three groups approved by the Home Office and most likely to qualify to bring in refugees.

Last night the Home Office said Mr Harrison denies implying in any way that Alert would get special status.

November 8: Letter sent from the Red Cross states 'the 200 refugees with the Leeds European Refugee Trust will meet the United Kingdom criteria for asylum seekers who can be given entry visas as victims of war with desperate needs.'

It is signed by Hansrudi Brawand, Head of the Delegation Ljubljana. International Federation of ICRC and Red Crescent Societies, and nominated by the International Federation of the Red Cross in Geneva.

November 11: Refugees arrive by Red Cross coaches at the Werzen Pass on the Austrian/Slovenian border. Some have been on the road for two weeks.

Border guards instructed by Austrian authorities not to allow buses across, since Britain has not guaranteed entry for the refugees.

Frantic phone calls to London. Courier hired by Alert leaves Vienna with IM2A temporary visa application forms. Cost £185. Some 131 refugees and 60 British volunteers spend first night in the coaches.

November 12: British immigration office set up in a local tourist office by the volunteers. IM2A forms are completed by midnight with six volunteers working in shifts with interpreters.

The refugees include 54 women, 45 men and 82

children. Around 20 had been released from detention camps. All say they have lost their homes to Serbian forces. Three children need urgent medical treatment.

By nightfall the refugees are in hotels paid for by the Austrian government and unknown donors.

November 13: Visa forms are taken by car to the British embassy in Vienna and sent by diplomatic bag to London. A decision is expected by 11 am on Monday, November 16.

Most of the volunteers return home because of the delay.

November 16: Mr Beesley contacts London and is informed no decision is to be made until following day.

Mr Clarke announced in the Commons that only six refugees with relatives in Britain will be granted visas. Cases of two people waiting for medical treatment being reviewed.

November 17: The Home Office contacts Alert and says another eight refugees, a family of four orphans, a 17-year-old boy with a failed kidney, and his 14-year-old sister, will be reconsidered if they agree to pay hospital bills and provide proof they can do so.

Heavy snow begins to fall on the mountain.

Source: Slater (1994: 159).

continued

You are a keen student of geography and you are planning to do geography at A-level. Your teacher gave the above cutting out in November, 1992 as part of some work on migration and refugees. You also heard news reports on this particular refugee incident. You have had an extended discussion over several lunch times with two friends about the good solution, the right solution. One friend believes your country should not take any more refugees, the other believes more should be allowed to settle.

You decide to try to clarify your own thoughts and feelings on the situation by making some notes under the headings (1) Reasons For, (2) Reasons Against and (3) your feelings when faced with each of the points for and against.

You then use the notes to draft a letter to your local MP giving her or him an outline of your thinking and feeling on the subject and explaining why you think and feel as you do.

After you have written your draft, your teacher happens to hand out a copy of the parable of the Good Samaritan, show you a video 'Why Human Rights?' and use a card-sorting activity (5c) on arguments for and against restricting entry to refugees from a video pack, 'Refugees in Today's Europe'. These resources enable you to evaluate your letter and perhaps lead you to redraft it.

Conclusion

The education of geography teachers into values education through both developments in their own subject and other influences has been a very significant part of the history of geography teaching since the 1970s. There were important books which helped us on our way. When taking an MA seminar or developing an in-service workshop today, I would use Graham Haydon's *Teaching About Values: a New Approach* (1997). His analysis of teachers as transmitters and as educators provides another defence against accusations of indoctrination, as well as bringing together the two ideas of (1) thinking with content to reach knowledge and understanding and (2) thinking with others to understand values through dialogue and discussion.

The implications of the postmodern turn in geography, which has yet to influence geography education significantly, have not been part of this chapter. Yet postmodernism calls into question accepted notions of geography as writing about and understanding reality, while it also questions current notions of citizenship which I regard as positive. John Morgan (2000) draws attention to the interest which geographers, in recent years, have shown in the role geography itself plays in the construction of citizenship, within which lie concepts of identity, inclusion and exclusion. He questions the concern of some to protect stable identities and cultures through more traditional concepts of citizenship.

Just as I sum up the last thirty years of developments in values education in geography teaching and related developments in concepts of citizenship education, we are about to enter a new phase. By 2010, the implications of postmodern work and its contribution to ideas of citizenship will be worked through. At the same time, the conversation between specialists and generalists in education will continue to enrich and question concepts of values and their relation to citizenship as an educational aim.

Acknowledgement

I should like to acknowledge the usefulness, in particular, of Meryl Welsh's (1978) unpublished MA dissertation 'The contribution of geography to citizenship education', University of London Institute of Education.

FOR FURTHER THINKING

1   What do we mean when we say that geography, or any subject, is value-laden, indeed is value-loaded?
2   Citizenship is an 'empty concept'. How do you prefer to 'load it up'? Where does this place you in ideological conceptions of education running from the liberal to the reconstructionist?
3   Ask your classes what they mean by 'good citizenship' and discuss their suggested meanings with them in order to relate these to their understanding of geographical topics.

References

Agyeman, J. (1995) *People, Plants and Places*, Crediton, Devon: Southgate.
Agyeman, J. (1997) 'The multicultural ecosystem', in Frances Slater, David Lambert and David Lines (eds) *Education, Environment and Economy: Reporting Research in a New Academic Grouping*, London: University of London Institute of Education, Bedford Way Papers, pp. 99–114.
Barker, W.H. (1927) *Geography in Education and Citizenship*, London: University of London Press.
Cox, M. (1993) 'To what extent does environmental concern influence the culture and lifestyle of A level geography students?', unpublished MA dissertation, University of London Institute of Education.
Crick, B. (1975) 'Basic concepts for political education', *Teaching Politics*, vol. 4, pp. 153–68.
Crick, B. (1976) 'Procedural values in political education', *Teaching Politics*, vol. 5, pp. 10–24.
Crick, B. and Porter, A. (eds) (1978) *Political Education and Political Literacy*, London: Longman.
Doyle, W. (1992) 'Curriculum pedagogy', in P.W. Jackson (ed.) *Handbook of Research on Curriculum*, New York: Macmillan.
Entwhistle, H. (1971) *Political Education in a Democracy*, London: Routledge & Kegan Paul.
Entwhistle, H. (1974) 'Education and the concept of political socialisation', *Teaching Politics*, vol. 3, pp. 101–9.
Fien, J. and Slater, F. (1985) 'Four strategies for values education in geography', in D. Boardman (ed.) *New Directions in Geographical Education*, Brighton: Falmer, pp. 171–86.
Fry, P. (1987) 'Dealing with political bias through geography education', unpublished MA dissertation, University of London Institute of Education.
Gilbert, R. (1984) *The Impotent Image: Reflections of Ideology in the Secondary School Curriculum*, Brighton: Falmer.
Halstead, J.M. (1996) 'Liberal values and liberal education', in J.M. Halstead and M.J. Taylor (eds) *Values in Education and Education in Values*, Lewes: Falmer.
Harvey, P.K. (1991) 'The role and value of "A" level geography fieldwork: a case study', unpublished Ph.D. Thesis, University of Durham.
Haydon, G. (1997) *Teaching about Values: a New Approach*, London: Cassell.

Hopkin, J. (1998) 'The world view of geography text books: interpretations of the national curriculum', unpublished Ph.D. thesis, School of Education, University of Birmingham.

Huckle, J. (1981) 'Geography and values education', in R. Walford (ed.) *Signposts for Geography Teaching*, London: Longman, pp. 147–63.

Kohlberg, L. (1984) *The Psychology of Moral Development* San Francisco: Jossey Bass.

Lambert, D. (1999) 'Geography and moral education in a supercomplex world: the significance of values education and some remaining dilemmas', *Ethics, Place and Environment*, vol. 2, Number 1, pp. 5–18.

Lester, A. (1995) 'Conceptualising social formation: producing a textbook on South Africa', unpublished Ph.D. thesis, University of London Institute of Education.

Lister, I. (1997) 'The aims and methods of political education in schools', *Teaching Politics*, vol. 6, pp. 1–18.

Marsden, W. (1998) 'The school journey movement to 1940', *Journal of Educational Administration and History*, vol. 30, Number 2, pp. 79–95.

Morgan, J. (1997) 'Geo-graphing: writing the wor(l)d in geography classrooms', in F. Slater, D. Lambert and D. Lines (eds) *Education, Environment and Economy: Reporting Research in a New Academic Grouping*, London: University of London Institute of Education, Bedford Way Papers, pp. 57–70.

Morgan, J. (2000) 'To which space do I belong? Imagining citizenship in one curriculum subject', *The Curriculum Journal*, vol. 11, Number 1, pp. 55–68.

National Curriculum Council (1990) *Curriculum Guidance 8. Education for Citizenship*, York: NCC.

Namafe, C. (1997) 'Cultural difference in responses to environment', in F. Slater, D. Lambert and D. Lines (eds) *Education, Environment and Economy: Reporting Research in a New Academic Grouping*, London: University of London Institute of Education, Bedford Way Papers, pp. 115–34.

Porter, A. (1986) 'Political bias and political education', *Teaching Politics*, September, pp. 371–84.

Porter, A. (1993) *Impoverished Concepts of Citizenship in the Debate on the National Curriculum*, London: Centre for Multicultural Education, University of London Institute of Education, Occasional Paper no. 8.

Qualifications and Curriculum Authority (1998a) *Spiritual, Moral, Social and Cultural Guidelines*, QCA/98/271, London: QCA.

Qualifications and Curriculum Authority (1998b) *Education for Citizenship and the Teaching of Democracy in Schools*, Final Report of the Advisory Group on Citizenship, 22 September 1998, QCA/98/245, London: QCA.

Qualifications and Curriculum Authority (1999) *Geography, Work in Progress: Draft 22 January*, in QCA's Work in Progress to Develop the School Curriculum, Materials for Conferences, Seminars and Meetings, Pack B. QCA/99/370, London: QCA.

Reid, L.A. (1986) *Ways of Understanding and Education*, London: Heinemann.

Rickinson, M. (1999) 'The teaching and learning of environmental issues through geography: a classroom-based investigation', unpublished D. Phil. dissertation, University of Oxford.

Roberts, M. (1995) 'Teaching styles and strategies', in W. Kent, D. Lambert, M. Naish and F. Slater (eds) *Geography in Education Viewpoints on Teaching and Learning*, Cambridge: Cambridge University Press.

Slater, F. (1982) *Learning through Geography*, London: Heinemann.

Slater, F. (1994) 'Education through geography: knowledge, understanding, values culture', *Geography*, vol. 79, Number 2, pp. 147–63.

Slater, F. (1995) 'Values: towards mapping their locations in a geography education', in W. Kent, D. Lambert, M. Naish and F. Slater (eds) *Geography in Education Viewpoints on Teaching and Learning*, Cambridge: Cambridge University Press.

Snook, I. (1972) *Indoctrination and Education*, London: Routledge & Kegan Paul.

Stradling, R., Noctor, M. and Baines, B. (1984) *Teaching Controversial Issues*, London: Arnold.

Superka, D.P. *et al.* (1976) *Values Education Source book*, Boulder, Colo.: ERIC, Clearing House for Social Science/Social Studies Education.

Taylor, M. (1998) *Values Education and Values in Education, a Guide to the Issues*, commissioned by ATL, London: Association of University Teachers and Lecturers.

Welsh, A.M. (1978) 'The contribution of geography to citizenship education', unpublished MA dissertation, University of London Institute of Education.

Wharton, G. (2000) *Managing River Environments*, Cambridge: Cambridge University Press.

Yangopolous, S. (1997) 'Developing sixth form students' understanding of the relationships between environment and development issues', in F. Slater, D. Lambert and D. Lines (eds) *Education, Environment and Economy: Reporting Research in a New Academic Grouping*, London: University of London Institute of Education, Bedford Way Papers, pp. 135–54.

Chapter 5

Finding its place

Contextualising citizenship within the geography curriculum

Graham Butt

The promotion of citizenship to the status of a foundation subject within the National Curriculum marks a significant point within the history of curriculum development in England and Wales. From the perspective of the recent review of the National Curriculum (DfEE/QCA 1999a) and for 'Curriculum 2000' (DfEE 1999) for post-16 students, the relationship which now exists between geography and the five cross-curriculum themes originally identified in 1991 is a complex one. The elevation of citizenship education from among these themes to a place within the statutory curriculum at key stages 3 and 4 reorientates this relationship, and encourages geography teachers to examine their role in its delivery.

There is evidence that for many years the attitude of the Department for Education and Employment (DfEE), and of its previous incarnations, towards the promotion of cross-curricular themes within schools was at best ambivalent. This attitude contrasted sharply to that held within the Education Departments in many countries in the European Union (EU), the Commonwealth and beyond, where the case for citizenship education has been established for some time. Marsden (1995: 155) also reminds us that in the UK various political lobbies have used cross-curricular themes 'to serve extraneous ends, which essentially have involved instruction, control and "conversion" of young people into passive and placid subjects, rather than the education of autonomous, reflective and critical-thinking citizens'.

This chapter traces the development of citizenship education in the UK with particular reference to its relationship with the changing geography curriculum and complements Chapter 2 by Bill Marsden in this volume with regard to the evolution of citizenship education. The chapter seeks to clarify those areas where geography and citizenship have shared educational interests and understandings, but also indicates some of the tensions and pitfalls that result from injudiciously forcing the two together. The 'location' for citizenship within the current Geography National Curriculum (DfEE/QCA 1999a) is a major focus for the latter section of this chapter. An over-riding consideration is the existence of a variety of different conceptions of citizenship education – a form of education which in the past has often been used to promote national, as opposed to global, citizenship and which has significant connections to cultural, ethnic and national identities, precisely Marsden's point.

The changing fate of citizenship education and its links to the geography curriculum

Driver and Maddrell (1996: 371) believe that 'citizenship' is: 'a word which appears in various incarnations throughout the history of the twentieth century, and has played a prominent, almost talismanic, role in discourses of geography education in many parts of the world'. It is certainly true that in the UK definitions of citizenship, and of citizenship education, have shifted over the past century and a half, particularly in response to the aftermath of two world wars. Marsden (1995 and Chapter 2 of this volume) succinctly outlines ways in which geography and citizenship education combined during this period; in the early nineteenth century the concept of good citizenship was tied to notions of being a good Christian, but shifted towards a closer association with nationalism following the passing of the Education Act in 1870. As a result geography (and history) delivered a version of citizenship education which openly promoted patriotic and imperialist sentiments in the classroom. Indeed, the geography textbooks used in many state schools tacitly encouraged young working-class males to emigrate to the colonies, an act which was seen as an honourable expectation of 'true citizens' of the British Empire (Driver and Maddrell 1996). However, despite the influence of nationalist and imperialist notions of citizenship held within many geography textbooks at this time Walford (1996: 441) reminds us that:

> it is simplistic (and a misrepresentation of the evidence) to cast geography teachers of the late nineteenth and early twentieth century simply as jingoists, despite some of the ways in which they characterised race and reflected some particular contemporary political apprehensions.

By the mid-1930s the discourse on citizenship had become focused on Britain's emerging Commonwealth rather than on its Empire, with a greater emphasis seen in geography textbooks on citizens' rights, responsibilities and influences on international communities. Marsden (1995), for example, describes the growth before the Second World War of liberal versions of citizenship education which paralleled the development of the League of Nations. He notes the work of geography educationalists such as Welpton who

> as early as 1914 argued for a social geography that presented the world not as grasped by a geographer, but as grasped by a citizen, and sought understanding not only of physical conditions, but more of the lives of people on the earth.
>
> (Welpton 1914: 125)

and Unstead whose series *Citizen of the World* encouraged children to be empathetic towards peoples from other lands (Unstead 1928). Fleure (1936) was also influential in promoting ideals of world citizenship, pacifism and anti-imperialism, spurred by his belief that school geography could reveal how imperial powers had previously exploited less fortunate nations. In the late 1930s the League of Nations and Association for Education in Citizenship visualised geography and history teaching as being central to the promotion of a global outlook in citizenship education that incorporated neither nationalism nor imperialism. The League produced publications such as *Geography*

Teaching in Relation to World Citizenship (1935), but was criticised in the UK for expressing views that all nations should be seen as equals. The inter-war years had therefore seen a shift from the extremes of imperialist geography and citizenship education towards an emphasis on the positive roles that citizens could play in helping to eradicate intolerance and cultural ignorance.

By the late 1940s, Matless (1996) argues, geography's contribution to citizenship education shifted again and primarily lay in its association with landscapes and the aesthetics of place. The passing of legislation for the introduction of National Parks and other recreational spaces created a reconception of citizenship within the framework of the national space – again geographers were called upon to provide appropriate academic content, which drew upon physical geography, coastal studies and fieldwork. The plans for national reconstruction after the Second World War would also require the education of citizens towards a new appreciation of landscapes, urban and rural life, communities, modern domesticity and recreation – all of which Matless (1996: 425) refers to as reflecting 'geographical citizenship'. Here the focus of citizenship education was predominantly at the national scale, with a knowledge and concern for national landscapes and environments being offered as one of its cornerstones.

Despite the rise in the 1960s and 1970s of a more internationalist attitude within geography education, perhaps particularly associated with Third/Developing World studies and the growth of development education, a strongly national focus was largely maintained towards citizenship education in schools. This may partially explain why the main influence of citizenship education on geography education has been upon the role of the citizen at the national scale, emphasising the importance of the individual's loyalty to the nation-state.

Citizenship in the National Curriculum

Reflecting on the process of creating the National Curriculum for England and Wales, following the Education Reform Act (ERA) of 1988, it is apparent that in the early 1990s each of the five cross-curricular themes (careers, citizenship, economic and industrial understanding, environmental education, and health) faced a difficult birth and an uncertain infancy. Established in 1987, the National Curriculum Council (NCC), which was set up to administer the introduction of curriculum reforms, soon ran into conflict with the then Secretary of State for Education, Kenneth Baker. It sought to expand its brief and consider the place of cross-curricular themes not explicitly covered in the narrowly subject based National Curriculum. Duncan Graham, Chair and Chief Executive of the NCC from 1988 to 1991, commented that 'ministers believed that work on the whole curriculum could result in a major distraction that might allow the [education] establishment to fight back' (Graham and Tytler 1993: 20) – in itself an interesting comment on the whole process of centralised curriculum development at that time. The lack of political will to promote cross-curricular themes, and the fear that these themes might take attention away from the prime purpose of creating a strongly subject-based National Curriculum, destroyed any prospect of introducing a whole curriculum perspective or even a curriculum with a clear sense of its broad education goals. It was left to individual teachers to determine whether and how their schemes of work could promote citizenship education.

The Report of the Commission on Citizenship (Speaker's Commission on Citizenship 1990) directly influenced thinking on the development of curriculum guidance (NCC 1990) and helped to provide a blueprint for the future of citizenship education within the National Curriculum. Both documents were eclectic in the range of themes they touched upon and although clear in their view that active citizenship should result from citizenship education the opportunities offered for such activities were narrowly restricted. In retrospect the thinking behind these documents was flawed. Neither publication suggested that political activity was a desirable outcome of citizenship education and both mixed largely incompatible elements of civic republicanism and liberal individualism (see Box 5.1).

Equally no account was taken of the tension between citizenship within the context of the nation-state and the 'multiple citizenships' which individuals possess across the wider world. There was little awareness in NCC (1990) that people are citizens at local, regional, national and international scales and that for many people these multiple citizenships, identities and loyalties present confusing dilemmas. For example, a second-generation British Asian Muslim, who has family connections to Pakistan but whose immediate family has always lived in Birmingham, may frequently experience tensions about his or her multiple citizenship (such as, say, a German Jew in Berlin, or a French Algerian in Marseilles may face). It is worth remembering that this was around the time that Norman Tebbit introduced his myopic 'cricket test'.

Among the cross-curricular themes *Education for Citizenship: Curriculum Guidance 8* (NCC 1990) was 'the most disappointing document of all' (Marsden 1995: 163) and represented a fear within the DES that citizenship education might be overtaken by aspects of peace

---

Box 5.1 Roots of citizenship's tensions

The liberal individualist tradition emphasises human rights for every individual. As such it promotes each person's right to enjoy freedom of association, peaceful assembly and protest. Liberal individualists believe that they should have the right to take an active and informed part in the political life of their society at the local, national and international scales, without fear of repression or abuse. The freedom of any individual to question the ways in which governments, businesses and other organisations use their power is strongly supported.

The civic republican tradition focuses strongly on participation by individuals (or groups) in the functioning of their immediate society. It is therefore typified by the involvement of people in the organisation, administration, support and functioning of schools, the local community and civic institutions. In comparison to the liberal individualist tradition, the focus is placed more centrally on responsibilities rather than rights.

Both of these traditions contain both internal and external tensions. It is therefore interesting that the Report of the Commission on Citizenship (Speaker's Commission on Citizenship 1990) and *Education for Citizenship: Curriculum Guidance 8* (NCC 1990) include elements from both the liberal individualist and civic republican traditions, but make no case for the resolution of the contradictions they present.

education, development education and global education. Lip service was paid within the document to more modern and enlightened approaches to citizenship education, with phrases such as 'global education' and 'international co-operation' included. However close inspection reveals that the conception of citizenship was very much based upon the 'citizen' being subject to laws, rules and obligations. The three stated objectives of citizenship education in the curriculum – looking at the nature of community; roles and responsibilities in a democratic society; and the nature and basis of duties, responsibilities and rights – were expressed only as passive educational goals. Here the role of geography would be limited to offering guidance on pluralism and globality, rather than educating students about issues of global citizenship such as international co-operation and inter-dependence, sustainability and human rights. Machon (1991) was therefore able to refer to the document as 'reasonable' and 'decent' but could raise little enthusiasm for its confusing eclecticism and its tone of misplaced self-assurance.

The positive influence of the Dearing Report, government change and 'Curriculum 2000'

It was only following the Dearing Report (Dearing 1994), and the change of government in 1997, that the concern to express more clearly the values of the curriculum and the function of citizenship education in the National Curriculum became prominent. The first incarnation of the National Curriculum, with its overloaded content and complex assessment arrangements, gave little space in which to develop any of the cross-curricular themes which, as a result, were largely left to wither on the vine. Perhaps the best that can be said of *Curriculum Guidance 8* (NCC 1990) is that it highlighted problems of opening up issues of national identity, citizenship, society and politics within a centrally deter-mined National Curriculum.

The announcement in November 1997 by the Secretary of State for Education, David Blunkett, that an advisory group was to be established to strengthen the education for democracy and citizenship in schools was therefore a welcome development. This decision, preceded by the publication of the White Paper *Excellence in Schools* (DfEE 1997) earlier that year, saw the creation of a citizenship working group chaired by Professor Bernard Crick. The group was to report in time for the DfEE and QCA to incorporate its findings into the planned review of the National Curriculum for the year 2000. The group's final report was published in September 1998 (QCA 1998) and was to be influential in the production of the first statutory Order for citizenship in the National Curriculum, to be implemented at key stages 3 and 4 from September 2002.

The advisory group defined citizenship education as follows:

> the knowledge, skills and values relevant to the nature and practices of participative democracy; the duties, responsibilities, rights and development of pupils into citizens; and the value to individuals, schools and society of involvement in the local and wider community . . . both national and local and an awareness of world affairs and global issues, and of the economic realities of adult life.
>
> (QCA 1998: 4)

It highlighted three strands of education for citizenship, namely:

1 *Social and moral responsibility.* Children learning from the very beginning self-confidence and socially and morally responsible behaviour both in and beyond the classroom, both towards those in authority and towards each other.

2 *Community involvement.* Learning about and becoming helpfully involved in the life and concerns of their neighbourhood and communities, including learning through community involvement and service to the community.

3 *Political literacy.* Pupils learning about the institutions, problems and practices of our democracy and how to make themselves effective in the life of the nation, locally, regionally and nationally through skills and values as well as knowledge – this can be termed *political literacy*, seeking for a term wider than political knowledge alone.

Importantly the report contained a section which made suggestions about how citizenship education might be delivered in combination with other subjects and referenced 'obvious and advantageous overlaps with elements of both the content and approach of other subjects, most notably History, Geography and English' (QCA 1998: 52). Section 7.5 took this further with respect to geography when it stated:

> In Geography, the emphasis of place, space and environment and the study of places, themes and issues from the local to the global, offers significant opportunities to learn about conflicts and concerns, to extend knowledge about political groupings and the activities of pressure groups and voluntary bodies and to evaluate the consequences for people, places and environments of decision-making. There is a particular opportunity to understand how people and places are inextricably linked and interdependent, thus to learn about and experience citizenship from the local to the global. The processes of enquiry in Geography, as in History, can also contribute to pupils' development of the understanding, skills and confidence needed to take informed action. Pupil involvement in fieldwork can enhance such learning and despite the pressure of the timetable, many schools in Key Stage 3 have Environmental Studies programmes.
>
> (QCA 1998: 53)

In essence the group sought to establish an entitlement to citizenship education which would take no more than 5 per cent of curriculum time and which was mindful of the fact that previous cross-curricular themes had failed to make a significant impact on schools. History and geography were highlighted as subjects through which concepts of citizenship could be presented in key stage 3, while at key stages 1 and 2 citizenship education could be covered in PSE or PSHE. A case was also made by the group for the continuation of citizenship education within post-16 education and training.

The changing significance of citizenship education in the National Curriculum

It has been argued that the last fifteen years have shown a perceptible change of focus of interest among educational policy makers within government, away from concerns about the quality of school education and towards education for the well-being of society (Broadfoot *et al.* 2000). In simplified terms this changing focus can be expressed in the form of a table (see Table 5.1).

Table 5.1 Citizenship: the changing focus

Time period	Focus of concern	Locus of concern	Relationship to the pupil
Mid-1980s onwards	Knowledge	School curriculum	External to the pupil – decisions about what is to be taught and learned
Early 1990s	Pedagogy	Teacher–pupil relations	Mediated by the pupil – decisions about the organisation of teaching and learning
Late 1990s	Values	The pupil as citizen	Internal to the pupil – decisions about the child's developing identity as a citizen

Source: after Broadfoot *et al.* (2000: 73)

While this table offers an oversimplified account of what has happened within the curriculum for English and Welsh schools during this period the trend it identifies is an interesting one. The 1980s were a time of increasing concern among policy makers and the government about the perceived inabilities of schools to provide children with 'appropriate' subject knowledge, understanding and skills. This resulted in the eventual passing of the Education Reform Act of 1988 and the creation of a National Curriculum through which the curricula of state schools could be centrally determined and assessed. Concerns about international competitiveness, future economic stability and the impacts of globalisation also fuelled a belief among the New Right that a National Curriculum was an essential means of keeping pace with other nations.

Following the implementation of the National Curriculum the focus of concern shifted somewhat to consider standards of teaching, learning and assessment, particularly within primary schools. In the early 1990s the use of OfSTED inspections to determine whether teaching and learning methods were appropriate in schools, and the introduction of the literacy and numeracy hours, showed major centralised prescription of pedagogic practice. However, the period from the mid-1990s until the new millennium saw another shift – the shift towards considerations of pupils as 'citizens'. As Broadfoot *et al.* (2000: 72) state: 'In the late 1990s anxiety was being expressed about the pupils themselves, their apparent lack in many cases of moral and civic values and consequent indiscipline inside and outside school. The specific teaching of "citizenship" was widely advocated.'

What is the focus for citizenship education in the context of geography education?

Comparatively little material has been published which offers geography teachers clear, concise and tangible support when considering their role in helping to deliver citizenship education. The aim of the last section of this chapter is therefore twofold: (1) to consider recent writings on citizenship education and indicate how these might be used when planning to teach geography; and (2) to specifically place these ideas into the context of the statutory Order for Citizenship (DfEE/QCA 1999b) and the revised Geography National Curriculum (DfEE/QCA 1999a).

Recent writings on citizenship education and how these might be used when planning to teach geography

The work of Lynch (1992) provides some guidance for geographers about issues of democratic citizenship within culturally diverse communities through his focus on prejudice reduction, global interdependence and human rights. While he is primarily concerned with how education for citizenship can assist newly democratic nations in developing the values and institutions necessary to sustain internal democracy and promote global interdependence, he is also aware that teachers within established democracies may need to help students reinterpret their (often outmoded) democratic traditions. Importantly he attempts to go beyond the provision of education for national citizenship to create a recognition of the need for global citizenship education.

Lynch (1992: 17) puts forward six key reasons why education for citizenship at local, national and international levels is important. Each of these still has very clear connections to contemporary geography and geography education, despite their publication in the early 1990s:

- the growth in the number of democratic governments;
- the decline in military confrontation between East and West;
- the surge in competition for the world's resources;
- the recognition of the catastrophic rapidity of environmental decline;
- the search for a means to overcome the poverty of the Third World;
- the increasing importance of the international role of education in both North and South.

Recently, considerable guidance has also been published by a variety of organisations for the promotion of citizenship and democracy education within the whole curriculum. These publications often make reference to geography, but contain rather limited practical advice for teachers. Following the publication of the first statutory Order for citizenship (DfEE/QCA 1999b) the Development Education Association published guidance for teachers on active global citizenship, the role of initial teacher education in the promotion of citizenship education, and frameworks for the international dimension in education. Some regional Development Education Centres have launched initiatives in citizenship education for teachers, have explored citizenship through projects such as GeoVisions, and have opened debates on civil society, world citizenship and the role of education. Many of these activities have served to raise awareness, but also indicate the often contested and unfocused nature of contemporary thought within this area.

Oxfam has arguably provided the most helpful cross-curricular support for the promotion of global citizenship education through pamphlets such as *A Curriculum for Global Citizenship* (Oxfam 1997), which highlights specific knowledge and understanding, skills, and values and attitudes, as shown in Box 5.2. Many geography teachers would consider that these points have direct and tangible links to the type of geography education that could be experienced by students in schools.

Other writers have provided helpful models of citizenship education which could be applied within a range of curriculum subjects (see for example Osler and Starkey 1996), or have used such models to write specifically for the context of geography education. Common themes are clearly identifiable as important to geographers – for example if

---

Box 5.2 A curriculum for global citizenship

Knowledge and understanding
- social justice and equality
- diversity
- globalisation and interdependence
- sustainable development
- peace and conflict

Skills
- critical thinking
- ability to argue effectively
- ability to challenge injustice and inequalities
- respect for people and things
- co-operation and conflict resolution

Values and attitudes
- sense of identity and self-esteem
- empathy
- commitment to social justice and equality
- value and respect for diversity
- concern for the environment and commitment to sustainable development
- belief that people can make a difference.

Source: Oxfam (1997)

---

one considers Tables 5.2 and 5.3 below, the first by Rawling (1991) offering support for geographers teaching aspects of citizenship for *Curriculum Guidance 8* (NCC 1990), and the second by Walkington (1999) for primary geographers addressing global citizenship education at the time of the publication of the Crick Report (QCA 1998), there are some striking similarities.

Although presented for different audiences, at different times, and in response to different visions of citizenship education, certain broad perspectives on citizenship and geography education are often repeated. As Walkington (1999) herself concludes, there are several areas where common ground is shared. These can be classified within specific concepts and key themes (such as interdependence, sustainability, justice and equity), methodology (such as the inquiry-based approach, role play and simulation), skills (such as handling information for decision making, critical thinking), and values and attitudes (such as empathy).

But of what practical help is advice such as that offered by Rawling and Walkington? Such writers are quick to indicate the broad themes, content, skills and attitudes that global citizenship education should espouse, but are less convincing about practical ways in which these might be conveyed in the classroom. The different conceptions of citizenship can leave the geography teacher at a loss when trying to ensure that what is planned for the classroom actually promotes sound citizenship education *and* geography education. This problem is particularly prevalent if the curriculum is

Table 5.2 Geography and citizenship (after Rawling 1991)

Content/context	Key concepts	Skills
• decision making at all scales (people, place and environment) • responses to work, employment and leisure • environmental issues • relationships between countries • international groupings	• decision making • conflict/co-operation • similarity/differences • human welfare • equality/inequality • development/ interdependence • responsibilities/rights	• issues of people/place, environment • analysing different viewpoints • groupwork • range of maps/scales

Table 5.3 Geography and citizenship (after Walkington 1999)

Approach	Skills
• an emphasis on challenging or combating preconceived ideas • searching for underlying processes • taking a holistic approach to studies • using issues to structure learning such as environmental issues or those concerning justice • co-operative learning strategies	• comparison (e.g. being able to see similarities and differences) • critical thinking • decision making • working in groups

Concepts	Values
• sustainability • Interdependence • change • place • cultural diversity	• a sense of place • a sense of community • empathy

understood primarily in terms of content to be covered. For example, Carter and Bailey suggest that topics such as 'the nature of inner city decline and possibilities for regeneration', and the provision of 'a systematised knowledge of the configurations of . . . [the students'] own country and of the world' (1996: 19, 18), are important to both citizenship and geography, but give no guidance on their planning and teaching. It is perhaps easier to tick off the 'geography' than the 'citizenship', the latter being left up to the student to interpret. Similarly we are told that students 'as citizens' can increasingly 'respond in informed ways to world events' (1996: 18) through studying geographical and citizenship themes, but no examples are given of the types of educational experiences that might promote such involvement. As Carter and Bailey (1996) correctly state, it is vital that students grow up to experience greater freedom and independence within their environment, and to appreciate how political, cultural, social and economic factors may place restrictions on their lives; however, the most appropriate ways of educating future citizens into this understanding are less clear.

The Geography Advisors and Inspectors Network (GAIN) of the Geographical Association produced guidance on how geographers may be advised to adopt an

Table 5.4 Geography and citizenship: National Curriculum advice

Citizenship *Key stage 3*	Geography *Key stage 3*
Knowledge and understanding about becoming informed citizens.	*Breadth of study.*

1b. the diversity of national, regional, religious and ethnic identities in the United Kingdom and the need for mutual respect and understanding.	6f. population distribution and change, including:
	  i. the global distribution of population
	  ii. the causes and effects of changes in the population of regions and countries, including migration
	  iii. the interrelationship between population and resources.

1i. The world as a global community, and the political, economic, environmental and social implications of this, and the role of the European Union, the Commonwealth and the United Nations.	*Knowledge and understanding of places.*
	3b. to describe the national, international and global contexts of places studied.
	3e. to explain how places are interdependent, and to explore the idea of global citizenship.
	
	Knowledge and understanding of environmental change and sustainable development.
	5a. describe and explain environmental change and recognise different ways of managing it.
	5b. explore the idea of sustainable development and recognise its implications for people, places and environments and for their own lives.
	
	Breadth of study.
	6f. see above
	6h. changing distribution of economic activity and its impact, including:
	  i. types and classifications of economic activity
	  ii. the global distribution of one or more economic activities
	  iii. how and why the distribution has changed and is changing, and the effects of such changes.
	6i. development, including:
	  i. ways of identifying differences in development within and between countries
	  ii. effects of differences in development and the quality of life of different groups of people.
	  iii. factors, including the interdependence of countries, that influence development.
	6j. environmental issues, including:
	  i. how conflicting demands on an environment arise
	  ii. how and why attempts are made to plan and manage environments
	  iii. effects of environmental planning and management on people, places and environments.

Table 5.4 (continued)

Citizenship Key stage 3	Geography Key stage 3
	6k. resources issues, including: i. the sources and supply of a resource ii. the effects on the environment of the use of a resource iii. resource planning and management.

Sources: DfEE/QCA (1999a: 24–5; 1999b: 14). © Crown copyright. Reproduced under the terms of HMSO Guidance Note 8.

Note: No specific links are made to geography at key stage 4 as the subject does not exist at this stage of the National Curriculum. Reference is made to Local Agenda 21 with reference to the 'wider issues and challenges of global interdependence and responsibility, including sustainable development' (1j). However, the themes within key stage 4 of the citizenship curriculum progress from those in key stage 3 and still maintain a relevance to geography.

issues-based approach to citizenship and sustainable development following the publication of the Final Report of the Advisory Group on Citizenship (QCA 1998). This considered a series of 'dimensions' (context, change, choices and decisions, futures, people and viewpoints) and 'questions' for particular issues within the Geography National Curriculum (DFE 1995) at each of the three key stages. Interestingly, themes with strong people–environment links were chosen for the exemplars – use of a park, investigating a river, and quarrying a limestone area. But, it could be asked, what about the students' social, economic, cultural and political environments? Do geography lessons studiously avoid these? If so, geography weakens its case to 'deliver' citizenship education.

The context of the statutory Order for citizenship (DfEE/QCA 1999b) and the revised Geography National Curriculum (DfEE/QCA 1999a)

The programme of study for citizenship at key stage 3 makes two specific references to links with the Geography National Curriculum (DfEE/QCA 1999a). These are shown in Table 5.4.

To appreciate more fully the connections between the geography and citizenship documents, and to consider the possible assessment of such connections, the attainment target for citizenship at key stage 3 is reproduced in full below:

Pupils have a broad knowledge and understanding of topical events they study; the rights, responsibilities and duties of citizens; the role of the voluntary sector; forms of government; provision of public services; and the criminal and legal systems. They show how the public gets information and how opinion is formed and expressed, including through the media. They show understanding of how and why changes take place in society. Pupils take part in school and community-based activities, demonstrating personal and group responsibility in their attitudes to themselves and others.
(DfEE/QCA 1999b)

Box 5.3   Example: the case of Rover Car Company, Longbridge, West Midlands, UK

Citizenship 1i, Geography 3b, 3e, 6h

Context

Develop a pupil-centred exercise designed to explore the cause and effect of the break-up of the Rover Car Company by its parent company BMW. BMW is based in Munich, Bavaria, in Germany. The rationalisation of the Longbridge works, the decision to sell the profitable Land Rover works at Solihull, and to maintain car production at Cowley, could be considered. Students examine the processes by which multinational companies, governments, workers and unions sought to influence events following BMW's announcement in March 2000 of its decision to sell its Rover subsidiary.

The responsibilities, power and rights of the major 'players' within these processes are explored. Students could be given access to prepared information cards on some, or all, of the following players: the Chair of BMW, the Chair of Rover, the Chair of Alchemy, the Chair of the John Towers group (the Phoenix Consortium), the Rover union leaders, Rover car assembly workers, the Trade and Industry Secretary, components manufacturers and representatives of those living and working in the West Midlands.

Activity

Scene setting on the car assembly industry to establish student understanding of how the manufacturing sector functions. General background on the Rover Car Company, followed by a mapwork exercise to clarify its location and major markets. Similar activities could also be carried out for BMW. The operation of multinational car companies within the global context could then be emphasised.

A historical account is then provided for students of the decisions/statements made by BMW, Rover, the British government, unions and interested purchasers of the Rover Group in the days following the announcement by BMW of the break-up of the Rover Car Company. Supported by information cards on the major 'players', students examine the possible motivations for, and reactions to, these decisions. A focus is placed upon the national 'March for Rover' held in Birmingham on 1 April 2000, which attracted 80,000 marchers.

Students are supplied with local and national newspaper extracts about the rationalisation of the branch plant at Rover Longbridge and the 'March for Rover'. They analyse these extracts for bias and values, and refer back to the work they have completed on the roles, responsibilities, power and rights of the key 'players'. Students are finally encouraged to consider the cause and possible effects of closure, alternative futures for those employed by Rover, the impact of decision making within a multinational company, and the influence of different 'players' within the process. They are encouraged to discuss other options for Rover, and to consider possible outcomes.

This unit of work is designed to illustrate the global nature of car production; the political, economic and social impact of decision making by multinational companies; the impacts on people/citizens locally (West Midlands), nationally (UK) and internationally (EU and global); the interdependence of places; and the impact of changing distributions of economic activity. Issues of power and powerlessness are explored as they relate to citizens in the UK, as well as issues concerning rights and responsibilities – from the shopfloor worker, to company chair, to government minister.

How does a geography teacher successfully approach planning the combination of citizenship and geography to ensure a meaningful educational experience for students at key stage 3? An example of how such an activity might be planned, with specific reference to the citizenship Order, the attainment target for citizenship at key stage 3, and the Geography National Curriculum, is described in Box 5.3. This outline plan offers suggestions about how 'subject' content, concepts, skills, and values and attitudes could be incorporated into the curriculum. However, it must be stressed that it only provides an illustration of how the Orders may usefully combine the three elements, rather than 'covering' an entire programme of cross-curricular work.

Curriculum options

The geography teacher who plans to use an activity like the one shown in Box 5.3 is presented with a number of curriculum options. The materials can either be used to focus strongly upon the Geography National Curriculum at key stage 3 (Gg 3b, 3e, 6h), or can be 'weighted' to also help students understand issues of citizenship (Cn 1i). The potential for cross-curricular work on bias, use of images, the media, and rights and responsibilities is considerable.

The issues surrounding the break-up of Rover are complex, but can only begin to be appreciated if students understand the possible effects of such rationalisation on people at the local, regional, national and international scales. It is important that students understand the 'real-life' effects of decisions made by multinational companies and governments, and the consequences that result. The location, and meaning, of 'power and powerlessness' should be stressed. In all of this the geography of the decision making is critical; distance is functionally related to costs, space is defined in political terms state by state and power accrues to those with the ability to move capital, goods or labour. So BMW can withdraw investment across national borders, skilled labour is 'footloose' (and unskilled is not) and a company's assets may be intellectual, like the plans for the new Mini that exist electronically, rather than material, like elderly production lines.

'Reminders'

Although many geography teachers may be comfortable about using most of this activity they will need to develop the ciitizenship perspective and their students will need to be supported in some of the thinking associated with unfamiliar aspects of both this and its geography. For example students may need support in:

- understanding the roles, responsibilities and power of the 'players' involved (e.g. what knowledge and understanding do students already have of union leaders, company chairs or ministers?);
- understanding the roles, responsibilities and power of the institutions involved (e.g. unions, government ministers, company chairs);
- clarifying the process of decision making undertaken by multinationals and governments;
- clarifying the possible motivations behind decisions made by multinationals and governments;
- being explicit about the dynamic part that geography plays;
- understanding the political, economic and social need for full employment in regions, and the effects of substantial reductions in employment in the car assembly and components industries;
- understanding the cause and effect of industrial inertia;
- clarifying their own values as well as the (assumed) values of others.

Conclusions

It is increasingly apparent that if geography is to maintain its relevance as a subject within schools in the twenty-first century it is going to have to develop and evolve, reflecting not only an academic and research-driven agenda from within the subject but also a greater appreciation of the rapidly changing world outside. The demand for geography educationalists to consider more fully the place of citizenship within their teaching has recently been given a new impetus by the publication of the statutory Order for citizenship (DfEE/QCA 1999b) which now has clearer links to the geography curriculum. Ironically this development has been striven for internationally within geography education for some years, as witnessed by the publication of the IGU *International Charter on Geographical Education* (CGE/IGU 1992) back in 1992. This charter clearly stated the need for geography education to have at its centre considerations of values and attitudes, human rights, international understanding, environmental ethics and social justice. Marsden (1995) also considers that in the future geography education must recognise that many issues within geography are essentially inter-disciplinary, although these can perhaps be most successfully addressed from geography's unique perspective.

At present we do not have a consensus on what citizenship education is, or should be, from the perspective of the geographer. The need to resolve this situation becomes pressing as the tensions between our local, national, international and global identities and actions become greater day by day. At a time when the growth in the use of the internet, email and satellite television is blurring certain kinds of spatial boundaries, geography teachers need to be alert to the sharpening of others. A global world does not mean that geography is somehow 'clear' (see Harvey 2000). On the other hand there is no sense in simply preserving geography behind outdated or backward-looking subject boundaries. 'Curriculum 2000' provides an opportunity to find out what geography has to contribute to citizenship education.

FOR FURTHER THINKING

1   This chapter offers a practical example, the case of Rover at Longbridge, to indicate how the geography and citizenship Orders might be combined. Which other aspects of the Geography National Curriculum could provide opportunities for similar curriculum combinations?
2   How far can the citizenship Orders enhance the promotion of learning about citizens' rights, responsibilities and power through geography?
3   To what extent is an understanding of citizenship essential to the development of a meaningful appreciation of geography within the National Curriculum?

References

Broadfoot, P., Osborn, M., Planel, C. and Sharpe, K. (2000) *Promoting Quality in Learning: Does England Have the Answer?* London: Cassell.

Carter, R. and Bailey, P. (1996) Geography in the whole curriculum. In Bailey, P. and Fox, P. (eds) *The Geography Teachers' Handbook*. Sheffield: Geographical Association, pp. 11–27.

CGE/IGU (1992) *International Charter on Geographical Education*. Freiburg: Commission on Geographical Education of the International Geographical Union.

Dearing, R. (1994) *The National Curriculum and its Assessment: Final Report*. London: SCAA.

DFE (1995) *Geography in the National Curriculum*. London: HMSO.

DfEE (1997) *Excellence in Schools*. London: DfEE.

DfEE (1999) *Learning to Succeed: a New Framework for Post-16 Learning*. London: DfEE.

DfEE/QCA (1999a) *Geography*. London: QCA.

DfEE/QCA (1999b) *Citizenship*. London: QCA.

Driver, S. and Maddrell, A. (1996) Empire, emigration and school geography: changing discourses of Imperial Citizenship 1880–1925. *Journal of Historical Geography* 22 (4) pp. 373–87.

Fleure, H. (1936) Geography. In *Education for Citizenship in Secondary Schools*. London: Association For Education in Citizenship.

Graham, D. and Tytler, D. (1993) *A Lesson for Us All: the Making of the National Curriculum*. London. Routledge.

Harvey, D. (2000) *Spaces of Hope*. Edinburgh: Edinburgh University Press.

League of Nations (1935) *Geography Teaching in Relation to World Citizenship*. London.

Lynch, J. (1992) *Education for Citizenship in a Multi-cultural Society*. London: Cassell.

Machon, P. (1991) Subject or citizen? *Teaching Geography* 16 (3) p. 128.

Marsden, B. (1995) *Geography 11–16: Rekindling Good Practice*. London: Fulton.

Matless, D. (1996) Visual culture and geographical citizenship: England in the 1940s. *Journal of Historical Geography* 22 (4) pp. 424–39.

NCC (1990) *Education for Citizenship: Curriculum Guidance 8*. York: NCC.

Osler, A. and Starkey, H. (1996) *Teacher Education and Human Rights*. London: Fulton.

Oxfam (1997) *A Curriculum for Global Citizenship*. London: Oxfam.

QCA (1998) *Education for Citizenship and the Teaching of Democracy in Schools: Final Report of the Advisory Group on Citizenship*. London: QCA.

Rawling, E. (1991) Geography and cross curricular themes. *Teaching Geography* 16 (4) pp. 147–54.

Speaker's Commission on Citizenship (1990) *Encouraging Citizenship*. London: HMSO.

Unstead, J. (1928) The primary geography schoolteacher – what should he know and be? *Geography* 14 (4) pp. 315–22.

Walford, R. (1996) Geographical education and citizenship: afterword. *Journal of Historical Geography* 22 (4) pp. 440–2.

Walkington, H. (1999) *Theory into Practice: Global Citizenship Education*. Sheffield: GA.

Welpton, W. (1914) The educational outlook on geography. *The Geographical Teacher* 7 pp. 291–7.

Part II

Curriculum issues

Chapter 6

The seduction of community
To which space do I belong?

John Morgan

The General Election in May 1997 saw a radical shift in political power in Britain. After eighteen years of Conservative government a self-defined 'New' Labour government came to power. For New Labour, the challenge was to set about 'modernising' Britain. The challenges for the renewal of Britain included the development of top-quality public services, especially in education and health, tough action on crime, forging a new partnership with business, introducing radical constitutional reform, and reconfiguring the UK's relationship with Europe. While Labour made it clear that it accepted many of the changes in economic and social policy made by the previous governments, it stressed that such policies had been socially divisive, leading to unacceptable levels of inequality, exclusion, insecurity and polarisation (Hay, 1999). In direct opposition to Margaret Thatcher's (in)famous statement that there is 'no such thing as society', the Labour government (and especially Prime Minister Blair) stressed its commitment to a set of core values or a distinctive political morality that underpinned its policies (Driver and Martell, 1998). Blair announced his aim as nothing less than 'to define a new relationship between citizen and community for the modern world'. The moves to make education for citizenship a statutory part of the school curriculum must be read as part of this modernising 'project'.

This focus on the importance of community has been expressed in various policy pronouncements. Thus in schools there is talk of community-based participation, partnerships between local authorities and business, and efforts to encourage parents to take more responsibility for schooling. New Labour's **communitarianism** asserts a relationship between individual and society. In Blair's famous phrase, everyone is part of 'one nation, one community'. This chapter is an attempt to 'unpack' the idea of community and how it relates to the work of school geography teachers. It does not attempt to offer teachers a blueprint for using geography as a means of educating for citizenship, but it does seek to highlight why 'geography matters'.

Smith (1993: 105) argues that community is 'the least specifically defined of spatial scales, and the consequent vague yet generally affirmative nurturing meaning attached to "community" makes it one of the most ideologically appropriated metaphors in contemporary public discourse' (See Box 6.1). Smith's comment has important implications for any attempt to use geography as a means to teach education for citizenship, since citizenship necessarily entails the assumption of belonging to a community. The important question then becomes: *which* community, or *whose* community? This is particularly pertinent in the light of claims that we live in a time when the ever-increasing levels of globalisation and informationalisation of everyday life have led to a 'growing disorientation in many people's sense of place' (Luke and Ó'Tuatail 1998: 72). In such circumstances, Harvey (1996) asks: 'To what space/place do we belong? Am I a citizen of the world, the nation, the locality?'

Box 6.1 Discourse

The main idea underlying the argument in this, and other chapters, is **discourse**. The French philosopher Michel Foucault suggests that discourse captures the idea that 'facts' can be conveyed in different ways and that the language used to convey these facts interferes with our ability to decide what is true and what is false. A discourse is a group of statements that provides a language for talking about a particular kind of knowledge about a topic. To use the language of **semiotics** (the study of signs and systems of signs), discourses are practices of signification, providing a framework for thinking about and understanding the world. Thus 'citizenship' is a discourse. When we are called upon to be 'citizens', we are called to adopt a particular range of behaviours and ways of belonging. We may be called to be 'British citizens' or 'citizens of planet earth', but underlying both these calls are sets of beliefs and assumptions about the nature of the world. However, as the chapters in this book illustrate so well, there is no agreement over the exact nature, content and meaning of citizenship. It is a contested concept, a contested discourse, in every sense of both words.

If discourse sets the limits within which ideas and practices are considered to be natural or commonsensical, these limits are not fixed. They are subject to challenge, negotiation and transformation. This raises the point that Foucault stressed in his writing – that discourses are inextricably linked to power. To be in a position to define and influence how a topic gets talked about is itself to exercise power. For instance, the publication of the *Orders for Citizenship* in the National Curriculum by the British government is an act of power: it makes its particular way of talking about citizenship influential. Its view of citizenship becomes a powerful or dominant discourse. On the other hand, interest groups like Oxfam and the Development Education Association produce alternative statements about the type of citizenship education they would like to see and so challenge aspects of the dominant discourse and seek to replace it with other features. For instance the focus on the nation within the dominant discourse could be replaced with a more explicit concern with developing global citizenship. Similarly, whereas the National Curriculum documents stress the importance of active citizenship, other groups might seek to emphasise the need for political literacy or rights over duties. In such ways the discourse of citizenship is contested and subject to debate.

Foucault's writings are not particularly accessible and in three major works from 1961 to 1975 he sought to exemplify the ideas signalled here in studies of the evolution of society's view of madness, medicine and penal systems. These works are: Madness and Civilisation (1961), *The Birth of the Clinic* (1963) and *Discipline and Punish* (1975). He moved beyond these studies into broader theoretical considerations, for example in *The Archaeology of Knowledge* (1969).

This chapter suggests that the specific function that geography plays in the construction of citizenship is to perform a type of 'mapping' that enables young people to locate themselves in relation to other people and other places. Thus Ross (2000) suggests that the social subjects, such as geography and history, 'inevitably define who "we" are, and what "our society" is, generalizing about activities, creating boundaries, borders and categories. . . . And the "we" is not just an amorphous collection of individuals, but becomes the class, the school, the district, the nation' (p. 154).

Thus, in the academic division of labour, geography's particular role is to define social space and territory, since it is concerned with boundaries, zones of activity and notions of regionality. The argument here is that, rather than simply providing pupils with an accurate and 'truthful' representation of the world, geography teachers are involved in the active *construction* of pupil's 'maps of meaning'. Further, the maps of meaning that are constructed in school geography lessons cannot be seen as innocent and free from power relations. For instance, to reinforce the idea that pupils primarily 'belong' to a national space necessarily means that they are less likely to identify themselves as 'Europeans'. That such identifications are political is particularly apparent when debates about Britain's place in the European Union still rage.

The argument, then, is that school geography provides young people with answers to the question 'to which space do I belong?' Sometimes this is done explicitly, but more often the everyday practices of teaching and learning position students in the world, defining them as belonging to a locality or nation and differentiating them from 'others'. In reality, these 'belongings' are made to appear as 'natural', but in fact require a good deal of discursive work. In school geography this is achieved through the use of scale to study the world. In school geography as practised in Britain the idea that events or processes can be studied at different scales has become axiomatic in definitions of what makes good geography teaching. Thus pupils are introduced to study at 'local', 'national' and 'global' scales. There is always some confusion as to the actual definition of these scales (for instance, does a study of the region count as 'local'?), and debates continue about whether to start with the 'local' and move on to large spatial scales or vice versa, but in general the 'three-scale model' is widely accepted. While this appears natural and commonsensical, in fact the production of scale is a political act, since it defines what can and cannot be said about an event. For instance, is the closure of a coal mine in South Yorkshire to be regarded as a local, national or global event? The answer is, of course, that it all depends at which scale we choose to define it. The local scale may focus on the effects of closure on individuals and families or the impact on the physical environment. The national scale would likely focus on the role of capital and the government's role in choosing whether or not to subsidise the pit, and this would probably require some understanding of wider forces of change in the global economy as these affect prices of energy and patterns of demand. Thus, a particular event – the closure of a coal mine – has different meanings according to whether we study it as a local, national or global event. It is not difficult to see the same processes operating in geography classrooms, where events and processes take on very different meanings according to the scale of study chosen by the teacher. I hope the argument that geography teachers, rather than simply reflecting the world to pupils, are actively involved in constructing or constituting the world, is becoming clearer, the argument being the geography teachers are becoming involved in 'cultural production' (see Box 6.2).

Box 6.2 Geography teaching as cultural production

The approach I am adopting here is the idea of geography teaching as a form of 'cultural production'. Just as societies need to produce materially in order to continue, so they must also produce culturally. They need *knowledges* to keep production going, and geography is one part of this set of *knowledges*. While geography may provide some people with technical skills, its more general function is concerned with providing people with an understanding of their location in the world. Cultural production produces concepts, systems and apparently 'natural' understandings to explain who we are collectively and individually, who others are, and how the world works.

Geography teachers can therefore be thought of as 'cultural workers'. They are actively engaged in producing knowledge about the world. This account would appear to suggest that geography is a seamless, monolithic structure, passing down 'ready-made' ways of understanding the world. In reality, cultural production is a 'messy' process. There are competing 'stories' that struggle to make themselves heard. Different teachers, occupying different social locations, represent different 'stories' and pupils must work hard to 'make sense' of the various 'stories' they encounter. While some accounts of the world are more influential than others, the process of cultural production is never guaranteed, and is never finished.

Imagining community in school geography

In this section, the focus is on the various 'stories' about community that are told in school geography. Rather than provide singular narratives about community, I suggest that in school geography answers to the question 'to which space do I belong?' revolve around three different uses of community – the local, the national and the global.

Local community

One of the important ways in which school geography seeks to locate pupils is through their belonging or attachment to a locality. Bale (1987: 57) summarises the way in which the local environment can be used as a resource for teaching:

> The local environment provides children with first-hand insights into the world which cannot satisfactorily be simulated in the classroom. It provides a situation for field work and practical exploration and investigation. At the same time the locality provides many clues as to the interdependent nature of the world – the fact that aspects of other countries of the world are in our own homes, schools and streets.

In Nicholas Tate's 1996 address to the Geographical Association in his capacity as chief executive of the Qualifications and Curriculum Authority, he stressed the importance of the local in providing pupils with a sense of identity. He suggests that a 'sense of local identity' consists of three main elements: a sense of the distinctiveness of a particular place; a sense of identification of that place; and a sense of belonging to a community with shared purposes. While the idea of teaching for a sense of community is for Tate apparently unproblematic, a closer examination reveals some important issues. O'Byrne (1997) usefully notes that localities exist on a series of dimensions. These include:

- the **historical**, in which a particular village or hamlet is still identifiable and definable even though it is now part of a larger city;
- the **political** dimension, based on an 'imaginary line' which defines the constituency, borough, ward which an area comes under;
- the **social** dimension, which refers to local interaction of residents as they live and work;
- the **cultural** dimension which refers to the customs, traditions, ways of life of the people in an area.

What this suggests is that any attempt to teach about the locality is based on a selection about what is important about that locality. None of the dimensions of locality can be seen as 'fixed' or permanent. They require constant maintenance and reconstruction. As geographers such as David Harvey (1993) have argued, the construction of place is an active process that takes place through broader relations of power. There are a number of important issues in teaching about localities in geography education. For instance, should the objective dimensions of a locality be stressed or should the focus be the subjective dimension of a place? Social and cultural geographers have stressed how a focus on place as a spatially bounded locality can obscure the internal divisions, conflicts and struggles that take place within it. This suggests that teaching about the local community cannot be divorced from broader political debates, examining the divisions that exist within local communities, between men and women, between different social classes and ethnic groups. In short, localities reflect broader relations of economic and political power. Doreen Massey (1999) has encouraged geography teachers to unpack or 'deconstruct' ideas of the local community in order to develop a more open or 'progressive' sense of place. In her version, rather than seek to draw boundaries around places and stress their unity and cohesiveness, the trick is to trace the webs of social relations that stretch out around the globe. Consider, for instance, a typical street in inner London:

> An 'Indian' restaurant here, run by a Bangladeshi family whose relatives may have been recent flood victims in Bangladesh, an East African news agency there, part of a national chain run by a family of refugees from Uganda, descendants of indentured Indian labourers, whose immediate fortunes are bonded into the recession of the British economy and the actions of the German Bundesbank, and whose children are spoken to by an African-American expressive culture. Overhead, a plane carries (if she is lucky) a Somali woman, who has lived in border refugee camps for several years, and who may seek housing in Camden, the housing officer perhaps being the son of a Jamaican woman who arrived in Britain in the 1950s to work on the buses. In another street, a heterosexual black man visits an AIDS project, staffed by gay men who were inspired to establish the project through the political activism of American groups.
>
> (Bhatt, 1994: 152)

This 'open' way of imagining a locality contrasts with representations that stress the boundedness or 'closed' sense of locality. It suggests extensive and fluid notions of community rather than a sense of community that entails belonging to a particular place. The educational implications of different ways of imagining localities warrant further consideration. I have suggested that one of the important ways in which school geography seeks to locate pupils is through their belonging or attachment to a locality. This locality is almost always defined as a community. As McDowell (1999) notes, community is a term that almost always carries with it connotations of warmth and solidarity. Of course, there are times when community becomes a negative thing, usually when it is linked to conservatism and oppressive tradition (for example, where belonging to a place is based on ethnic affiliation). Geographers are increasingly wary of the seductions of community when it is rooted in place, and stress the ways in which communities are constructed to exclude certain groups of people. In any case, a sense of belonging to a locality is only one of a number of possible identities offered to pupils through school geography.

While geography teaching provides pupils with a means of locating themselves as belonging to a locality, this locality is usually imagined as belonging to a larger unit or imagined community – the nation. It is often argued that geography developed as a subject in order to provide pupils with an understanding of their role as British subjects, and as such as part of an Empire that played a powerful part in the shaping of the world (Ó'Tuatail, 1996). It might be argued that this particular role in 'instilling a spirit of national strength and pride' became less important in the period after 1945, but the role of geography in the promotion of national identity has been revised in the moves to establish a 'National Curriculum' from the mid-1980s. The 'National' Curriculum for geography can be read as an attempt to reimagine and refashion the nation. Constructing national identities involves emphasising attachment to place. Penrose (1993) has argued that there are three components to the concept of 'nation'. First, nations are composed of a distinctive group of people who 'belong' to it. Second, these people occupy a distinctive territory or place. Third, there is, at some level, a bond between people and place that melds them together. Penrose goes on to argue that the achievement of political power requires a successful project of the 'nation', and that considerable effort is devoted to promoting this 'belonging'. Donald (1992) suggests that we should see the role of schooling, along with other institutions such as the media and state broadcasting, as involved in this cultural production of the nation. Indeed, his argument was that the National Curriculum should be regarded as an attempt to get children to imagine themselves as part of the British nation.

According to this view, school geography is actively involved in the construction of the 'nation'. It does so by repeatedly reinscribing the boundaries of the nation. On a small-scale level, the everyday use of data that are collected and presented by nation-state, the reproduction of maps that divide the world according to states, and the use of textbook accounts that stress the sovereignty of nation-states all serve to naturalise the idea of the 'nation'. The focus on Britain simultaneously signifies to pupils that they belong to that space and that 'other' people belong elsewhere. For example, the requirement that pupils learn a great deal about the economic activities and social and physical features of places in Britain can be regarded as an act of 'writing' the nation. It literally inscribes the pupil in a shared space (invariably pupils' geographical knowledge of their 'own' country is much greater than that of other countries). In his study of school geography and history textbooks, Ahier (1988) demonstrates the textual strategies that textbook writers use to give their readers their sense of place in the world. He argues that the textbooks play an important role in the construction of a geography of 'them' and 'us': 'the presentation of *others* in the texts is tied into the location and differentiation of *ourselves*' (p. 164).

The debate about the role of the National Curriculum in promoting certain forms of identification in pupils continued throughout the 1990s. It was given impetus in Nicholas Tate's address to the Geographical Association in April 1996. Tate urged geography teachers to teach a distinctly 'British' geography. He suggested that while geography lessons should encourage a global sense of identity in relation to environmental matters, this should not prevent students developing their sense of national identity. Tate argued that: 'A world of social and geographical mobility, frequent job changes and family breakdown is a world in even greater need of those things that bind people into distinctive communities.'

Tate argued that 'we have heard relatively little about purposes of education that relate to the way in which it can contribute to social cohesiveness, to maintaining, transmitting, and if necessary, rebuilding a sense of community'. Tate thus sees education as a vehicle through which a sense of national identity can be built. It is easy to see how, in Tate's terms, geography has a part to place in a wider project of social integration. In his speeches and articles Tate has returned to the themes of 'belonging' and 'nationhood'. Jones (1997) argues that this can be read as a yearning to hold on to what has been lost in the face of economic, social and cultural change. Education, in the form of an integrating National Curriculum, can act as a bulwark against these changes. Jones identifies Tate as a 'Neoconservative' who 'accepts the existence of the capitalist order, but who is concerned that it leads to the destruction of the traditional symbols and practices on which a meaningful social life depends' (p. 153).

Jones argues that the National Curriculum can be read as part of a wider project to establish a 'common culture' whose features are strongly Anglo-centric. The National Curriculum can be seen as a cultural form that seeks to unify students at a time when national unity is being radically pluralised through processes of economic and cultural globalisation. As Goodson (1994) argues, when we talk about a National Curriculum, it is appropriate to ask whose 'nation' we are talking about, since a curriculum is always an act of 'social prioritising'. Against this reading of the National Curriculum, it might be possible to argue that school geography can provide young people with a more inclusive concept of the nation, through incorporating elements of multiculturalism and recognising the internal diversity of the national space (Phillips *et al.*, 1999).

Global community

Commentators such as Jones and Goodson argue that the establishment of a 'National' Curriculum must be seen in the light of challenges to the integrity of the nation-state posed by globalisation. Indeed, it might be argued that increasingly school geography is concerned with the construction of identities required for life in a 'global community'. It is perhaps inevitable that in an era where we are bombarded by images of a 'borderless' world and the possibilities of the 'global village', the school geography curriculum should reflect such ideas. Gough (1999) has discussed the relationship between discourses of globalisation and curriculum development. He suggests that globalisation represents 'noise' that forms the background to any curriculum work. The school geography curriculum reflects ideas about globalisation both directly and indirectly. The direct way in which globalisation is reflected in the curriculum is through textbooks and syllabus representations. Thus there tends to be a focus on the 'global economy' and on the ways in which different stages of economic production are increasingly occurring over longer distances. Examples of transnational corporations such as Ford and Nike are used to illustrate these processes. In addition, there is a tendency to focus on global issues (such as global warming and the refugee crisis). The overall effect of these representations is to provide pupils with a map of the contemporary world which stresses the links and interdependency between people and places. These are supported by more indirect ideas about globalisation through the use of technologies such as the internet which serve to reinforce the idea that the world is 'shrinking' and that instantaneous communication can take place between distant places. The overall effect of this work in geography classrooms is to suggest to pupils that they are members of what Urry (2000) calls a 'putative global community'. Urry suggests the following list of responsibilities that go with such membership:

- to find out the state of the globe, both through national sources of information and image and especially through sources which are internationalised;
- to demonstrate a stance of cosmopolitanism towards other environments, other cultures and other peoples. Such cosmopolitanism may involve either consuming such environments across the globe; or refusing to consume such environments because of a concern for the wider impact;
- to engage in forms of behaviour with regard to culture, the environment and other places which are consistent with the various conceptions of how to live sustainably;
- to respond to images, icons and narratives which address people as highly differentiated citizens of the globe rather than as citizens of a particular nation, ethnic group, gender, class or generation;
- to seek to convince others that they should also seek to act on behalf of the globe as a whole which is suffering collectively;
- to act in terms of the global public interest rather than in terms of local or national interests.

Readers might like to consider the extent to which such responsibilities are reinforced in geography classrooms.

Since there is a tendency in the school curriculum to treat knowledge as 'truth', globalisation is generally presented as a 'fact' – it is happening here and now. This message is easily supported by the use of examples of products consumed by pupils such as Nike trainers or Coca-Cola. Thus school geography provides pupils with a map of the contemporary world economy. However, globalisation is a socially constructed discourse by which certain groups seek to represent the world. There is a danger that we see the school geography curriculum as *reflecting* a globalised world rather than as actively involved in *constituting* it (see Gibson-Graham, 1996; Barnes, 1996). In addition to ideas that suggest that globalisation is a 'fact', and that simply map the shifting contours of the world economy, we can recognise other forms of discourse about globalisation that offer alternative perspectives on the extent and desirability of globalisation, and suggest very different models of global citizenship from those linked to new technologies. For instance, Oxfam's *A Curriculum for Global Citizenship* (1997) makes explicit its commitment to forms of education based on anti-racist development education and environmental education. It stresses a knowledge and understanding of social justice and equity, skills such as the ability to challenge injustice and inequalities, and values such as a commitment to the 'belief that people can make a difference'. So if geography does suggest to young people that they need to recognise their location in a 'borderless' world, it does not do so in a singular and uncontested way. School geography is a site where young people learn about globalisation and learn to accept the challenge of living in a rapidly changing, uncertain world. In these conditions, new types of knowledge, skills, attitudes and values are needed. However, different approaches to the idea of a global community are to be found in the classroom, with very different implications for citizenship.

Where does this discussion of the various 'stories' about community that are told in school geography leave us? Not with a clearer sense of definition, but with an increased awareness of the contested, ambiguous and contradictory nature of community. Community is symbolic, and communities are always 'imagined' (Anderson, 1991). It is perhaps possible to think of communities as a necessary fiction, through which attempts are made to make sense of the world. If we think of community in this way, the work of geography education can be thought of as concerned with the construction of 'maps of meaning'. The classroom becomes a place where links are forged and new identifications are constructed.

In this section I have suggested that school geography provides pupils with different answers to the question 'to which space do I belong?' These answers tend to focus on ties of locality, nation and the global. In different classrooms, and in the same classrooms at different times, these different constructions of community are being played out. However, the ways in which community is constructed are not innocent. It is not simply a matter of favouring one scale over the others, or of letting them all happily co-mingle in the classroom

Geography matters?

It is significant that education for citizenship is being promoted at a time when there is much talk about the break-up of older forms of community (linked, for example, to the decline of industrial activities) and the establishment of new forms of community (through, for instance, the internet). The question of which spaces we belong to is increasingly important when (according to many social theorists) we live in a fast-changing, globalised world. This chapter has argued that school geography provides a set of resources through which young people can anchor themselves in these unstable and uncertain conditions. My intention has been to stress the importance of school geography in the construction of citizenship. In classrooms, geography teachers are involved in the drawing of boundaries and the opening up of different perspectives. This chapter suggests that geography matters, and that as teachers we need to ask what types of 'geographical imagination' we are constructing (Crang, 1999). However, cultural geographers have pointed to the ways in which young people's 'geographical imagina-tions' are also shaped by the symbols, images, texts and media which bombard them daily with images of the world. It might be argued that the practices of everyday consumption of goods and images are more important in creating new 'spaces of identity' (Robins and Morley, 1995) than the lessons taught in school geography. Indeed, many commentators have argued that pedagogy is no longer (if it was ever) confined to the classroom, and is increasingly found in the products of Hollywood, television, the internet and computer games (see Goldman and Papson, 1999, on the forms of citizenship promoted by Nike). This suggests the need for geography teachers to engage in a form of 'border pedagogy' (Giroux, 1992) in which pupils are given the opportunities to explore the complexities of their own histories and geographies, to examine the nature of the links between themselves and other people in different places, and to critically explore the boundaries of their own communities in order to decide to which spaces they belong.

FOR FURTHER THINKING

1   Discuss ways in which pupils can be encouraged to distinguish between 'open' and 'closed' understanding of their localities.
2   Spend some time examining the contents of your KS3 coursebook; in particular, try to identify (a) how the text is used to convey *them* (or *others*) and *us*, and (b) ways of using the text to encourage pupils to understand the *discourse*. Finally, (c) are there any real alternatives to the discourse that you have described?
3   Draft a KS3 scheme of work entitled: 'To which spaces do I belong?' Try to include concepts included in this chapter such as 'community' and 'globalisation' and incorporate how new technologies such as the internet have introduced new forms of 'community'.

References

Ahier, J. (1988) *Industry, Children and the Nation*, London, Falmer Press.

Anderson, B. (1991) *Imagined Communities*, London, Verso.

Bale, J. (1987) *Geography in the Primary School*, London, Routledge and Kegan Paul.

Barnes, T. (1996) *Logics of Dislocation*, New York, Guilford Press.

Bhatt, C. (1994) 'New foundations: contingency, indeterminacy and black translocality', in Weeks, J. (ed.) *The Lesser Evil and the Greater Good*, London, Rivers Oram Press.

Crang, P. 1999 'Local-global', in P. Cloke, P. Crang, and M. Goodwin (eds) *Introducing Human Geographies*, London, Arnold, pp. 24–34.

Dicken, P. (1998) *Global Shift: Transforming the World Economy*, London, Paul Chapman.

Donald, J. (1992) *Sentimental Education*, London, Verso.

Driver, S. and Martell, L. (1998) *New Labour: Politics after Thatcherism*, Cambridge, Polity Press.

Foucault, M. (1961) *Folie et déraison. Histoire de la folie à l'âge classique*, Paris, Librarie Plon. (Published in English as *Madness and Civilisation*, New York, Random House, 1965.)

Foucault, M. (1963) *Naissance de la clinique*, Paris, Presses Universitaires de France. (Published in English as *The Birth of the Clinic: an Archaeology of Medical Perception, London, Tavistock Press, 1973.)*

Foucault, M. (1969) L'Archéologie du savoir, Paris, Gallimard. (Published in English as *The Archaeology of Knowledge*, New York, Pantheon, 1972.)

Foucault, M. (1975) *Surveiller et punir*, Paris, Gallimard. (Published in English as *Discipline and Punish: the Birth of the Prison*, New York, Vintage Press, 1979.)

Gibson-Graham, J.-K. (1996) *The End of Capitalism (as We Knew It)*, Oxford, Blackwell.

Giroux, H. (1992) *Border Crossings*, London, Routledge.

Goldman, R. and Papson, S. (1999) *Nike Culture*, London, Sage.

Goodson, I. (1994) *Studying Curriculum: Cases and Methods*, Buckingham, Open University Press.

Gough, N. (1999) 'Globalization and school curriculum change: locating a transnational imaginary', *Journal of Education Policy*, 14, pp. 73–84.

Harvey, D. (1993) 'Class relations, social justice, and the politics of difference', in S. Pile and M. Keith (eds) *Place and the Politics of Identity*, London, Routledge, pp. 41–66.

Harvey, D. (1996) *Justice, Nature and the Geography of Difference*, Oxford, Blackwell.

Hay, C. (1999) *The Political Economy of New Labour*, Manchester, Manchester University Press.

Herod, A., Ó'Tuatail, G. and Roberts, S. (1998) *An Unruly World? Globalization, Governance and Geography*, London, Routledge.

Jones, K. (1997) 'Tradition and nation: breaking the link', *Changing English*, 4, pp. 149–59.

Luke, T. and Ó'Tuatail, G. (1998) 'Global Flowmations, Local Fundamentalisms, and Fast Geopolitics: "America" in an accelerating world order' in Herod *et al.*

Massey, D. (1999) 'The social place', *Primary Geographer*, April, pp. 4–6.

McDowell, L. (1999) *Gender, Identity and Place: Understanding Feminist Geographies*, Cambridge, Polity Press.

O'Byrne, D. (1997) 'Working-class culture: local community and global conditions', in Eade, J. (ed.) *Living the Global City: Globalization as Local Process*, London, Routledge.

Ó'Tuatail, G. (1996) *Critical Geopolitics*, London, Routledge.

Oxfam (1997) *A Curriculum for Global Citizenship*, Oxford, Oxfam.

Penrose, J. (1993) 'Reification in the name of change: the impact of nationalism on social constructions of nation, people and place in Scotland and the United Kingdom', in J. Penrose and P. Jackson (eds) *Constructions of Race, Place and Nation*, London, UCL Press, pp. 27–49.

Phillips, R., Goalen, P., McCully, A. and Wood, S. (1999) 'Four histories, one nation? History teaching, nationhood and a British identity', *Compare*, 29, pp. 153–69.

Robins, K. and Morley, D. (1995) *Spaces of Identity*, London, Routledge.

Ross, A. (2000) *Curriculum: Construction and Critique*, London, Falmer Press.

Smith, N. (1993) 'Homeless/global: scaling places', in J. Bird, B. Curtis, T. Putnam, G. Robertson and L. Tickner (eds) *Mapping the Futures: Local Cultures, Global Change*, London, Routledge, pp. 87–119.

Urry, J. (2000) *Sociology beyond Societies: Mobilities for the Twenty-first Century*, London, Routledge.

Chapter 7

'Where shall I draw the line, Miss?'

The geography of exclusion

Crispin Jones

Boundaries, borders, frontiers and marches

The quotation in the title of this chapter came from a geography lesson that I was recently watching in an inner London comprehensive school. The pupil was drawing the boundary of the European Union (EU) on a map that the newly qualified teacher had given him. Apart from the relevance or otherwise of the exercise, what interested me was that he, like many other British people, was very vague about the eastern boundary of the Union, despite having been given a list of member states of the EU. The pupil's lack of knowledge is revealing and not unsurprising. Nor was he helped by the map being out of date, again not surprising given the spate of changes in Central, Eastern and South-eastern Europe since 1990. More pertinently, the idea of boundaries, borders, frontiers, marches, call them what you will, is most complex once one moves away from commonsense assumptions.

The key aspects of these linked concepts is that all the words are indicative of the limits of authority and power, with those inside the states subject to both and those outside the states free of both but a potential threat to them. In many periods of history, the area between two authorities has often been vague, as terms like the Welsh Marches indicate. Marches were areas of contestation, as indeed other frontier and borderlands were and still are. As state power consolidated in Europe, authority in such areas became more definite though rarely as strong as in more central areas of the state. Authority was still weak in such areas and remained so in Europe until well into the nineteenth century; indeed areas still exist in Europe (e.g. in the Caucasus) and elsewhere where centralised authority is limited.

However, boundaries do not just define nation states as simple lines on maps. They are also useful indicators of inclusion and exclusion and, as such, comprise a range of unclear constructs with which young people need to work. And maps are, of course, not just about the clear, precise and simple delineations of boundaries. They are also representations of ideological perceptions of the world (Black, 1997). A school atlas in Greece stresses Byzantium, one in Serbia the aspirations of a greater Serbia. The layouts are similar, the motherland first, followed by the rest of the world in descending importance (and scale) for that state. Atlases that take a different view have to make this clear in their title as, for example, does Crow's *Third World Atlas* (1983). Children thus learn early on about not just the centrality and importance of their own state but also its supposed clear and precise boundaries. As Norman Davies notes,

> although most European nations are aware that their present territory was once ruled by foreign powers, dominated by different cultures or inhabited by alien peoples . . . present day nations and regimes have a strong inclination to believe that they and their forebears have possessed their present territory since time immemorial.
>
> (Davies, 1999, p. 39)

Education's supporting role here is important, for as nationalism grew in the nineteenth century across Europe, so too did mass education, which had as one of its roles the duty to ensure that children were and are 'thoroughly indoctrinated with the notion that every inch of ground within their national frontiers was eternally "theirs" and hence inherently "French" or "German" or "Polish" or whatever' (ibid).

Even so-called progressive politicians have supported such chauvinistic ideas; nationalism is a powerful and unifying political ideology. At the beginning of the French Revolution, Danton reiterated the view that France had 'natural boundaries' within which, presumably, French people lived or had the right to live. He claimed: 'The limits of France are marked out by nature. We shall reach them at their four points; at the Ocean, at the Rhine, at the Alps, at the Pyrenees' (quoted in Doyle, 1989, p. 200).

Such an indoctrination process is not what most cartographers have in mind when they draw their maps but these products still play a role in giving an apparent clarity to concepts of national and international inclusion and exclusion, as recent debates about appropriate map projections demonstrate. Young people's mental maps may appear to lack the clarity of a printed map but their purpose is the same – to locate the important, to help work out what is ours, what is not and what is contested. For most of these key areas geography (and especially urban and historical geography) is one of the few curriculum areas where such key issues can be usefully explored with young people. This chapter covers three key aspects of exclusion, social and otherwise, namely: insiders/outsiders, migration and socio-spatial patterning. The chapter explores the potential contribution geography makes to these three critical aspects of social exclusion. In this exploration the term exclusion draws heavily upon the work of Tony Giddens, and from the 'Third Way' (Giddens, 1999) rather than from the New Labour government's Social Exclusion Unit's somewhat limited and insipid reworking of this complex and useful concept (Social Exclusion Unit, 1997, 1998a and 1998b).

Insiders and outsiders

Racism and social exclusion thrive on the patterning of the world, at whatever level, into a simple binary grouping of 'them' and 'us', insiders and outsiders. Outsiders – 'them', 'the Other' – are not only different from insiders, they are potentially dangerous to the insiders – 'us'. But the outsiders do help to bind the insiders together. As Franco Moretti notes: 'A hostile Other [is] the source of collective identity' (1999, p. 29). In the British case, the construction of a British identity from existing English, Scots and Welsh conflicting identities was a response to a range of dangerous 'Others'. Linda Colley demonstrates this in her careful analysis of eighteenth- and nineteenth-century British history, showing that Britain was an invented nation forged, above all, by war. Time and time again, war with France brought Britons, whether they hailed from Wales or Scotland or England, into confrontation with an obviously hostile Other and encouraged them to define themselves collectively against it. They defined themselves as Protestants struggling for survival against the world's foremost Catholic power. They defined themselves against the French as they imagined them to be, superstitious, militarist, decadent and unfree. And increasingly as the wars went on, they defined themselves in contrast to the colonial peoples they conquered, peoples who were manifestly alien in terms of culture, religion and colour.

(1996, p. 5)

It was this British national identity that was strengthened by two world wars in the last century that is now being eroded as its foundations fade in the new century. The British no longer share a Protestant oppositional culture in any meaningful sense, save for the Ulster Protestants in Northern Ireland. The French and the Germans are now Britain's allies, if not its friends, and the once colonial 'Other' has become an integral part of modern British society. The EU is a pale substitute for the objects of the xenophobic fears of the past but it has to do. With less need of a British identity formed in the old manner, the national identities that had been subsumed have now re-emerged in the current devolution movements. What this means in the creation of new boundaries and new 'Others' may be unclear, but needs to be engaged with.

At an international level, similar divisions continue to hold great power over perceptions of the rest of the world. The North/South divide is well established as a heuristic concept and geography teachers, especially when moving into the area of development education, have long tried to break down stereotypes of the developing world of the 'Africa never discovered the wheel' variety. How successful this work has been may be questioned but it still remains one of the few curriculum areas where such negative stereotypes are regularly challenged in our schools.

Of equivalent importance is the insider/outsider debate in relation to Europe. Where Europe is and who is a European are complex questions that are seldom explicitly addressed in the curriculum and, as a consequence, long-standing, ideologically drenched definitions have persisted. Indeed, why do we need such definitions if not to exclude? Europe was invented as an oppositional concept, especially in relation to Christianity's struggle with Islam (Coulby and Jones, 1995, pp. 41–58). As a consequence, medieval Christendom and modern Europe, to a very large extent, have similar borders, maintain similar sets of insiders and outsiders and so share old worries. Echoes of these persistent themes are perhaps exemplified by current debates about Turkey's wish to join the EU and the anti-Islamic aspects of the terrible violence in Bosnia, Kosovo and Chechnya. No wonder the pupil did not know where to draw the line.

Nor is it just an issue in schools. Students of mine at the Institute of Education have similar difficulties. Small groups of postgraduate students have been asked over the years to define the borders of Europe and always find problems with the eastern boundary. Although the Urals is the preferred choice it is always accompanied by other definitions which offer alternative perspectives. Again, Turkey causes particular problems and so do the states of the Caucasus region.

The issues here are not only about where the borders are, but more importantly why Europe is where it is. In particular, as noted earlier, it is Europe's eastern boundary that is so contested, in part because it has mainly been from the East that peoples moved into Europe's rich heartland. Such images and accounts have been a dominant paradigm in historical accounts of population movements in the Western Eurasian peninsula (Davies, 1997). More recently and at a smaller scale, the ecological terminology of ethnic succession and conflict were employed by the Chicago School (for example Burgess, 1926; see Box 7.1) to describe processes in cities in the twentieth century. In doing so the School captured an uncritical geographical imagination for the century that followed.

Box 7.1 The Chicago School

The Chicago School is the name given to a powerful tradition within sociology that has had a profound effect upon other social sciences, including geography. The University of Chicago established one of North America's first sociology departments in 1892 and in the decades that followed this School left an indelible mark upon the form and focus of much social enquiry. The School's methodology claimed to be empirical and pragmatic, setting itself apart from the abstract theorising of European counterparts. Direct observation produced classic works such as Zorbaugh's *The Gold Coast and the Slum* (1929) but other, now well-established research methods like participant observation were also pioneered. These qualitative approaches were matched by William Ogburn's quantitative mapping and this draws attention to the School's concern with cities.

Ernest Burgess's famous work dealing with Chicago's social structure made the journey to another discipline – geography. This empirical work dealt with Chicago, a single case study, at a particular point in time. From this case study more theoretical generalisations were made. Analysis of these usefully draws attention to how pragmatic work, whatever its ideological claim to neutrality might be, is always theoretically underpinned. In this instance that basis is an unsophisticated Social Darwinism (see p. 127) describing social processes in ecological terms and with explicit racist descriptions of Chicago's immigrant population at the time. In the *Growth of the City* (1926, p. 37), for example, Burgess describes the existence of distinct areas of the city in the following terms:

'Yet interesting occupational selection has taken place by nationality, *explainable more by racial temperament* or circumstance than by old-world economic background, as Irish policemen, Greek ice-cream parlors, Chinese laundries, Negro porters, Belgian janitors, etc.' (my emphasis).

This brief reference has a number of crucial lessons for geography teachers. The *first* is to acknowledge the interrelatedness of disciplines and, *secondly*, that fashionable belief systems frame all academic enquiry; in the 1920s the above expressions would have excited little comment. But *finally*, and perhaps most significantly, is the reminder that a critical stance should always be taken, even with work that a discipline has canonised. In the area of citizenship no caution is more vital.

However, if the eastern borders of Europe are contested, the debate is seldom investigated or reflected upon in work done in Britain's schools. This is because conventional definitions have held sway for a very long time in our schools. As a British school atlas of the late 1830s put it:

> According to the decisions of modern science, Europe is bounded on the south by the Mediterranean sea, on the west by the Atlantic ocean, which includes the Azores Islands and Iceland; Greenland being considered a part of North America. On the north, its boundary is the Arctic Ocean, comprehending the remote islands of Spitzbergen and Nova Zembla. Towards the east, the limits of Europe seem even yet to be inaccurately defined. Its natural and geographical boundaries might easily be obtained by tracing the river Ousa from its source to its junction with the Belaia, thence along the Kama to the Volga, which would constitute a striking natural division, to the town of Sarapta, whence a short line might be carried due west to the river Don, which would complete the unascertained line of demarcation. But this great outline, through the petty governments under the dominion of Russia, science has hitherto been prevented from adopting.
>
> (Russell, c.1838, p. iii)

Only a modest change of language would make the definition one that many people would accept (and teach) today. For example, in the 1990 *Cambridge Encyclopedia*, Europe is defined as the

> Second smallest continent, forming an extensive peninsula of the Eurasian landmass, occupying c.8% of the Earth's surface, bounded N and NE by the Arctic Ocean, NW and W by the Atlantic Ocean, S by the Mediterranean Sea, and E by Asia beyond the Ural Mts.
>
> (Crystal, 1990, p. 423)

This is almost Russell's definition, expressed more crisply and, by appearing scientific, appearing less questionable. Moreover, Russell's reference to Russia has contemporary resonance, as current events in Chechnya and other states in the Caucasus reveal. Earlier in this chapter it was suggested that maps, despite their seeming precision, are socially constructed. The prose accompanying the maps may disguise this but cannot completely conceal their social origins. Even the *Cambridge Encyclopedia* definition does not comment on why other extensive peninsulas of the Eurasian landmass do not merit continental status, for example the interestingly named Indian sub-continent. However, there is more to this than merely retaining unquestioningly the Russell boundaries. This is because running alongside such definitions are widely held value judgements about relative *worth* which still persist, despite being implicit and less easily recognised now. In these value judgements, those people lucky enough to live in Europe, however defined, have greater moral, economic and cultural value than those in other areas of the globe. To return to Russell:

> This portion of the globe, though least in dimension, is of more importance than any other, not merely to its own inhabitants, but to all who think commerce, science and

the arts, of any advantage to mankind. In modern times it has been the seat of literature; and its natives have been justly distinguished for their power, wisdom, courage and strength of intellect: of which, imperishable monuments may be found in the extent of their dominions, the purity of their religion, the principles of their legislation, and the comprehensiveness of their laws.

(Russell, c.1838, p. iii)

A sentiment not far removed from those of certain contemporary tabloid newspapers! It is also a tacit rephrasing of the idea of the barbarians at the gate, a concept that could be said to define Europe and European perspectives on the rest of the world. Moreover, recent changes in international relations, following the collapse of Communism in Europe, have introduced or reaffirmed ideas on insiders and outsiders, based on a division of Europe that has seemingly replaced the old Cold War divide into its replacement, the EU/non-EU divide.

Such a view of insiders and outsiders is more than a somewhat abstruse debate about boundaries. It also has within it stereotypes as to who is an insider and who is an outsider that are now only loosely based on that artificial division, if indeed they ever had a factual basis. If an insider in Europe is a European, what exactly does that term mean and at what point in the curriculum are children given a definition? The point of the question is that without examination, children are likely to maintain a view of Europeans as white, Christian peoples, a perspective that encourages a view of black Europeans or European Muslims as outsiders, the latter point being crucial to the horrors in Bosnia and Kosovo of the late 1990s.

These views are not just broad 'European' ones. They would hold true for many in England too in relation to their own part of the state in which they live. It is a view that is fostered by politicians, the mass media and also, perhaps unwittingly, by some in education. English tabloid newspapers, like some of their peers in other European countries, are clear about insiders and outsiders. This 'fog in Channel, Continent isolated' mentality is apparently shared by many in Britain. But what is new in England is devolution. A fascinating change in intra-national perceptions of who is an insider and who is an outsider has occurred in Britain apparently as a result of devolution. What are teachers in English schools now to teach about the geography of Scotland and Wales, the English's seemingly new 'near abroad'? Asking children in a secondary school in 2000 to list what they knew about Wales produced very short lists. To ask the same question in a Welsh classroom about England would have very different results. In other words, there is a danger of building a new insider/outsider category unless deliberate efforts are made in schools and elsewhere to maintain an inclusive view of Britain. This prospect could usefully be compared to changes in the curricula in the Baltic states where, prior to the implosion of the Soviet Union, the curricula were Russian. With the collapse of the Soviet Union the situation has reversed: now Russian and things Russian have all but disappeared from the curricula even though the country remains a major trading partner and the land of allegiance of many in the successor states (Coulby, 1997). Significantly, access to citizenship rights in these states frequently contains an element of language, the deliberate effect being to disenfranchise Russian speakers whose families may have lived in those states for generations (Smith, 1990).

In the English classroom therefore, pupils may well begin to be confused about their place in the world, certainly in Europe and potentially even within the United Kingdom. Some may also feel excluded, on the other side of one sort of boundary or another, a topic rarely discussed in lessons. Here is a real opportunity for geography teachers.

Movement and migration

The second aspect of exclusion that is relevant here is migration. Migration and its consequences remain critical but are seldom explored in the manner required in our schools. The reasons for this are obvious. A migrant is usually perceived to be a tolerated 'outsider' who may or may not be accorded 'insider' status in terms of rights. These rights might include the right to settle, to work, to family reunification, to vote, to become naturalised or to become a full citizen. However, the term 'migrant' itself is slippery. Movement from where to where – and for how long – makes anything but an operational definition of migration almost impossible. As Box 7.2 implies, words like 'permanent' are crucial but are themselves evasive. At what temporal point does a person's movement become permanent? And who makes that definitional decision, the migrant, some state official or some combination of both? And which definition has the most social power and impact?

As Box 7.2 shows, there are many ways in which movement and migration can be classified. It shows that most of us are migrants of one sort or another but, more to the point, we are all descendants of migrants. We forget this at our peril. The concept of 'indigenous' is again a socially constructed term, and ideologically loaded. At what point the descendants of migrants become indigenous is the critical question. Yet many people emerge from our schools still thinking that the population can be divided into two neat categories. In Britain and Ireland we have forgotten our migrant past in an effort to rewrite history in our contemporary image, a recurring feature of life in the area that Norman Davies has called 'The Isles' (Davies, 1999).

Moreover, taxonomies like those put forward in Box 7.2 only reveal the operational nature of the concept of migration. Much more significant than the type of movement is its motivation. The study of push and pull factors underlying migration is a well-known but nonetheless useful and revealing aid to an understanding of this motivation. Equally important but little investigated are the non-movers, those who remain behind when the migrants leave and who are present when they arrive. Migration generally depletes the resource base of the sending society and increases that of the receiving country (Berger and Mohr, 1975).

Migration is seldom seen in this positive light in our classrooms. Academic definitions apart, many children see migrants as an alien category, an excluded 'them'. In the British case they are currently seen as black, to the point that the term 'immigrant' has passed into popular meaning as a black person rather than a migrant who has entered the country. To maintain exclusion over time, terms like 'first generation' and 'third generation' are applied, nearly always to people who are seen as non-white by the dominant host and white majority, helping to perpetuate exclusion and sustain racism and xenophobia. The new wave of migration by those fleeing persecution has meant that there are larger numbers of asylum seekers and refugee children in British classrooms. Current government plans for their dispersal across the country means that schools will

---

Box 7.2 Migration or movement: a 'commonsense' UK typology

International movement
- Holidays in 'far-off places'
- Roma nomadic movement
- Weekends in country X, weekdays in country Y
- Cross-national commuting

Intra-national movement
- Weekend at home 1, weekdays at home 2
- From home to work in same village/town
- Urban commuting
- Ex-urban commuting
- Move permanent residence
  - down the street
  - within the town
  - across the city
  - within the region
- Roma nomadic movement

Transnational 'commonsense' migration
- Seasonal migration from place A to place B and return
- Move permanent residence across the world
- Move permanent residence to another state
- Roma nomadic movement

Intra-national migration
- Move permanent residence
  - across the city
  - within the region
  - within the state
- Roma nomadic movement

---

accommodate these new children without having a clear idea as to why they are there. The potential for exclusion is high.

Again, the task for the geography teacher is clear. The movement of people and its explanation are likely to be covered in geography lessons or not at all. The dynamic of world demography *is* migration and settlement. It is also a continuing dynamic in Britain that too often is seen as recent, as aberrant and upsetting of some imaginary status quo. Yet our classrooms are full of movement and migration that are seldom discussed and even more rarely explained. As an example, more languages are spoken in London than anywhere else in the world: children in its schools speak more than 307 languages, and one-third of its 850,000 pupils do not speak English at home (Baker and Eversley, 1999).

Similar linguistic variety, albeit on a smaller scale, would be found in most British cities. It is not new – think of English place names – and it is a continuous process and has made Britain the complex demographic state that it is today.

Continuous migration has also led to the complex socio-spatial patterning of our cities. Again, many pupils see this as a recent rather than a recurrent feature of urban life and, if left unchallenged and unexplained, such a view will encourage and perpetuate social exclusion.

Socio-spatial patterning and exclusion

Charles Booth's socio-economic maps of London, with different streets in different colours, from black where what he called the criminal classes lived to the gold of the wealthy, still have a value today. They attempt to visualise the stark socio-spatial patterning of cities and it is fascinating to look at them today with young people both to assess their utility and to discuss the changes that have (or have not) taken place since they were first constructed in the 1880s. They are early attempts to delineate social exclusion accurately.

The founder of the Chicago School (see p. 101), Robert Ezra Park, moved the analysis further, stating 'the processes of segregation establish moral distance which makes the city a mosaic of little worlds which touch but do not interpenetrate' (Park, quoted in Moretti, 1999, p. 89). Both he and Booth make a clear case for moral as well as physical distance between the excluded and the included, a distinction which continues to bedevil much discussion of the subject, best summed up by the phrases 'the deserving' and 'the undeserving poor'. The distinction supports partial inactivity and encourages condemnation, perspectives which are not unknown in our schools.

Such patterning returns us to the discussion about boundaries, 'them' and 'us', with which this chapter started. The focus is now on the inequalities within the state, especially within the city. Walter Benjamin described it perceptively:

> A city is uniform only in appearance. Even its name takes on a different sound in the different neighbourhoods. In no other place – with the exception of dreams – can the phenomenon of the border be experienced in such a pristine state as in cities.
>
> (Benjamin, quoted in Moretti, 1999, p. 80)

It is a rich lode for teachers to explore. London's linguistic richness mentioned earlier is echoed in the city's internal form. Areas like Brixton, Green Lanes, Notting Hill, Southall and Tower Hamlets contain specific cultural groups that have many of the characteristics first described by the Chicago School in terms of territoriality and boundaries and the School's racism has echoes too. This urban mosaic, its boundaries, sustained by space and implicit morality, exist within many city classrooms. At the urban level, such ideas have long been explored by geographers like David Harvey (Harvey, 1973, 1989a and 1989b) but these investigations have seldom been followed through into the space of the urban school itself. It is an important area for geography teachers to explore. *A lack of explanation supports discrimination, racism and xenophobia.* A lack of understanding confirms patterns of exclusion and inclusion within the classroom and the school setting. Helping young people better understand this is a further major responsibility for geography teachers.

Towards social inclusion

Can such a challenge be met? There is evidence that the challenge is being accepted. At a recent RGS/Institute of British Geographers annual conference, Ron Martin was reported as saying that geography was in danger of losing focus. He asserted that geographers needed to tell the world what shapes social and physical environments and that they needed to be involved in practical social policy work as human geography is about big social questions (Brown, 2000). It was a view that was echoed by other conference speakers. As a major discipline in higher education and an important school subject, geography does not just seek to understand social exclusion, it must seek to end it.

FOR FURTHER THINKING

1   Critically examine ways in which studying geography can help provide pupils with explanations that can reduce discrimination, racism and xenophobia.
2   This chapter provides useful guidance on the pitfalls to avoid when teaching migration and urban patterns and processes. Identify other topics in geography where a lack of awareness of the origins or the underpinnings of a model could lead to similar pitfalls.
3   In the previous chapter, scale was a key idea. In this chapter the idea of borders and boundaries is crucial. How explicit are your schemes of work with both sets of ideas?

References

Baker, P. and Eversley, J. (1999) *Multilingual Capital*. London: Battlebridge Publications.
Berger, J. and Mohr, J. (1975) *A Seventh Man*. Harmondsworth: Penguin.
Black, J. (1997) *Maps and History: Constructing Images of the Past*. London: Yale University Press.
Booth, C. [1891–1903] (1969) *Life and Labour of the People of London*. London: Hutchinson.
Brown, P. (2000) 'Lost in sacred space'. *Guardian Higher*, 11 January, p. 5H.
Burgess E. (1926) *The Growth of the City*. Chicago: University of Chicago Press.
Colley, L. (1996) *Britons: Forging the Nation, 1707–1837*. London: Vintage.
Coulby, D. (1997) 'Language and citizenship in Latvia, Lithuania and Estonia: education and the brinks of warfare'. *European Journal of Intercultural Studies*, 82.
Coulby, D. and Jones, C. (1995) *Postmodernity and European Educational Systems*. Trentham.
Crow, B. (1983) *Third World Atlas*. Milton Keynes: Open University Press.
Crystal, D. (ed.) (1990) *The Cambridge Encyclopedia*. Cambridge: Cambridge University Press.
Davies, N. (1997) *Europe: a History*. London: Pimlico.
Davies, N. (1999) *The Isles: a History*. London: Macmillan.
Doyle, W. (1989) *The Oxford History of the French Revolution*. Oxford: OUP.
Giddens, A. (1999) *The Third Way*. Cambridge: Polity Press.

Harvey, D. (1973) *Social Justice and the City*. London: Edward Arnold.

Harvey, D. (1989a) *The Condition of Postmodernity: an Enquiry into the Origins of Cultural Change*. Oxford: Blackwell.

Harvey, D. (1989b) *The Urban Experience*. Oxford: Blackwell.

Moretti, F. (1999) *Atlas of the European Novel: 1800–1900*. London: Verso.

Park, R.E., Burgess, E.W. and Mckenzie, R.D. (eds) (1967) *The City*. Chicago: University of Chicago Press.

Russell, J. (*c*.1838) *A Complete Atlas of the World*. London: Fischer Son and Co.

Smith, G. (1990) *The Nationalities Question in the Soviet Union*. London: Longman.

Social Exclusion Unit (1997) *Social Exclusion Unit: Background and Structure, December, 1997*. London: Social Exclusion Unit.

Social Exclusion Unit (1998a) *Truancy and School Exclusion: Report by the Social Exclusion Unit*. London: HMSO.

Social Exclusion Unit (1998b) *Bringing Britain Together: a National Strategy for Neighbourhood Renewal*. London: HMSO.

Zorbaugh, W.H. (1929) *The Gold Coast and the Slum*. Chicago: University of Chicago Press.

Chapter 8

A very British subject

Questions of identity

Gwyn Edwards

Do we have a national identity worth bothering with?

(Toynbee 2000)

Since its launch in 1988 the National Curriculum in the United Kingdom has been a site of ongoing controversy and contestation. A persistent and increasingly significant facet of the debate concerns the interrelated themes of citizenship and identity. Questions of identity, in particular, loomed large in both the initial implementation and subsequent rewritings of the National Curriculum. Indeed, it could be argued that they were in fact its *raison d'être*. For, in justifying the imposition of a centrally prescribed National Curriculum on an educational system that had always valued and defended the autonomy of teachers, Kenneth Baker (Secretary of State for Education) stated:

> I see the national curriculum as a way of increasing our social coherence. There is so much distraction, variety and uncertainty in the modern world that in our country today *our children are in danger of losing any sense at all of a common culture and a common heritage*. The cohesive role of the national curriculum will provide our society with a greater *sense of identity*.

> (Baker 1987; my emphasis)

Questions of identity were, and continue to be, particularly prominent in the ideological battle over the history curriculum. This battle has been well documented (Phillips 1996; McKeirnan 1993; Crawford 1995) and further elaboration is not necessary here. It is sufficient to say that Chris McGovern, director of the History Curriculum Association, asserted that changes to the History National Curriculum proposed by the Qualifications and Curriculum Authority, if adopted, would 'destroy history as a subject that has traditionally given school-children a sense of national identity' (cited in *The Guardian*, 5 April 1999). Indeed, in response to the proposed changes, the History Curriculum Association launched an alternative manifesto in a 'final attempt to restore to the children of this country their birthright – a sense of identity' (ibid.).

The identity debate was further fuelled by Dr Nick Tate, Chief Executive of the Qualifications and Curriculum Authority. In a series of speeches and articles during the 1990s, he constructed and reiterated a discourse which envisages the school curriculum as a means of fostering a common culture, creating a more cohesive society, and 'maintaining, transmitting, and if necessary rebuilding a sense of community' (cited in *TES* 1996a). Central to this discourse is an insistence that pupils should develop a clear sense of national identity, which according to him is 'one of the few lodestars left at a time of rapid change and flux' (ibid.). This, he asserts:

> means giving priority in the curriculum to English and British history . . . to the geography of the British Isles; to the literary inheritance in English; to the English Language as it is spoken and written in these islands; to the British political system; and to the study of the Christian religion and the Judaeo-Christian roots of our shared values.
>
> (ibid.)

Tate's attention has focused predominantly on the teaching of history and English. But in an address to the annual conference of the Geographical Association in April 1996, he suggested that in the face of a homogenised global culture geography too should help foster a sense of national community. Furthermore, he invited the conference to consider whether or not the geography curriculum after 2000 should incorporate a requirement to study 'the geography of either England or the United Kingdom as an entity in itself' (cited in *TES* 1996b). His suggestion was significant in that, unlike history and English, there had previously been no explicit attempt to appropriate the geography curriculum in England for the purpose of engendering national identity.

In contrast, the statutory Order for geography in Wales established from the beginning the need to 'develop knowledge and understanding of Wales' (CCW 1991, p. 7). Consequently the whole of Wales was designated as the Home Region and, therefore, would be 'the study for all pupils living in Wales' (ibid.). Moreover, it was envisaged that this study of geography would encourage the pupils 'to explore their own identity in relation to the community in which they live, and the wider community of Wales' (ibid.). Additionally, the non-statutory guidance provided a detailed list of ways in which the 'Welshness' of the geography curriculum could be realised in the classroom.

Although not subject to the requirements of the National Curriculum, Scotland is showing a similar trend. A Review Group set up by the Scottish Consultative Council on the Curriculum recommends in its report that 'the distinctive nature of the Scottish experience should be at the centre of the Scottish curriculum' (SCCC 1999a, p. 21). In line with this recommendation, the Scottish Consultative Council on the Curriculum itself, in a recent review of the Environmental Studies component of Curriculum 5–14, advocates geographical studies that 'maintain a focus on the geography of Scotland by including, where appropriate, comparative reference to the Scottish context in relation to geographical aspects elsewhere, and by including at least one topic with a specific Scottish focus' (SCCC 1999b, p. 29).

It seems, therefore, that rather than inculcating a greater sense of collective British identity, as was intended by some of its advocates, the National Curriculum (as it applies to England, Northern Ireland and Wales) and its equivalent in Scotland has legitimated, and is actively fostering, a resurgence of national identities which are, to some extent, at odds with the notion of 'Britishness'.

The emergence of identity as a site of contestation in the school curriculum in the 1990s coincided with, and is partly constitutive of, a burgeoning interest in citizenship education. A commitment to the notion of citizenship education, in some form or other, has a long, if chequered, history in the United Kingdom. However, it is only in recent years that citizenship education has established itself high on the political agenda. It came to prominence in the early 1990s in response to the perceived inadequacies of a subject-based National Curriculum. 'Citizenship' was identified by the National Curriculum Council as one of five cross-curricular themes designed to 'tie together the broad education of the individual subjects and augment what comes from the basic curriculum' (NCC 1990, p. 2). Additional support for citizenship education at this time came from the the House of Commons Commission on Citizenship. Support, too, came from the National Commission on Education (1993) which in its report considered 'the teaching of citizenship of great importance' and recommended its inclusion in a compulsory core that would take up 50 per cent of the curriculum in Key Stage 1 (ages 5–7) and 70 per cent in Key Stages 2 and 3 (ages 7–14).

It therefore came as no surprise that shortly after its election victory in May 1997 the New Labour government pledged to 'strengthen education for citizenship and the teaching of democracy in schools' (DfEE 1997, p 35). To this end, the Citizenship Advisory Group was set up, under the chairmanship of Professor Bernard Crick. Following an initial report in March 1998, the Advisory Group's final report was published in July 1998 (Advisory Group on Citizenship and Education for Democracy 1998) with the intention that its recommendations would be incorporated into the review of the National Curriculum then being undertaken by the Qualifications and Curriculum Authority. Specifically, it recommended that 'citizenship be a statutory entitlement in the school curriculum . . . established by setting out specific learning outcomes for each stage . . . [that] should be tightly enough defined so that standards and objectivity can be inspected by OFSTED' (ibid. p. 22). This recommendation was duly heeded and from 2002 citizenship education will be a statutory requirement for all secondary school pupils in England.

Perhaps uncritically, there has been a tendency to link the current educational concerns with identity and citizenship almost exclusively to a neo-conservative 'cultural restorationist' agenda (see Box 8.1). But the fact that these concerns have not only continued but have intensified and become more politicised since New Labour came to power calls for an alternative explanation. David Blunkett, the Secretary of State for Education, for example, recently commented on the fact that 'Americans reinforce their

---

Box 8.1 Cultural restorationism

This term was coined by Stephen Ball (1990) to describe the endeavours of the New Right within the British Conservative Party to reclaim and reassert traditional forms of educational practice during the 1980s and early 1990s. Ball argues that a cultural restorationist agenda was in the ascendant throughout this period across the whole range of educational policies, but particularly in the areas of curriculum, assessment pedagogy and teacher education. The most obvious and far-reaching consequence of cultural restorationism was the establishment of a traditional subject-based National Curriculum – what Ball calls the curriculum of the dead – that the New Right initially promoted, and then sought to utilise, as a means of preserving what is considered to be 'our' cultural heritage and national identity.

identity in ways we never have'. In comparison, he argued, 'We have tended to down-play our culture, and we need to reinforce our pride in what we have' (cited in *The Guardian*, 14 May 1999). Indeed, as reports in the media testify, the issue of national identity is now a major cause of confrontation both between and within the main political parties.

It is my contention that debates about national identity and citizenship in the school curriculum emanate from wider anxieties about the future of nation-states during a period of unprecedented political, economic and social transition. Over the last 200 years the nation-state has become the norm of modern political organisation and, as such, plays a key role in identity formation 'through its regulative logic and emotional attributes' (Smith 1979, p. 2). Moreover, in the contemporary world it is normal to associate citizenship almost exclusively with rights provided and protected by, and a reciprocal loyalty to, the nation-state. But it is now widely acknowledged that the nation-state is being progressively undermined by new and complex patterns of global interconnectedness. As nation-states gradually become 'enmeshed in and functionally part of' larger networks of 'global transformations and flows' (Held *et al.* 1999, p. 49), there is a corresponding diminution in their capacity to act independently within their own borders, especially in economic affairs. And the capacity for independent action is being further eroded by the 'willing surrender' (Held 1989) of power by national governments to supranational organisations and institutions. Moreover, from within, nation-states are being increasingly challenged through claims for varying degrees of self-determination by nationalist and regionalist movements which do not feel their interests, aspirations and identities are being adequately met (Marquand 1991). This weakening of the power and legitimacy of the nation-state has two important effects. First, it destabilises our sense of who or what we are, both collectively and individually, and, second, it renders problematic our long-established taken-for-granted understanding of citizenship.

Historically, education played a crucial role in the establishment and consolidation of nation-states, particularly through the deliberate inculcation of shared national consciousness and identity. In Europe, the emerging nation-states consolidated their power base by imposing 'the language and culture of the capital' (ibid., p. 32) upon the territory over which they claimed jurisdiction. As Held *et al.* (1999, pp. 337, 338) point out, this 'involved, where necessary, controlling the kind of cultural messages and symbols available to the public' and 'the control, suppression and eradication of competing identities and peripheral nationalisms'. State organisations and cultural practices, they contend, 'were consciously used to construct national histories, define national identities and inculcate national allegiances' (ibid.). Commenting on the role of education in the establishment of France as a nation-state in the nineteenth century, Graff (1987, p. 276) observes:

> The school's task included not only national and patriotic sentiments but estab-lishing unity in a nation long divided by region, culture, language, and persisting social divisions of class and wealth. Learning to read and write involved the constant repetition of the civic national catechism, in which the child was imbued with all the duties expected of him: from defending the state, to paying taxes, working, and obeying laws.

Geography as both an academic discipline and a school subject made its own unique, and not insignificant, contribution to the emergence and consolidation of European nation-states. As Hooson (1994, p. 3) reminds us, geography became institutionalised in Europe 'at a time of competitive nationalisms, the final scramble for colonies, mass emigration, free trade, urbanization and universal education'. Consequently, he argues, the founding scholars 'were inescapably caught up in the web of particular preoccupations, priorities and perceptions of their home country' (ibid.). Geography, too, was deeply implicated in the subsequent imperialist ventures of the newly established European nation-states. Hudson, for example, claims that 'the study and teaching of . . . geography . . . was vigorously promoted at that time largely, if not mainly, to serve the interests of imperialism in its various aspects including territorial acquisition, economic exploitation, militarism and the practice of class and race domination' (cited in Godlewska and Smith 1994, p. 4). Taylor (1993, p. 187) takes this argument further. For him:

> Geography's relation with imperialism is much more than as an actual or potential instrument for imperialist ends. . . . The whole period of producing Geography as a European science is imbued with assumptions of imperialism. . . . As new worlds were discovered and old worlds reinterpreted, a dominant world view emerged of a white, civilized centre and a barbaric, subjugated periphery of non-white natives.

The view expressed by Taylor is consistent with the argument of Edward Said as set out in his seminal work on Orientalism (see Box 8.2). Said (1978) conceptualises Orientalism as a discourse created by European institutions which legitimated and supported the occupation, subjugation and exploitation of the Orient by western imperial powers for their own political and economic ends. Its predominant discursive strategy was the assertion and reiteration of the superiority of Europe over the Orient, 'the one rational, mature, normal, the other irrational, backward, and depraved' (Peet 1998, p. 14). He goes on to argue that this discursive binary not only gave justifiable grounds for the colonisation of the Orient but also created a highly stigmatised 'Other' against which Europe's own identity could be established, strengthened and, if necessary, reaffirmed.

Box 8.2 Orientalism

Orientalism is a complex, multifaceted idea developed by Edward Said in his two classic works, *Orientalism: Western Conceptions of the Orient* (1978) and *Culture and Imperialism* (1993). As understood by Said, Orientalism is a mode of discourse with supporting institutions created by European scholars, writers and artists through which European culture constructed the Orient sociologically, militarily, ideologically, scientifically and imaginatively during the post-Enlightenment period. In doing so it provided the 'Other' through which the superiority of European culture could be established and confirmed. Initially arising within a set of cultural practices, the discourse of Orientalism was subsequently appropriated and transformed by European imperialist powers to legitimate and defend the occupation, subjugation and exploitation of the Orient for their own political and economic ends.

It is now common for the essence of this argument to be applied to identity formation in general. As Said (1995, p. 332) himself contends, 'the construction of identity . . . involves establishing opposites and others whose actualities are always subject to the continuous interpretation and reinterpretation of their differences from us'. Guibernau (1996, p. 49) likewise claims that 'groups tend to define themselves not by reference to their own characteristics but by exclusion, that is by comparison to "strangers"'. As Bowie (1993, p. 190), for example, observes: 'It is in opposition to Englishness that Welshness is defined'. If the argument that identity is primarily constituted through the process of 'othering' is valid, then geography, inevitably, plays a key role in identity formation.

Examples of geography's past complicity in identity formation through the negative representation of others are not difficult to find. The *Century Geographical Reader 6* (undated but present-tense references to the Queen places it somewhere in the Victorian period) provides a potent and salutary illustration.

Initially, the reader is oriented to a particular reading of colonialism through a discourse which emphasises the 'independence' of Britain and, in contrast, positions other countries as its 'possessions', 'dependencies' and 'colonies'. There then follow descriptions of 'the physical and political characteristics of several [colonised] countries, their industries, commerce and manufactures, and the manners and customs of their inhabitants' (Preface). The people of India are described as 'one of the strangest collections of human beings that ever peopled a country' (p. 39). Moreover, 'violent race hatred exists among [them], no bond of patriotism unites them [and] they hate one another more than they dislike foreigners' (ibid.). British colonialism is then justified on the grounds that

> the people of India feel the benefits of a firm and steady rule. Property is safe; the robbers, who of old infested the country in gangs, strangling lonely travellers, and the pirates who used to sail up the great rivers, burning villages and murdering the inhabitants have been put down.
>
> (ibid.)

But this is not all. Britain has made 'railways, roads, works for irrigating . . . the land' (ibid.) and, additionally, 'it has provided schools and colleges for the natives (p. 44). Thus, the book concludes, the people of India have 'reason to be satisfied with British rule' (ibid.).

Throughout the book, equally distorted images of the 'Other' are presented. The Burmese, we are told, 'are most marvellously lazy and conceited . . . good for nothing but steering a boat or driving a car' and the Negroes in Jamaica, 'as elsewhere, show a great disinclination to work' (p. 201). The Bushmen of South Africa, we learn, 'are among the lowest and most degraded members of the human race' and while 'property they have none, . . . they lose no opportunity of stealing that of other people' (p. 77). Likewise, the natives of Australia 'are still in a savage state' and 'attempts to civilise them have failed' (p. 115). Moreover, they 'were at first a great source of trouble to the settlers. They stole and killed the colonists' sheep and horses, and were in consequence shot down in great numbers' (p. 116).

The way in which this text establishes the intellectual, moral, technical, administrative, legislative and entrepreneurial superiority of Britain – subliminally if not overtly

– through the negative representation of the 'Other' is obvious and needs no further elaboration. Books as explicitly racist as this have, of course, long disappeared from the shelves. But it could be justifiably argued that they have left a residual stain on geography education that is proving difficult to remove. Winter (1996), for example, provides an insightful deconstruction of the portrayal of a place and its inhabitants taken from a popular and widely used Key Stage 3 textbook written specifically to meet the requirements of the Geography National Curriculum. For the purpose of her analysis she focuses on a double-page spread entitled 'Kenya – what is the Maasai way of life?' She begins with the claim that by being defined as an 'economically developing country', and then being compared with a 'developed' country like the UK, a deficient image of Kenya is constructed. The Maasai, she argues, are cast as a 'museum piece', on show to the western gaze 'because of their "curiosity" features' (ibid. p. 377). The text, she contends, is dominated by a 'white male, western voice' which denies the Maasai any say in the representation of 'their places, history, stories and lives' (ibid.). Silent too are other voices that legitimately could be heard in the study of this place, such as 'the Kenyan government; the tourists; the cattle ranchers and the safari travel firms' (ibid.). Nor, she informs us, is mention made of the current political, economic and social changes that are impacting significantly on the Maasai way of life. On the contrary 'a picture of a static way of life is presented' (ibid.).

Winter's analysis is both timely and important in that it brings to the fore an inherent problem for geographers in representing place. Despite the efforts of positivist geography to persuade us otherwise, there is no epistemological vantage point from which the world can be described objectively. By whatever means presented, accounts of places, and of the people who inhabit them, are always positional and, therefore, contestable. This recognition of the positionality and contestability of geographical knowledge has important implications for the study of places, at whatever scale and in whatever context. While we can never be entirely freed from the shackles of our own subjective perspectives, we can at least be 'sensitive to what is involved in representation [and] in studying the Other' (Said 1978, p. 327).

The working party that produced the original Geography National Curriculum sought to rehabilitate the study of place partly in response to widespread criticism that pupils had inadequate place knowledge and partly in the belief that it had been marginalised by thematic approaches. The outcome was that in addition to acquiring prescribed locational knowledge, pupils were required to study specific places at local, regional and national scales. Moreover, although in the rewritings there have been some minor adjustments and shifts of emphasis, and a significant reduction in the amount of prescription, the emphasis on place study has been maintained. Noticeably lacking, however, has been any acknowledgement of wider debate concerning the contested meaning of place in geography or the problem of its representation. Consequently, the Geography National Curriculum provides no theoretical rationale or practical guidance for the study of place. Indeed, it appears that the meaning of place is taken to be self-evident. But as Daniel (1992, p. 314) suggests: 'Place should be seen as a fluent not a fixed concept, not a settlement in the field of enquiry but a contested terrain'.

It is my contention that the Geography National Curriculum from its inception, and throughout its subsequent development, has been constructed on an understanding of place that is both empirically and theoretically flawed, and that this in turn has implications for questions of identity and citizenship. My criticisms are twofold. First, places are confined to a rigid hierarchy of localities, regions and countries. But, as Donat (1967, p. 9) argues, 'places never conform to tidy hierarchies of classification. They all overlap and interpenetrate one another and are wide open to a variety of interpretations'. To compound the problem, localities and regions are invariably defined in relation to countries. In turn, the study of countries, and regions within them, has been structured almost exclusively around a crude economically developed – economically developing dualism. On the basis of this dualism the world is clinically divided and neatly parcelled into two distinct entities. On the one hand are those countries that have reached a desirable state and, therefore, are considered developed. On the other, are those that have not yet made it and are, by implication, developing.

The study of place primarily, if not exclusively, through the framework of this dualism has three adverse consequences. First, it essentialises the dualism and, thereby, renders it unproblematic. Second, it privileges a predominantly western view of the world, thus limiting the opportunities for studying places from a range of positions and perspectives. Third, it perpetuates 'the error of developmentalism' (Taylor 1989) by assuming a world consisting of a large number of relatively autonomous nation-states which in terms of economic – and, by implication, social and political – change are following, or should follow, a common trajectory based on the experience of those parts of the world deemed to be developed. Imperialism, Crush (1994, p. 337) claims, 'was an act of geographical violence through which space was explored, reconstructed, re-named and controlled'. This is no less true of developmentalism. As Said (1978, p. 327) points out, 'even if we disregard the Orientalist distinctions between "them" and "us", a powerful series of political and ultimately ideological realities inform scholarship today . . . if not the East/West division, then the North/South one, the have/have nots one', and, it could be added, the developed/developing one.

My second criticism is that places, at whatever scale, are conceived as unique, naturally bounded, homogeneous, relatively stable entities. Admittedly there is acknowledgement that places are interdependent. However, the assumption is that places exist as discrete entities prior to, and distinct from, their subsequent interdependence. It is now widely recognised that within the context of rapid globalisation this conception of place is highly problematic. The boundaries that once differentiated places as distinct and separate entities are being rapidly dissolved by an incessant global flow of information, goods, ideas, images and people. Moreover, places are increasingly vulnerable to the environmental risk, crime and terrorism that occur on a global scale. It is now recognised that places, rather than being unique and interdependent, are becoming more and more reciprocally constituted. Indeed, there are those who argue that this has always been the case.

An understanding of places as open and porous and reciprocally constituted in and through a myriad global networks, flows and interactions has implications for the way that identity formation is conceptualised. Oakes (1993, p. 48), for example, argues that 'identity has never been neatly provided by a naturally bounded place, but has always been negotiated within a complex and often confusing mesh of interaction across multiple geographical scales'. This suggests that identities are more in-between, fragmented and diverse than the essentialising discourse of a common national identity would imply.

I argued earlier that the Geography National Curriculum lacks a coherent rationale and gives insufficient guidance for place study, and I illustrated through the work of Winter how this has led to a perpetuation of Eurocentric representations of places and people. Johnston (1996), however, provides a useful rationale for the study of place that could be easily adapted and applied in schools. According to him, places are: social creations; self-reproducing; controlled and changed by people; not isolated and self-contained; often formally bounded; and potential sources of conflict. It is beyond the scope of this chapter to examine in detail the implications of Johnston's rationale for the study of place. But the way in which places are social creations and potential sources of conflict, albeit discursive, can be illustrated through the following vignette.

Writing in *The Field*, the Conservative politician Norman Tebbit declared:

> Our continental neighbours use 'insular' as a term of abuse, but we in Britain have every reason to be thankful for our insularity. Our boundaries . . . are drawn by the sea – some might say by providence. Unlike those of most other nations they have not been drawn, rubbed out and redrawn time and time again. . . . The blessing of insularity has long protected us against rabid dogs and dictators alike.
>
> (Tebbit 1990, p. 78)

The image evoked here is of a stable, enduring, timeless Britain, protected by the sea from the political turmoil that afflicts her quarrelsome and abusive continental neighbours. Moreover, the use of the words 'providence' and 'blessing' implies that the protection afforded by the sea is attributable to some kind of divine intervention and thus creates an aura of holiness. This suggestion of divine intervention resonates strongly with Margaret Thatcher's recent assertion that 'God separated Britain from mainland Europe, and it was for a purpose' (cited in *The Guardian*, 22 December 1999).

Gordon Brown, the Chancellor of the Exchequer, writing in *The Guardian* interprets Britain's geographical location differently. For him:

> The geographic fact of our existence – an island nation open to the world – means that Britain has also been remarkably outward-looking. We are a nation of seafarers, traders, merchant venturers, and explorers – who have seen the open seas around us more often as a highway than a moat and who should be well equipped to meet the trade and technological challenges of a global marketplace.
>
> (Brown 2000)

Here the sea is envisaged as a source of opportunity and challenge, rather than as a means of protection. The emphasis is on openness and the future as opposed to insularity and the past; Cool Britannia as opposed to Rule Britannia. What is significant, however, is not so much the different symbolic meanings attributed to Britain's geographical location but the commonality of the discursive strategies used in the extracts. Both extracts homogenise and essentialise the nation-state. And both endeavour to establish a mythical bond between place and people. Both, too, project meanings onto place; meanings, moreover, which are embedded in political ideologies and which are evoked with political intent. Notable also in both extracts is the inclusivity of the language used.

Repetitive use of the words 'we', 'us' and 'our' creates a strong sense of shared identity and collective destiny.

The final report of the Advisory Group on Citizenship and Education for Democracy referred to earlier in the chapter concluded that:

> a main aim for the whole community should be to find or restore a sense of common citizenship, including a national identity that is secure enough to find a place for the plurality of nations, cultures, ethnic identities and religions long found in the United Kingdom. Citizenship education creates common ground between different ethnic and religious identities.
>
> (1998, p. 17)

This conclusion acknowledges the multinational, multicultural multi-ethnic and multi-faith composition of the United Kingdom but then implies that the numerous identities that could be constructed from this rich diversity should be subordinate to a common national identity. Such a view is not far removed from Kenneth Baker's (1987) concern that because of the 'distraction, variety and uncertainty in the modern world . . . our children are in danger of losing any sense at all of a common culture and a common heritage'.

Recent exhortations and endeavours to utilise the school curriculum explicitly for the inculcation of national identity are based on two questionable assumptions. The first is that it is possible for citizens of the United Kingdom, coming as they do from diverse cultures and nations, to align themselves to a common national identity and the second is that it is desirable for them to do so. The problem with the second assumption is that there are no grounds for believing that a national identity is intrinsically more valuable than any other identity, place-based or otherwise. As Toynbee (2000) observes: 'It is odd how many tin-eared politicians keep banging the drum of Britishness, utterly oblivious to how hollow it rings'.

The kind of identity that the National Curriculum was designed to inculcate derives from cultural nationalism which, Yoshino (1992, p. 31) contends, 'aims to regenerate the national community by creating, preserving or strengthening a people's cultural identity when it is felt to be lacking or threatened'. Cultural nationalism, Castells (1997, p. 65) argues, is a reaction against globalisation, against networking and flexibility and against the crisis of the patriarchal family – 'the three fundamental threats, perceived in all societies, by the majority of humankind, in this end of millennium'. It produces 'defensive identities' that function as 'refuge and solidarity, to protect against a hostile outside world' (ibid.).

As Chambers (1993, pp. 153–4) sees it:

> [W]e face the possibility of two perspectives and two versions of 'Britishness'. One is Anglo-centric, frequently conservative, backward looking, and increasingly located in a frozen and largely stereotyped idea of the national culture. The other is ex-centric, open-ended, and multi-ethnic. The first is based on a homogeneous 'unity' in which history, tradition, and individual biographies and roles . . . are fundamentally fixed in the national epic, in the mere fact of being 'British'. The other perspective suggests an overlapping network of histories and traditions, a

heterogeneous complexity in which positions and identities, including that of the 'national', cannot be taken for granted, are not interminably fixed but are in flux.

Geography educators, therefore, should be sceptical of any attempts to use their subject as a purveyor of nationalist sentiments. And this applies as much to the individual nations that make up the United Kingdom as it does to the United Kingdom as a whole. The implications of a '*Curriculum Cymreig*' and its equivalent in Scotland for a substantial number of Welsh and Scots whose identities are being forged in and through cultures, histories, allegiances and experiences other than those of the country in which they live should not be overlooked.

Whether we recognise it or not, education is caught up in the turbulence of exponential change the outcomes of which are beyond prediction. In the face of upheaval and uncertainty, it is not surprising that the governments of nation-states are keen to promote essentialist notions of culture, nation and identity. But little will be gained by foisting upon future citizens a homogenised, politically manipulated national identity based on a selective, mythologised version of the past. To do so is an affront to their personal autonomy and an infringement of the basis principles of democratic living. Rather, education should help young people acquire the necessary understandings, skills, dispositions and values to construct for themselves identities that will enable them to live their lives meaningfully, purposefully and co-operatively amidst the change and uncertainty they will increasingly encounter.

Education, Bailey (1984, p. 22) insists, 'liberates from the tyranny of the present and the particular and liberates for the ideal of the autonomous, rational moral agent'. We can, he contends, break 'the incestuous ties of clan and soil' (ibid.). Similarly, for Said (1994, p. 278) liberation 'is the transformation of social consciousness beyond national consciousness'. Geography education in the past has been — and to a large extent still is — a very British subject concerned with producing very British subjects. In future it should endeavour to be a very global subject concerned with empowering very cosmopolitan citizens. If geographers are genuinely committed to educating for democratic citizenship in the twenty-first century then nothing less will do.

FOR FURTHER THINKING

1   To what extent do you agree that the Geography National Curriculum is an agent for 'cultural restorationaism' (see p. 111)? Is it inevitable that a National Curriculum should assume such a role?

2   Examine your schemes of work. Do they, even if by omission, promote the idea that 'multicultural Britain' is a recent idea?

3   This chapter has been concerned with geography – 'a very British subject . . . producing . . . very British subjects' (p. 119). Consider where the English fit into this; do you agree with Jeremy Paxman's view that England seems to be a 'land of Lost Content' in which, unlike the Scots or Welsh, the English have 'extinguished their identity within the idea of being British' (Paxman, 1999, p. 13)?

References

Advisory Group on Citizenship and Education for Democracy (1998) *Education for Citizenship and the Teaching of Democracy in Schools* London: QCA.

Bailey, C. (1984) *Beyond the Present and Particular: a Theory of Liberal Education* London: Routledge & Kegan Paul.

Baker, K. (1987) Speech given at Manchester University, September 1987.

Ball, S. (1990) *Politics and Policy Making in Education* London: Routledge.

Bowie, F. (1993) 'Wales from within: conflicting interpretations of Welsh identity' in Macdonald, S. (ed.) *Inside European Identities* Oxford: Berg.

Brown, G. (2000) 'This is the time to start building a Greater Britain' *The Times* 9 January 2000.

Castells, M. (1997) *The Power of Identity* Oxford: Blackwell.

CCW (Curriculum Council for Wales) (1991) *Geography in the National Curriculum: Non-Statutory Guidance for Teachers* Cardiff: Curriculum Council for Wales.

Chambers, I. (1993) 'Narratives of nationalism: being "British"' in Carter, E., Donald, J. and Squires, J. (eds) *Space and Place: Theories of Identity and Location* London: Lawrence & Wishart.

Commission on Citizenship (1990) *Encouraging Citizenship: Report of the Commission on Citizenship* London: HMSO.

Crawford, K. (1995) 'A history of the right: the battle for control of National Curriculum History' 1989–1994 *British Journal of Educational Studies* Vol. 43, No. 4.

Crush, J. (1994) 'Post-colonialism, de-colonization, and geography' in Godlewska, A. and Smith, N. (eds) (1994) *Geography and Empire* Oxford: Blackwell.

Daniel, S. (1992) 'Place and the geographical imagination in education' *Geography* Vol. 77, No. 4, pp. 310–22.

DES (1991) *Geography in the National Curriculum (England)* London: HMSO.

DES (1995) *The National Curriculum for Geography (England)* London: HMSO.

DfEE (1997) *Excellence in Education* London: DfEE.

Donat, J. (ed.) (1967) *World Architecture 4* London: Studio Vista.

Epstein, A.L. (1978) *Ethos and Identity* London: Tavistock.

Godlewska, A. and Smith, N. (eds) (1994) *Geography and Empire* Oxford: Blackwell.

Graff, H.J. (1987) *The Legacies of Literacy* Bloomington, Ind.: Indiana University Press.

Guibernau, (1996) *Nationalisms: the Nation-State and Nationalism in the Twentieth Century* Cambridge: Polity Press.

Held, D. (1989) 'The decline of the nation state' in Hall, S. and Jacques, M. (eds) *New Times: the Changing Face of Politics in the 1990s* London: Lawrence & Wishart.

Held, D., McGrew, A., Goldblatt, D. and Perraton, J. (1999) *Global Transformations: Politics, Economics and Culture* Cambridge: Polity Press.

Hooson, D. (ed.) (1994) *Geography and National Identity* Oxford: Blackwell.

Johnston, R.J. (1996) 'A place in geography' in Daugherty, R. and Rawling, E.M. *Geography Into the Twenty-first century* Chichester and New York: Wiley.

McKeirnan, D.L. (1993) 'History in the national curriculum: imagining the nation at the end of the 20th century' *Journal of Curriculum Studies* Vol. 25, No. 1, pp. 33–51.

Marquand, D. (1991) 'Nations, regions and Europe' in Crick, B. (ed.) *National Identities: the Construction of the United Kingdom* Oxford: Blackwell.

National Commission on Education (1993) *Learning to Succeed* London: Heinemann.

National Curriculum Council (1990) *Curriculum Guidance 8. Education for Citizenship* York: NCC.

Oakes, T.S. (1993) 'The cultural space of modernity: ethnic tourism and place identity in China' *Environment and Planning D: Space and Society* 11, pp. 47–66.

Paxman, J. (1999) *The English. A Portrait of a People* London: Penguin Press.

Peet, R. (1998) *Modern Geographical Thought* Oxford: Blackwell.

Phillips, R. (1996) 'History teaching, cultural restoration and national identity in England and Wales' *Curriculum Studies* Vol. 4, No. 3, pp. 385–99.

Said, E. (1978) *Orientalism: Western Conceptions of the Orient* London: Penguin Books.

Said, E. (1993) *Culture and Imperialism* New York: Vintage.

Said, E. (1994) *Representations of the Intellectual* New York: Pantheon Books.

Said, E. (1995) 'Afterword' in *Orientalism: Western Conceptions of the Orient* Harmondsworth: Penguin.

SCCC (Scottish Consultative Council on the Curriculum) (1999a) *The School Curriculum and the Culture of Scotland: a Paper for Discussion and Consultation* Dundee: SCCC.

SCCC (Scottish Consultative Council on the Curriculum) (1999b) *Environmental Studies 5–14 Science, Society and Technology Guidelines: Consultation Draft* Dundee: SCCC.

Smith, A.O. (1979) *Nationalism in the Twentieth Century* Oxford: Martin Robertson.

Taylor, P. (1989) 'The error of developmentalism in human geography' in Gregory, D. and Halford, R. (eds) *Horizons in Human Geography* London: Macmillan.

Taylor, P. (1993) 'Full circle, or new meaning for the global' in Johnston, R.J. (ed.) *The Challenge for Geography* Oxford: Blackwell.

Tebbit, N. (1990) 'Being British, what it means to me: time we learned to be insular' *The Field* No. 272, pp. 76–8.

TES (Times Educational Supplement) (1996a) 'Rebuilding a sense of community' *TES* 19 April 1996.

TES (Times Educational Supplement) (1996b) 'Geography's turn for the "British culture" speech' *TES* 19 April 1996.

Toynbee, P. (2000) 'Puny view of Britain' *The Guardian* 20 January 2000.

Winter, C. (1996) 'Changing the dominant paradigm in the geography curriculum' *Curriculum Studies* Vol. 4, No. 3, pp. 367–84.

Yoshino, K. (1992) *Cultural Nationalism in Contemporary Japan* London: Routledge.

Chapter 9

Citizenship denied

The case of the Holocaust

Paul Machon and David Lambert

Introduction

In schools geography does not have much of a reputation for tackling overtly political issues, except perhaps in partial, coded and incomplete ways, as in the case of environmental issues (see Lambert, 1999a; also Chapter 10 by John Huckle in this volume). There is a risk that geography lessons claiming to 'carry' citizenship will do so in a similarly emasculated way, unless the suite of what is normally done in geography is *reconsidered* in the light of this explicit political concept, citizenship. Reconsideration includes both curriculum and pedagogical matters. The focus of this chapter is mainly on the former, specifically on content selection, and can be read as a case-study exploration of the kind of material not often selected for study in geography lessons. Taking the chapter as a whole, readers are invited to consider the nature of geography and its educational potential (see Box 9.1 'Geography and other disciplines'), together with the education and training needs of teachers intending to address ideas of the kind we discuss.

The ideas developed in this chapter pose the most difficult of questions for social scientists, including geographers, for they centre on the Holocaust. This seminal event in the creation of contemporary Europe, we argue, is simultaneously geographical *and* political, and possesses distinct pedagogic issues. We focus on the Holocaust for among its powerful political elements is a fundamental concern about rights to, and *exclusion from*, citizenship. The questions the Holocaust poses will always be hard to emasculate because they are so fundamental:

- What value does life have?
- Where are the roots of the human capacity for inhumane action?
- And, politically, what is the state's function in affording security to 'its' people?

Our chapter is in two parts. The *first* considers the political geography of the Holocaust; the *second* describes an educational encounter with the Holocaust by geography teachers in training during a field trip to southern Poland.

What the first part offers is a spatial interpretation of a particular (and relatively familiar) historic-political story – or *event* – emphasising what it reveals about citizenship. There are other stories or events we could have chosen of course: the geography of the Gulags springs to mind, for example, or even more contemporary horrors such as those

---

Box 9.1 Geography and other disciplines

All academic disciplines intend to

* *describe,*
* *account for* and
* *provide a critical 'take' on*

the observable world. If a discipline has developed a distinctive approach to what and how its practitioners have operated – and particularly if a shared body of understanding has been developed historically and is shared by those practitioners – then that discipline acquires a stature of its own. This status has risks, particularly the extent to which prevailing paradigms or practice can exclude some substantive work because 'it's not geography' and so must 'belong' elsewhere.

In addition, we also observe that some events – the Holocaust is one of them – do not really lend themselves to single-discipline approaches but rather call for a multidisciplinary approach in order to more fully describe, explain and pose awkward questions. Geography has always been effective at working alongside and even incorporating methodologies from other disciplines, indeed has prided itself on its ability to do so, especially across the apparent physical/human divide. Again, our argument is not with this but the extent to which disciplines meet challenges.

The challenge that confronts any discipline is the quality with which its three tasks are discharged – can it describe, explain and sustain critique? The Holocaust in particular (but not exclusively) provides exceptionally difficult questions for any social scientist, because of the enormity and the heinous nature of the events. Here we put our belief plainly: that any discipline (including geography) unable to cast at least some light on such events in a convincing way is fundamentally limited both substantively and methodologically. As such, it may not have much of a role to play in education.

---

that have occurred in the Balkans. In relation to the latter ('Europe's worst massacre since World War II'), Ó'Tuatail has recently remarked that

> The ethnic cleansing of Srebrenica was not an unusual act of violence in the post-Cold War world. In Afghanistan, Algeria, Azerbaijan, Cambodia, Chechnya, Croatia, Rwanda, Sri Lanka and many other places political, ethnic and religious conflicts have degenerated into bloody wars of often shocking brutality. . . . Yet geography made the violence of Srebrenica unique.
>
> (Ó'Tuatail, 1999, p. 120)

We have settled on the Holocaust partly because it is more familiar, both to teachers and students, than these other examples of genocide. There is a huge and growing Holocaust literature – playing its part in the formation of preconceptions that also need to be critically examined – the serious study of which may encourage students to use geographical perspectives to help account for and understand other significant events of this nature.

We then move to the second part of the chapter, to consider the difficulties encountered when student teachers were challenged to engage with the Holocaust while contemplating the geography classroom, and in particular teaching citizenship in that classroom. We note in Box 9.1 that events like this challenge disciplines and that it should be against such hard tasks that disciplines must pit themselves. The same can also be said for teachers, not least with reference to the training standards specified by the Teacher Training Agency: in terms of 'subject knowledge', and geography's new place as part-purveyor of citizenship education, how do new teachers of geography understand their role as subject specialists? What is subject expertise and how effectively does a geography degree prepare teachers to explore citizenship education through geography lessons?

And so to the Holocaust. Conventionally, this is perceived as history's property, although there have been notable achievements that have captured something of its spatiality like Martin Gilbert's *Atlas of the Holocaust* (1984) and a sense of place in Primo Levi's *The Truce. A Survivor's Journey Home from Auschwitz* (1979). But even these brilliant pieces employ space in a rather passive way, a canvas upon which this historically contingent event occurred. Yi-Fu Tuan (1999, p. 106) has observed that the discipline of geography is probably to blame for this, for it has had a blind spot toward questions of evil and 'the entire realm of morals and ethics'. Furthermore, he writes:

> A deeper reason for the neglect of moral questions is the geographer's indifference to events. Events, we seem to feel, are best left to historians. The event of war is prominent in history books. In geography books it is conspicuously absent. There is of course a geography of the American Civil War, but we have not written it. We map battle-fields – the cool and static aftermath of an event – rather than the clash of beliefs, alliances, and armies, in which courage, cowardice, wisdom, stupidity, good and evil are likely to be displayed.
>
> (ibid.: pp. 106–7)

Our argument is that space, geography's focus, should more properly be seen as a dynamic element that *structures* such 'events' by offering spatially differentiated choices to *agents* with spatially differentiated political power. This is not to replace the 'passive canvas' with a mechanistic dualism of structure and agency, but is to argue for their coexistence in complex, messy, dialectical and iterative ways that are constantly being made and remade. Consequently, spatially differentiated control of knowledge and action is one of the basic elements of political power, including its legitimisation and perpetuation across whatever space is defined as the state's own; it can therefore begin to account for the variations in political practice that can always be found. The Holocaust was an event in time, but it also happened in a particular space – indeed, in particular places within that space. Studying the spatiality of the Holocaust helps us understand *the event*.

Such political perspectives have echoes in contemporary curriculum concerns that can be illuminating. For example, from a Polish perspective Kortus notes in his discussion of the content of Polish school geography that 'the negative features of the geopolitical site of Poland in Europe are deeply implicated in the Polish conscience' (Kortus, 1990,

p. 11). It is also acknowledged that Polish geographers have contributed to the 'awakening of the Polish national and political conscience looking forward to a national independence and struggling for it' (ibid., p. 10). This 'awakening' was conducted *against* the conventional wisdom that Poland's geopolitical and geo-economic position was both weak and risky, with potential dangers from both the East (Russia) and the West (Germany).

As we show below, a similar structural relationship existed in pre-World War II Germany between its intellectuals and the development of a particular political consciousness, which included a distinct spatial expression. Such distinct geopolitical belief structures find a place in the school curriculum in all states, furthering the development of the consciousness and legitimating it. Retrospectively, the relationship between intellectual endeavour (such as that we explore more fully below in the context of the Holocaust) and education can be made to appear plain because of its location in another time and place. But if such relationships are always present, then the reflective geographer is invited to consider the significance of the contemporary reforms in England's education system, and in particular how this 'space' is perceived intellectually and in curriculum terms.

FOR FURTHER THINKING

1   What are the disciplinary 'roots' of geography which are conventionally incorporated into the geography we teach?
2   Reflecting on geography's post-war history in schools, what 'new' disciplines have been added to the geography that we teach?
3   Why are some disciplines, notably history and political theory, missing from geography teaching?

Part I A geography of the Holocaust

This section moves in four steps towards an account of the geography of the Holocaust. Particular attention is paid to how citizenship in the Third Reich was redefined.

a. Inclusive and exclusive citizenship

Why do we connect the study of the Holocaust and citizenship? To answer this it is useful to set the particular and horrific events against a larger background of the European experience of an evolving modernity (Slater, 1997, p. 329) and particularly the search for a legitimate state form.

Early theorising about the state (see Box 9.2) stumbled over the nature of the contract that could be agreed between individuals and the state, and the bargains that could be struck between the rights and duties of the two, given their hugely disparate powers. There were many reasons why bargains were hard to strike, not least the presence of entrenched and powerful groups who frequently needed revolutionary – or near-revolutionary experiences – to forcefully demonstrate that the location of social power

---

Box 9.2 The state

The state is one of the key concepts in political science.

Different political belief-systems would agree that the state is that set of institutions that has the authority to make and administer the rules that govern society within a defined territory – underlining the idea's spatiality. However, there would be violent disagreement about what *state functions* should be discharged in pursuit of the preferred *state form*.

Although state institutions, the armed forces, the civil service, the judiciary and so on (the *state apparatus*), are not a unified entity they can appear to be if the members (called *state agents*) of those entities are sufficiently uniform. This can occur in two ways, either by the state agents being drawn from the same section of society or the state's agents having a consensual view that is sufficiently homogeneous or *hegemonic*.

A state's authority to rule is based on the legitimacy with which it can claim to do so, hence political theory is a branch of *moral philosophy*. In practice legitimacy is claimed by states acting on behalf 'of the people' that, as we show, can be variously defined. States protect 'their' authority by having a 'monopoly of legitimate violence' but they also devote considerable attention to ensuring their legitimacy in the long term.

A telling comparison can be seen by conceptualising the state form of the UK (capitalist, individuated and with a representative democracy) and that of Nazi Germany in the late 1930s. In the former, control mechanisms (the law, courts, police and so on) are comparatively very rare because citizens willingly shoulder much civic responsibility themselves; this is termed a *soft control* state. In Germany the opposite was true – a *hard control* state.

---

could change. A politically effective development in the face of potentially revolutionary challenges was the construction of *nation-states* predicated on more or less nationalist ideologies; an ideology that could be employed to submerge otherwise important divisions between people.

Even so, political negotiations for the establishment of legitimate nation-states were difficult because state membership was hard to define. Definitions could include the possession of a particular language or adherence to a particular religion, categories over which individuals had some degree of choice rather than something that was attached to them at birth. It is a useful pedagogic device when conceptualising nation building in this early period to see the process as a homogenisation of categories like religion and language and the elimination (or at least the marginalisation) of exceptions to these larger patterns. Simultaneously state provision was also made uniform across the space to which the state laid claim. In this way the idea of national citizenship was born so that, for example, any French citizen could expect to receive the same treatment from the state, at the hands of the law for instance, as the rest of his compatriots. This would be true wherever in the Republic they ended up, providing that the state's authority was acknowledged in some categorical way. Alongside the homogenising requirements made by states of its citizens, other systems were also unified. Famously in France, these

---

Box 9.3 Social Darwinism

Darwin's account of evolution in the plant and animal kingdoms, and in particular the emphasis upon competition as a mechanism for evolutionary change, found a ready audience in much late nineteenth-century social thinking. This mechanism was 'read off' into human affairs, supporting in an apparently scientific way Europe's world-wide imperialist project that was the dominant geopolitics of the time.

The concept also found resonance in the classification of 'the world's races' that acquired a hierarchical structure. In its most extreme form this theory produced the notion of an Aryan super-race and the notion of the *Untermenschen*.

Much of the language that is still employed to discuss cultural and ethnic differences as racial is uncritically drawn from this social Darwinist legacy.

---

included nationalising time and, profound in the construction of capitalist states, codifying property relationships and especially landholding. Such changes transformed a bewildering array of locally understood custom and practice to nationally unified forms of measurement, cadastral maps and legally enforceable processes of private ownership and inheritance. Such developments produced an *inclusive* citizenry, by which is meant that individuals could choose to subscribe to what the state offered, on the understanding that not only rights but duties followed from this (Birnbaum and Katznelson, 1995).

By the end of the nineteenth century, social Darwinist (see Box 9.3) accounts of social behaviour, including politics, particularly when related to an imperialist project, produced a quite different state form. Such prescriptions produced an *exclusive* citizenry. Here states were defined by the exclusion of particular groups from membership of that state. This logic proved to be a particularly efficient populist model for legitimating state form, particularly as the basis of political power slipped away from small elites to rest upon the masses. The efficiency came from the idea's emotional and intellectual appeal – and an ability to cut across otherwise divisive categories, like social class and economic well-being. This efficiency led to gains in the ease with which political legitimacy could be maintained, with failure being attributed to 'outsiders' or those within who did not really belong. Politicians were quick to exploit the authority that came with nationalism and no earlier ideologies of the state escaped contact with it unscathed. What social Darwinism additionally offered was an organic view of the state with the irresistible imperative that it was 'natural'. This imperative extended to the hierarchical classification of 'races' with the subsequent outcome of differential rights to citizenship. This ideology is seen clearly in imperialism and developed its most dangerous and murderous form in the Holocaust.

b. Geopolitics

In Britain, Halford Mackinder is the best-known member of the geographic community whose work supported imperialism. In his writings he insisted that geography education should serve an imperial purpose: 'the ruling citizens of the world-wide Empire should be able to visualise distant geographic conditions . . . [and therefore we must] . . . aim to make our people think Imperially . . . and to this end our geographical teaching should be directed' (Mackinder, 1907).

In Germany Friedrich Ratzel was involved in a similar imperialist discourse that privileged the struggle for survival in an explicitly social-Darwinist fashion. In 'Political Geography' (1907) he argued that superior nations had the right to expand at the expense of the inferior in order to gain additional living space – *Lebensraum* – for themselves. These sentiments were later codified into a formal branch of the discipline, geopolitics, largely by the efforts of Karl Haushofer who began the journal *Zeitschrift für Geopolitik* in 1924.

Haushofer's close association with the emergent National Socialist (Nazi) Party (see Box 9.4) must not conceal the fact that such views, with all the attendant threats of political action, were not exclusively German but a normal part of the lexicon of all nationalist movements. Nor should we overlook the place of geopolitics in another broadly based project in German academic life, *Ostforschung* or research on the East (Burleigh, 1998). This interdisciplinary research was undertaken to demonstrate on historical, sociological, racial and linguistic grounds that large areas of central and eastern Europe were part of a far older German *Heimat* to which contemporary German expansionists could claim a right. An example of the sort of work undertaken by German geographers in this movement is shown in Figure 9.1, Map of the area settled by Germans and where their cultural influence is paramount (*Karte des deutschen Volks- und Kulturbodens*) by Albrecht Penck in 1925 (quoted in Rössler, 1990, p. 61, and Burleigh, 1998, p. 27).

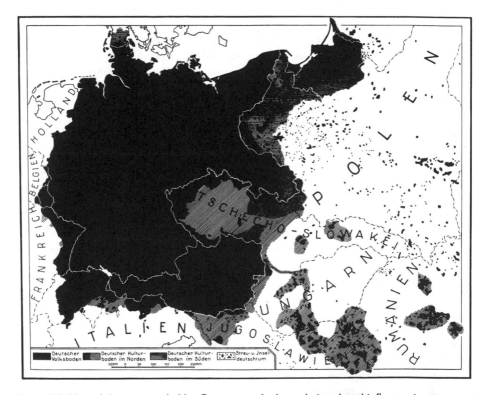

Figure 9.1 Map of the area settled by Germans and where their cultural influence is paramount

Source: Mechtild Rossler, *Wissenschaft und Lebensraum, Geographische Ostforschung im National-Sozialismus* (Berlin: Dietrisch Reimer Verlag, 1990), p. 61.

Box 9.4 Nazism

Nazism was a territorially distinct political ideology within fascism.

Fascism sought to find a 'middle way', avoiding the excesses of too individual democracies (but preserving their productive capacity) and collective states based upon 'artificial' criteria like class position (but preserving their communality). Fascism can usefully be seen as an oppositional ideology, disliking and hating rather than having optimistic long-term aspirations for all its peoples.

Nazism incorporated social-Darwinism into its distinctive fascist project, building a provenance for the race theory that was developed on mythology, pseudo-science including *Rassehygien* and *Lebensraum*.

Nazism can also be characterised as *aggressive nationalism*. That is to say that it was a fundamentally and uniquely murderous state form but one that had extremely sophisticated and explicit territorial ambitions built on nationalist thinking – Germany for the Germans (however either term was defined).

The journey we have taken so far sets the scene for the events that follow with much of Europe being transformed from a 'blank canvas' to an ideologically charged landscape occupied by people with differentiated rights to citizenship of an *exclusive* sort because it was defined on racial grounds.

c. The journey to the abyss

After the National Socialist Party came to power in the 1930s, the cluster of beliefs we have touched upon began to be enacted as policies. Studies have been made of the impact of these policies, for example changes to the family and the dramatically changed role of other elements in society such as the church (Ericksen, 1985), education and medicine. This is a familiar story – but made less so by characterising it as a *race war* (Davidowicz, 1975). Together, what all these changes did was to redefine citizenship in the German state by *exclusion*, with rights being withheld and additional duties being imposed upon some individuals. Sections of the included civil establishment actively contributed to the discharge of these new policies and felt equipped to do so because of their training in a pseudo-science allied to the *Ostforschung*, called *Rassehygien*. This was a systematic and apparently biologically founded racism that had been in the curriculum of medical schools (Weindling, 1989). Euthanasia had been an early product of such thinking (Müller-Hill, 1988, Aly *et al.*, 1994; Burleigh, 1994), but so too had been medicine's place as a state agent, for example authorising marriages on racial grounds (Proctor, 1988, p. 132); see Figure 9.2.

d. The Holocaust in space

Across Europe the curious traveller can still be surprised by the physical evidence of the period that ended in 1945. By this date, millions had been extirpated in the Nazi project of producing a 'citizenry' made uniform on racial grounds. The isolated names on uncomfortable gravestones in rural France give way to longer and more monumental

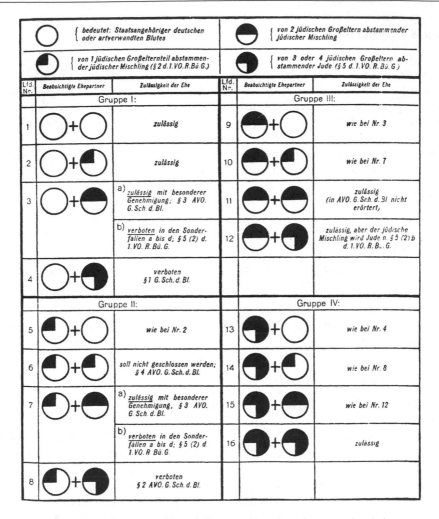

Figure 9.2 Overview of the admissibility of marriage between Aryans and non-Aryans; constructed by Dr Spanger of Reich Health Office

Source: *Zeitschriftfur Arztliche Fortbildung* 33 (1936): 115, reproduced in Robert N. Proctor, *Racial Hygiene: Medicine under the Nazis* (Cambridge, Mass.: Harvard University Press, 1988), p. 133.

lists in Dutch cities. The density of such encounters increases as one moves east, eventually into eastern Poland with the broad sweep of camps, from Stutthof on the Baltic to the vast industrial death camp of Auschwitz-Birkenau in the south. Further east still the evidence is present, but the techniques of death were less formal and apart from gross horrors captured in state monuments like those at Babi Yar and Slutsk, evidence exists in the *absence* of ethnic groups (Vishniac's '*vanished worlds*' – see Vishniac, 1983; Wiesel, 1993; Vishniac Kohn and Hartman Flacks, 1999).

This geography has an elective affinity with Nazism's belief systems, its geopolitics and *Lebensraum*. Our argument here, however, is that *space was actively involved in these processes* and it is to three brief, important illustrations of this that we now turn.

First, the process of elimination of racial groups was tackled systematically and geo-strategically. This remained true throughout the development of the Holocaust mechanisms even though these evolved piecemeal and innovatively, as one problem after another was resolved. What tied the evolving systems together was their increasing productivity. From the start two clear spatial patterns were established. The first was the clearance of rural areas and the decanting of those displaced into temporary zones in

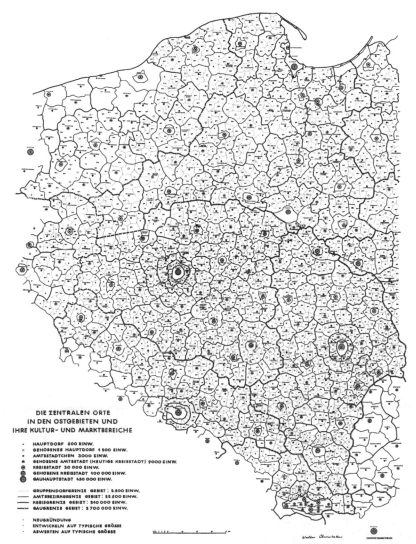

DIE ZENTRALEN ORTE
IN DEN OSTGEBIETEN UND
IHRE KULTUR- UND MARKTBEREICHE

Abb. 20:   Die zentralen Orte in den Ostgebieten und ihre Kultur- und Marktbereiche
(Christaller 1941)

Figure 9.3 Christaller's plan for the Germanification of northern Poland on 'rational' grounds

Source: Mechtild Rossler, *Wissenschaft und Lebensraum*, Geographische Ostforschung im National-Sozialismus (Berlin: Dietrisch Reimer Verlag, 1990), p. 148.

towns and cities – ghettos. Flows in and out of these ghettos were regulated so that they became instruments of death, but their primary purpose remained as holding areas on the way to the death camps. The second was at a larger scale and broadly from west to east, from holding areas like camps near Bergerac or Nancy to the death camps on Poland's eastern borders. Only once an area was *Judenfrei* were these camps and ghettos closed. Schwarz (1990) identifies hundreds of such sites, indicating their satellite relationship to larger centres. The choice of such sites was not accidental, but guided by economically rational decision-making processes like access to transport – particularly railways (Hilberg, 1985), as well as their isolation and the political views of the local population. These last two factors contributed to the comparative invisibility of the process across space. Only in the Soviet Union did these two patterns differ. There, the rural to urban movement was present, but the west to east movement did not occur because of the incompatibility of the rail systems. In their place *Einsatzgruppen*, special action groups, exterminated on the field of battle, where people lived or in the ghettos where they had been transferred. People were shot dead in their thousands.

Secondly, the *Ostforschung* project was acted out in various cultural ways. Landscapes were 'Germanised' by changes to the architecture (Adam, 1992, Chapters 11 and 12), by the creation of distinctive regional governments (Neumann, 1983) within an expanding Reich and by the sanctification of agriculture (Schoenbaum, 1996, Chapter 5). Academic geographers were involved in the planning and delivery of much of this work, legitimating what was being done by their scientific approach. The best known was Walther Christaller, the originator of Central Place Theory, an economically rational account of the distribution of settlements across landscapes that lent itself admirably to the Germanification of landscape. Working in effect as a planning consultant for Reich agencies, Christaller's proposals for northern Poland are shown in Figure 9.3.

Finally, there were differences in the experience of the Holocaust state by state: different state forms produced different views of citizenship – and its inclusivity and exclusivity. This can be glimpsed in the different survival rates state by state, or more properly region by region within states. There is no easy picture here because state fortunes changed over time and so states were exposed to a Holocaust mechanism of differing efficiency.

Hungary can stand as an example here (Braham, 1986, 1994; Cesarani, 1997). Prior to the final reverses on the Eastern Front, Nazism's fascist allies in Hungary, the Arrow Cross, dealt with 'their' Jews without interference from outside unpleasantly enough by isolation and marginalisation. However, once the alliance disintegrated Hungary was quickly occupied, and its Jewish population exposed to fully developed and murderous Holocaust mechanisms. This is shown in Figures 9.4, 9.5 and 9.6. Aided by effectively organised Arrow Cross (Hungary's fascist party) members, often working in official capacities, rural areas were quickly emptied and a substantial ghetto was established in Budapest. At this stage of the war (1943–4), Auschwitz was working fully and the journey into southern Poland was short. Only the liberation of Budapest early in 1945 (Máté, 1980) prevented the wholesale elimination of Hungarian Jewry.

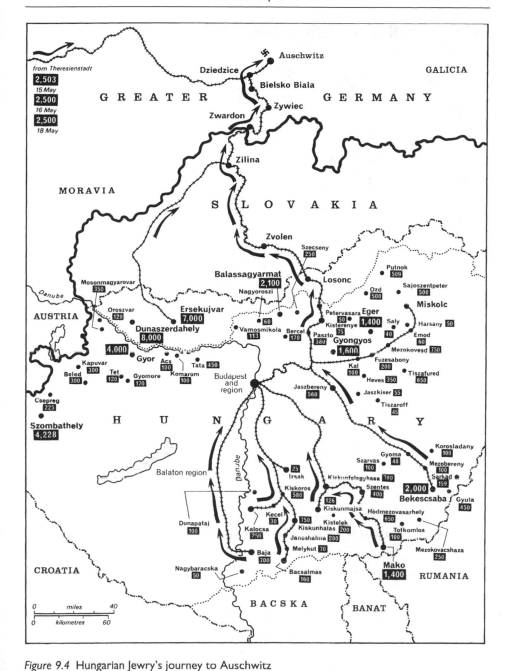

Figure 9.4 Hungarian Jewry's journey to Auschwitz

Source: Martin Gilbert, *Atlas of the Holocaust* (London: Michael Joseph and Routledge, 1982).

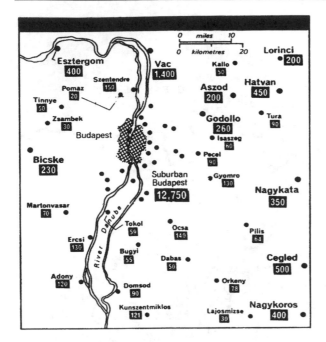

Figure 9.5 Deportations from Budapest's outlying districts into the city

Source: Martin Gilbert, *Atlas of the Holocaust* (London: Michael Joseph and Routledge, 1982).

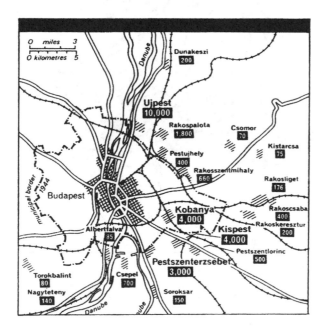

Figure 9.6 Deportations from Budapest's suburbs into the city

Source: Martin Gilbert, *Atlas of the Holocaust* (London: Michael Joseph and Routledge, 1982).

Part 2 A field trip to Auschwitz

This part of our story provides a description of a first-hand encounter by student teachers with the Auschwitz museum in southern Poland. It begins by outlining the framework within which they were expected to work. Secondly, it analyses some of the trip's outcomes, critically reflecting upon the challenges faced in this kind of work with student teachers. Finally, it concludes by recommending further developments of such work. The discussion raises, we believe, interesting questions concerning the preparedness of geography teachers, in terms of their 'subject knowledge', to make contributions of substance to discussions of citizenship in relation to the creation of contemporary Europe: the spatialities of the Holocaust event are as significant as they are interesting, but how convincingly can recently qualified geographers engage with such matters?

a. An educational encounter for teachers in training

It happened. It happened. It happened.

(Doel amd Clarke, 1998, p. 56)

A recent article in the *Times Educational Supplement* emphasised that although genocide was not just a mid-twentieth-century aberration (Newnham, 1999), but had parallels with contemporary ethnic violence, such events need to be understood in their particular geographical and historical contexts. Well, how easy is it to understand the Holocaust through its particular spatial context? In what ways can this be understood? Can the direct study of one – perhaps *the* prime site of mass murder – be of value to teachers and if so, in what ways? Our contention is that asking teachers in training to use and extend their disciplinary expertise to address these appallingly difficult questions contributes to their education, including how to handle such material in the classroom. Work such as this, we argue, crucial in the development of their capacity to construct with students notions of citizenship. The Holocaust is, to some, beyond representation, but *it happened* and pupils and students have a right to ask why. Indeed, they need to ask this. Thus, the broad focus of this chapter was adopted on the field trip and shared with the participants. Can geography be of service to teachers, student teachers and pupils trying to take in and understand the enormity of one of the most extreme events of the twentieth century? And again, if it struggles to do so, what does this say about geography and its capacity to educate in the field of citizenship?

The field visit was undertaken by a group of secondary PGCE students to Cracow, in southern Poland, in June 1999. The visit included an excursion to Oswiecim, the place now known to the world as Auschwitz-Birkenau. Between 1942 and 1945 this death camp killed and disposed of over 1.5 million people, mostly Jews. The purpose of the visit was to provide first-hand experience of this 'singular' (Doel and Clarke, 1998) twentieth-century event and to provoke creative and critical reflection upon some ideas and concepts associated with the teaching and learning of citizenship in geography: for example, inclusion and exclusion, racism, geopolitics and national identity. These important concepts were considered to be capable of being 'opened up' in an especially challenging manner through this geographical study. A field component in this venture was considered crucial for a number of reasons, some taking us beyond Harvey's (1991)

Box 9.5 The benefits of undertaking fieldwork

- Increased motivation and enthusiasm for the subject aided by novel milieu
- Acquisition of technical competency in a range of field, laboratory and data-handling skills
- Opportunity to relate to peers and teachers in new physical and social settings
- Exemplification of theoretical ideas and provision of case studies
- Some increase in conceptual understanding
- Creation of intellectual and physical challenges
- Strengthening of technical and specialised vocabulary
- Contribution towards personal and social development, and growth in confidence and self-esteem
- Growth in respect for others and emphasis on collaboration rather than competition

Source: Harvey (1991).

---

conventional justifications for fieldwork, familiar to most geographers (see Box 9.5). In this case, the intention was to build in explicit, first-hand experience, so that the student teachers could *bear witness* to the wretched place. Their 'task' was to understand the event and the place, but also to find ways of either representing it to others or using what they had learned in some way to serve an educational purpose.

The visit took place towards the end of the PGCE course, that is after the assignments had been handed in and immediately following the completion of practical teaching experience. The visit's programme included study visits of various aspects of social, political and economic change, including farming, heavy industry and tourism in and around the city of Cracow. But it was the visit to Auschwitz-Birkenau that was expected to have the greatest impact – and to create the biggest challenges to the student teachers in terms of their response to the experience as subject specialists.

The student teachers were expected to respond by way of a formal task, namely by producing in a compressed time scale a 'text' for use with secondary school students. Many students interpreted this to mean a 'case study', appropriate to whatever level they chose to work (from KS3 to 'A'-level), with 'activities'. However, discussion with the student teachers immediately before the visit prompted them to think more critically about why and how to use text with students (Lambert, 1999b), encouraging them to consider the possibility of producing a text that more fully exploited its *explanatory* potential.

This was a challenging task. There is a paucity of material on topics as difficult as the Holocaust in existing school *geography* textbooks and so few templates exist from which guidance can be drawn. The student teachers were encouraged to look to other disciplines, finding Neville's (1998) work to be a particularly good example of an explanatory historical text for school students. In addition, academic work on this topic in geography is relatively sparse and not particularly accessible, creating a potential knowledge vacuum among the student teachers. Nevertheless, information is available and the group was introduced to the geography of the Holocaust in a seminar run by one of the authors prior to the visit.

To produce an explanatory text on a complex matter at any level is a difficult and underrated skill in teaching. The task was specifically not to produce an 'activity', in which the 'pedagogic adventure' (Tochan and Munby, 1993) predominates, but to research and develop an aspect of subject knowledge, using their disciplinary expertise to provide an introductory description and an explanatory account, and then to clarify and make useful distinctions for the young learner. Such texts could be openly challenging, even a struggle to get through, but nevertheless worthwhile and stimulating for the reader as a result of the quality of their instruction. The task was, in a sense, designed to promote the development of what could be called 'subject didactics' (Lambert, 1999c), using a subject discipline to shed light on, and account for, events, concepts and processes and so help learners 'make sense of the world'.

In summary, the field visit explicitly mapped out a four-stage framework in which the student teachers were to operate. These four stages were:

- introduce to the student teachers some ideas and background concepts concerning the Holocaust. In particular it was thought important that the student teachers had the events **contextualised** in time and space. This was done mainly by a presentation prior to the trip, using the narrative at the start of this chapter.
- provide a meaningful and **appropriate experience** of the Auschwitz-Birkenau site at first hand. This would include a visit to the museum, an interpretation from a Polish tour guide and time to roam alone or in groups.
- allow time for **individual reflection**. Initially this would be a day or so during which the student teachers could think and talk with each other about their response to – and understanding of – the experience. This reflection was sometimes stimulated by questions posed by the tutors, encouraging the student teachers to think again about the context and the experience.
- require the **production of a piece of text**. This was required within a week of the group's return to London. It was acknowledged that although the student teachers had been asked to prepare for a pupil/student audience, in practice it would be the tutor who saw the work; this possibly had a distorting impact resulting, for example, from students making assumptions about what would be considered 'good work'.

b. The texts: analysis and reflection

Texts were produced by student teachers on a range of topics situated in southern Poland. We are concerned here only with those that tackled the Holocaust. The texts produced and examined here included:

1 'Auschwitz – a case study'
2 'How do you choose a location for a factory of death?'
3 'The Holocaust – memory or museum?'
4 '"Hidden" geography: Auschwitz and the Holocaust'

There is not space here to provide anything more than a glimpse of the ways in which the task was approached. The student teachers tried hard to respond to the task and their texts indicate that they were serious in their quest to use and understand at a variety of levels: personally, as geographers and as future teachers of citizenship themes. Attempts were also made to explain concepts such as the nation, nationalism, racism, fascism and genocide. A number of geographical interpretations of the Holocaust were offered but, as we shall indicate, the texts had severe limitations. Many of the authors, working in pairs, drew directly from their first-hand experience of having 'been there'. For example, from the fourth title above:

> The desire to expand eastwards ensured that the German [Nazi] extermination machine rampaged across Europe.

> At first glance, the horrific events that became commonplace at Auschwitz may seem to be completely irrelevant [to geography programmes of study], but when looked at in closer detail these events consisted of basic industrial processes of production and removal of waste in a system that was both effective and efficient.

The closing line moves us towards an aspect of 'geography' where the authors felt more confident. Indeed, the relatively sophisticated responses contained in the second title in the opening list were achieved by the authors choosing to concentrate on the familiar territory of rational economics (albeit of 'industrial murder'). For example,

> The factory scale was a 'Fordist' model of mass-production. The train journey to the camp is perfectly straight. There was no unnecessary journey, but for travelling to your death – a journey for which you bought a one-way ticket, and entered the camp by its solitary entrance. You would probably never leave. Hitler was famous for saying that if you tell a lie, you should make it a big one. As you enter the gates of Auschwitz, there is a slogan *Arbeit Macht Frei*; lies come no bigger.

> Auschwitz demonstrates the extremity to which nationalism can reach. Nationalism is propagated by mythology . . . for example . . . the great 'Other' – the perceived threat of a so-called common enemy (Jews etc) created an artificial homogeneity.
>
> The need to expand their 'operations' led to the establishment of a committee to discuss the most favourable location for such a camp, the need for expansion being one of the key factors. An additional committee was assembled in 1940 to discuss the idea of building a death camp in order to execute [*sic*] Jews, Gypsies, homosexuals and other members of society who did not comply with the Nazi expectation. The location of Auschwitz was not chosen randomly as there were several factors which determined the location of the death camp, some of which can be applied to many industries – for example, distance from raw materials, availability of power supply, transport links, location of markets, labour supply and capital – and others that are more specific for the location of a death camp.

Beyond the unsettling level of disinterest with which the reader is being asked to approach the Holocaust, the authors supplied many more detailed maps and statistical summaries that emphasised the scale of the Auschwitz-Birkenau operation. These included, for example, the links with the Nazi-founded chemical industries operated by

I.G. Farben at Birkenau (Borkin, 1979), again drawing attention to the economic geography implicit in the camp's location and adding to the sophistication of those pieces.

Explanatory accounts of the 'final solution' (*why* it happened, as opposed to *how* it happened), were more limited: typically, 'because the Nazis were racist' – although still managing to convey the scale of the evil harboured by the project: 'This research [*Ostforschung*] had "shown" that only the Germans could civilise the east. Poland had to be Germanified; it was the duty of the "other people" to disappear.'

As we have seen, the combination of beliefs in 'racial' purity and territorial ambition remains a lethal mix in Europe, Africa and elsewhere – to the present day. Little in the student teachers' writing captured this, indicating perhaps the extent to which the Nazi story is accepted, uncritically, 'as history'. It may also reveal a lack of fluency in being able to handle territorial and ethnic events such as wars and violent boundary disputes, and perhaps, as Yi-Fu Tuan (1999) speculated, an unwillingness to count moral questions (and questions to do with the state are, by definition, moral ones) as 'geography'. We conclude that moving from here to a more positive and lively conception of citizenship in geography – and an inclusive one – therefore poses challenges of the first order to geography teachers.

In the third piece of writing, the authors endeavoured to open up an intriguing issue known to many in the social sciences as the 'crisis of representation'. To do this they juxtaposed two accounts of equivalent length to 'offer entirely different views of Auschwitz, one as a tourist attraction' (quoting from Fallon, 1999) 'and the other as a concentration and death camp' (quoting from Halina Birenbaum, a survivor). The student teachers wrote:

> On visiting Auschwitz . . . one is very much 'told a story'. The fact that 500,000 people now visit each year somehow influences the experience one will have at Auschwitz. . . . You do not have to imagine the daily ritual of life that was done here; it is done for you. The way it is preserved gives us all the evidence we require to place it in our memories as a place symbolising terror. . . . It is designed to shock and achieves that amply.

From here the student teachers concluded that 'this raises questions about visiting the death camps in Poland', specifically about how the Holocaust is to be represented. For them, the issue is illuminated by contemporising the issue, for 'if we look at Kosovo we can see that the lessons of the Holocaust have not been learnt'. But the 'lessons' are not specified. The failure to learn is attributed to the lack of appropriate education and in particular the way in which 'evidence' is presented. From this they conclude that it must be right for the young to study Auschwitz, not least because it is 'harder to educate the young if the evidence is not prominent'. Such accounts do not allow that the butchers in both Auschwitz and Kosovo may have shared a belief in the rightness of their actions, and perhaps even in their political effectiveness (just what else can be learned from Auschwitz?), based on an exclusive view of citizenship. Again, the challenge of constructing alternative models of citizenship presents itself. The 'evidence', though necessary, may not in itself be sufficient to provide effective 'lessons'.

'The Holocaust – memory or museum?' was perhaps the least successful of the four texts for students, seeming to move away from the set task (to provide explanatory texts for students) and towards 'exploratory writing' for the benefit of the beginning teachers themselves. Nonetheless, this illustrated the need to consider the significant 'textual turn' experienced within the social sciences in recent years with regard to the narrative accounts produced by the disciplines. Geography at school level still largely retains the position that it is possible to secure objective, value-free knowledge of the world. In other words, it assumes that language is somehow capable of neutrally and truthfully describing reality. This approach is under fire from an increasingly influential critique that is captured in the following quotation from a critique of the field trip written by one of its participants:

> I would argue that much could be learned from an examination of the ways in which different subjects [the student teachers in this instance] construct the object of their disciplinary gazes [here, this is Auschwitz or the Holocaust]. . . . Some cultural and literary theorists argue that there is no escape from narrative, that we can only make sense of the world through telling ourselves and others stories about it. These are ideas that are worth exploring in relation to field visits.

Such a critique usefully begins to theorise the task being established here – is it possible to facilitate the development of theoretical structures in the young (that may run counter to conventional wisdom), so that when a narrative is strung together its storyline is not the only one available, but the subject of choice on ethical grounds?

c. Implications for teaching citizenship through geography

We are confident that geography teachers will be able to use the discipline to develop an understanding of citizenship with students; some of the work done with the student teachers in Poland indicated that this is the case. However, their work also usefully located some of the attendant risks and potential limitations that should warn against any complacency within the subject or its proponents about its capacity to open up citizenship as a political and moral concept.

Among the risks indicated by the student teachers' texts was the tendency for them to be written to show where the *geography* could be found. In other words, the Holocaust was offered as a vehicle to 'carry' geography, rather than the subject being employed to begin to describe, explain and pose difficult questions. The tokenistic fluency with which neo-classical industrial location theory could be 'read off' against the death camp's situation in southern Poland poses obvious moral and ethical questions – but could also waste the theory's explanatory power to reveal something of the decision-makers' *Weltanschauung*. When this was done confidently and competently theories were employed in ways that would raise good questions for pupils, and make useful distinctions in the evidence presented. For example, how was it possible for thousands of 'ordinary people', such as those working on the railways or in various capacities in the administration, to collude with such monumental evil?

The answer to this question lies, at least in part, in ideas of what constitutes the citizen and the role of the state. If geography can help pupils understand the lethal combination resulting from racist thinking and the occupation of space, it will have made a substantial contribution to citizenship education. The geography of the Holocaust shows that when racist assumptions had been 'legitimised' by science, and the German state had adopted territorial ambitions to the east, germanification followed and the 'final solution' became inevitable. However, if we are going to get anywhere close to realising such discussions in school geography, the collective of geographers in education may do well to ponder the difference between adopting citizenship to defend the place of geography in the curriculum, and developing the capacity of geography (and geography teachers) in order to enhance the curriculum experience.

There is a sense in which the previous paragraph points uncomfortably at the limits of geography. Our position is that geography (like any subject) is limited if it turns in on itself and chooses to serve only itself, shunning tough questions about its contribution to deeper moral thought. This is a call for geography teachers to work beyond the discipline's familiar subject territory and to be *less precious with regard to the sanctity of disciplinary boundaries*. When the focus of the student teachers' writing was primarily 'geographical' the accounts produced by the fieldworkers were, within limits, both interesting and convincing. Straying away from such a narrow focus produced far less convincing work; attempts to explain nationalism in some texts were, for instance, naïve and in one case dangerously misleading. In short, there were concepts that related to political theory, to political change and development, especially in Europe, that the student teachers in this small sample were unable to deal with other than in a partial and incomplete manner. The lack of political theory is perhaps the more intractable issue, probably requiring an educational intervention. The point, the significance of the issue can be illustrated briefly but starkly by a conversation overheard between two of the student teachers. 'How long had Poland been Communist?' one asked. '*Oh, since the early nineteenth century I think*,' came the reply.

FOR FURTHER THINKING

Four challenges for geography teachers

1   To establish a concept of citizenship that is positive, reflective and inclusive.
2   To enable learners to have ethical choices and not be confined, in some uncritical way, to the prevailing hegemony.
3   To be aware of the elective affinities of the theories that are assumed or employed – for example, central place theory.
4   To incorporate some knowledge of political theory into the range of subject matters encompassed by geography in schools.

Conclusion

Just as the chapter is in two main parts so too is our brief conclusion.

In the opening section an argument was developed, albeit briefly, that endeavoured to understand *how*, and with more difficulty *why*, the Holocaust happened, using the lens of geography. Although this seminal mid-twentieth-century event was unique, some more universal tendencies can be extracted:

- the attraction and risks of subscribing to *exclusive* definitions of citizenship;
- the centrality of the nation-state as a *geopolitical* concept, so deeply ingrained ideologically that it is hard to think in other terms; and finally,
- the chilling persistence in Holocaust accounts of notions of *rationality, modernity, efficiency* and *effectiveness*, all of which are valued constructs in much school geography, but treated there as though they were value-free.

In the second section we have exemplified some of the risks and limitations attendant upon geography teachers 'carrying' citizenship work in classrooms and have identified four 'challenges' where work and further thinking would be useful. What we are doing here, of course, is raising issues concerned with the initial and continuing education of teachers. Not least, this calls into question the narrow way in which 'subject knowledge' is expressed in the present standards for newly qualified teachers, primarily as knowledge of syllabuses. There is work to be done, but it is readily identifiable and, given the appropriate support, geography teachers will, as they have done before, incorporate in an accomplished way, new material into their work.

References

Adam P. (1992) *Arts of the Third Reich*. London, Thames and Hudson.
Aly G., Chroust P. and Pross C. (1994) *Cleansing the Fatherland*. Baltimore, Md., Johns Hopkins Press.
Birnbaum P. and Katznelson I. (1995) *Paths of Emancipation: Jews, States and Citizenship*. Princeton, NJ, University of Princeton Press.
Borkin J. (1979) *The Crime and Punishment of I.G. Farben*. London, Andre Deutsch.
Braham R. (1986) *The Tragedy of Hungarian Jewry*. New York, University of Columbia Press.
Braham R. (1994) *The Politics of Genocide*. New York, University of Columbia Press (two volumes).
Burleigh M. (1994) *Death and Deliverance*. Cambridge, CUP.
Burleigh M. (1998) *Germany Turns Eastwards*. Cambridge, CUP.
Cesarani D. (ed.) (1997) *Genocide and Rescue*. Oxford, Berg.
Dawidowicz L.S. (1975) *The War Against the Jews*. London, Penguin Press.
Doel M. and Clarke D. (1998) Figuring the Holocaust. Singularity and the Purification of Space. In Ó'Tuathail G. and Dalby S. (eds) *Rethinking Geopolitics*. London, Routledge.
Ericksen R.P. (1985) *Theologians Under Hitler*. New Haven and London, Yale University Press.
Fallon S. (1999) *Europe on a Shoestring*. London, Lonely Planet Publications.
Gilbert M. (1982) *Atlas of the Holocaust*. London, Michael Joseph.
Harvey P.K. (1991) The Role and Value of A Level Geography Fieldwork: a Case Study. Unpublished Ph.D. thesis, University of Durham.
Hilberg R. (1985) *The Destruction of the European Jews*. New York, Holmes & Meier (three volumes).
Job D. (1990) Geography and Environmental Education – an Exploration of Perspectives and Strategies. In Kent A., Lambert D., Naish M. and Slater F. (editors) *Geography in Education*. Cambridge, CUP.
Kortus B. (1990) Europe in the Teaching of Geography in Poland. In *Serie didattica Fascicolo 1*. Pubblicazioni della Cattedra di Geografia, Libera Università 'Maria SS. Assunta'.
Lambert D. (1999a) Geography and Moral Education in a Supercomplex World: the Significance of Values Education and Some Remaining Dilemmas, *Ethics, Place and Environment*, 2 (1), pp. 5–18.
Lambert D. (1999b) Rediscovering Textbook Pedagogy: the Need for Research on the Use of Textbooks in Geography classrooms. *Issues for Research in Geographical Education. Research Forum 1*. London, ULIE/IGU.

Lambert D. (1999c) Teaching through a Lens: the Role of Subject Expertise and Teaching in the Fields of Social and Environmental Education. A paper read at the International Conference on Teacher Education, Hong Kong Institute of Education, February 1999.

Levi P. (1979) *The Truce. A Survivor's Journey Home from Auschwitz*. London, Penguin Press.

Mackinder H.J. (1907) *On Thinking Imperially. Lectures on Empire*. Sadler M.E. (ed.). London, privately printed.

Máté G. (1980) *Budapest Szabad!* Budapest, Móra Könyvkiadó.

Moon B. (1998) *The English Exception? International Perspectives on the Initial Education and Training of Teachers*. Universities Council for the Education of Teachers, Occasional Paper No. 11, London.

Müller-Hill B. (1988) *Murderous Science*. Oxford, OUP.

Neumann F. (1983) *Behemoth. The Structure and Practice of National Socialism, 1933–1944*. New York, Octagon Books.

Neville P. (1998) *The Holocaust*, Cambridge Perspectives in History, Cambridge, CUP.

Newnham D. (1999) Please Sir . . . What Does Genocide Mean? *Times Education Supplement*, 4 June 1999, pp. 4–7 www.tes.co.uk/tp/90000000/PRN/network/library/library.html

Ó'Tuatail G. (1999) The Ethnic Cleansing of a 'Safe Area'. The Fall of Srebrenica and the ethics of UN-governmentality, in Proctor J. and Smith D. (eds) *Geography and Ethics: Journeys in a Moral terrain*. London: Routledge.

Proctor R.N. (1988) *Racial Hygiene. Medicine Under the Nazis*. Cambridge, Mass., Harvard University Press.

QCA (1998) *Education for Citizenship and the Teaching of Democracy in Schools*. London, QCA.

Rohde D. (1999) *Endgame: The Betrayal and Fall of Srebrenica, Europe's Worst Massacre Since World War II*. New York: Farrah, Strauss and Giroux.

Rössler M. (1990) *Wissenschaft und Lebensraum. Geographische im Nationalsozialismus*. Berlin, Dietrisch Reimer Verlag.

Schoenbaum D. (1996) *Hitler's Social Revolution*. New York, Norton Press.

Schwarz G. (1990) *Die Nationalsozialistischen Lager*. Frankfurt, Campus Verlag.

Slater D. (1997) Geopolitics and the Postmodern: Issues of Knowledge, Difference and North-South Relations. In Benko G. and Strohmayer U. (eds) *Space and Social Theory*. Oxford, Blackwell.

Tochan F. and a Munby H. (1993) Novice and Expert Teachers' Time Epistemology: Wave Function from Didactics to Pedagogy. *Teaching and Teacher Education*, 9 (2), pp. 205–18.

Tuan Y. F. (1999) Geography and Evil: a Sketch. In Proctor J. and Smith D. (eds) *Geography and Ethics: Journeys in a Moral terrain*. London, Routledge.

Vishniac R. (1983) *A Vanished World*. London, Penguin Press.

Vishniac Kohn M. and Hartman Flacks M., (eds) (1999) *Children of a Vanished World*. Berkeley, University of California Press.

Weindling P. (1989) *Health, Race and German Politics Between National Unification and Nazism, 1870–1945*. Cambridge, CUP.

Wiesel M. (ed.) (1993) *To Give Them Light*. London, Viking Press.

Chapter 10

Towards ecological citizenship

John Huckle

Citizenship education contributes to education for sustainable development, through developing pupils' skills in, and commitment to, effective participation in the democratic and other decision-making processes that affect the quality, structure and health of environments and society and exploring values that determine people's actions within society, the economy and the environment.

(QCA, 1999)

The students we teach in geography classrooms are growing up in a world of stark contradictions. While prevailing forms of development continue to bring considerable benefits such as greater life expectancy, more gender and racial equality, and some extension of political freedoms, there is growing evidence of ecological degradation, economic instability, social exclusion, loss of cultural diversity, and psychological insecurity. In varying ways, and to varying extents, most of the world's people are living in ways that are ecologically, economically, socially, culturally and personally unsustainable. They urgently need an accountable, equitable and environmentally sustainable system of global governance and citizenship to tackle the problems created by unsustainable development and to hasten the transition to more sustainable futures.

This chapter focuses on ecological democracy and citizenship in the context of globalisation and the need for a global democracy. After reminding readers of the evidence that we are not living sustainably, it proceeds to examine how dialectical materialism, regulation theory and critical theory can help us to understand our current predicament and recast school geography in a more relevant and enabling form. These related ideas help to move geography towards a reappraisal of the relations between society and nature, and to move society towards new forms of global governance that incorporate a strong commitment to sustainability. A school geography that incorporates appropriate critical theory and pedagogy can do much to develop ecological and global citizenship and the chapter concludes by considering the opportunities available to teachers who wish to promote the kind of outcomes encouraged by new curriculum guidance.

An unsustainable world

The Human Development Report from the United Nations (UNDP, 1998) states that global inequalities are worsening. Twenty per cent of the global population accounts for 86 per cent of global consumption and one billion people have been left out of the consumption boom of the past two decades. Consumption has increased sixfold since 1980 years and doubled since 1990. People in Europe and North America now spend $37 billion a year on pet food, perfumes and cosmetics: enough to provide basic education, water and sanitation, basic health and nutrition for all those now in need of them and still leave $9 billion over. The 225 richest people in the world have combined wealth of more than $1 trillion, equal to the annual income of the poorest 47 per cent of the earth's population, some 2.5 billion people. Among the 4.4 billion people in developing countries, almost three in every five lack basic sanitation, one-third have no safe drinking water, one-quarter have inadequate housing, while one-fifth are undernourished.

The same report also informs us that the burning of fossil fuels has quintupled since 1950, and it is the wealthiest one-fifth of the world who consume more than 50 per cent of the total. The poorest one-fifth are responsible for just 3 per cent of carbon dioxide emissions. A child born in New York, Paris or London will (on average) consume, pollute and waste more in a lifetime than fifty children born in a developing country.

The Living Planet Report from the World Wide Fund for Nature (Loh *et al.*, 1998) suggests that humans have destroyed more than 30 per cent of the world's natural wealth since 1970. Consumption pressure from increasing affluence has doubled in the past twenty-five years and politicians have only been paying lip service to the idea of sustainable development. Half the accessible supplies of fresh water are used up: double the amount of 1960. In the same period (1960 to 2001) marine fish consumption has more than doubled; wood and paper consumption has increased by two-thirds; and carbon dioxide emissions have doubled.

Britain's young people are not isolated from such problems, and Box 10.1 shows one way to engage them in the classroom. The documentary *Eyes of a Child* shown on BBC 1 in June 1999 suggested that one in three children lives in poverty (in households with less than half average income); 20 per cent live in a household where nobody works; one in eight has behavioural problems; one in three 14-year-olds has tried drugs; and children commit 15,000 crimes each day. It is the poorest children who suffer most from the health problems associated with environmental pollution and are often most deprived of contact with the rest of the living world.

The root causes of unsustainable development lie in the way the world's economic, political and cultural systems are governed. People are not free and equal in determining the conditions of their own existence and therefore cannot realise their common interest in sustainable forms of development. Lack of democracy means that powerful minorities

---

Box 10.1 An ET's view of the world

Year 9 pupils imagine they are an ET (an extra-terrestrial creature) approaching planet earth. They call up information about the planet on their computer screen. This tells them about economic production and distribution on earth, the welfare of its people, and the state of its environment. Why are the people living in unsustainable ways and should they adopt the Blueprint for Change suggested in a recent issue of the *New Internationalist* (Ellwood, 2000)? Pupils debate the issues and alternative proposals for sustainable development on planet earth.

> ## Box 10.2 Dialectical materialism
>
> Dialectical materialism suggests that the world is best understood not as a complex of ready-made things but as a system of processes through which all things come into being, exist and pass away. Things like mountains, forests, people, cities, governments and schools are related and changing systems of processes and relations.
>
> Relations between things enable systems to function with powers to transform themselves and other systems. Things are the constitutive and constituted moments of systematic processes, or flows of matter, energy and information, and it is impossible to separate things from the network of systems within which they are embedded. Part and whole, organism and environment, nature and society, are all dialectically related; the one constitutes the other and there can be few grounds for knowledge that seeks to understand the one without reference to the other.
>
> Dialectics seeks to explain the general laws of movement or development in nature, society and thought and reflects four principles:
>
> - totality (everything is related);
> - movement (everything is constantly being transformed);
> - qualitative change (the tendency to self-organisation and complexity); and
> - contradiction (the unity and struggle of opposites).

control such key institutions of global governance as the UN, G8, OECD, NATO, IMF, World Bank and WTO. Regional, national and local politics are generally more democratic but here too powerful interests such as transnational corporations, high-level think-tanks and newspaper owners exert unfair influence.

There is mounting opposition to such a world and growing evidence that a more democratic and sustainable alternative is struggling to emerge. People and movements have the ideas, resources and political will that will make this happen and among geographers and other social scientists new and rediscovered ideas are playing a key role. Dialectical materialism (see Box 10.2) suggests how we might heal our relations with one another and the rest of nature while regulation and critical theory suggest how our responsibilities towards humanity and the biotic community might be balanced against our rights to self-determination within a new form of global democracy.

Dialectical materialism, realist nature and environmental politics

A geographical education that seeks to heal our relations with the rest of nature should be based on a philosophy that overcomes the modern separation of nature and society by adopting a dialectical, systematic and materialist approach to the bio-physical and social worlds. Dialectical materialism maintains that the world is by its very nature material. Everything that exists (including everything mental or spiritual) comes into being as a result of material causes and develops according to the laws of science. The rational discovery and application of scientific knowledge about the world enables people to make progress and realise higher states of development. The current challenge is to develop forms of knowledge, rationality and citizenship that can guide us towards sustainable development (Cornforth, 1961; Harvey, 1996).

Dialectical materialism explicitly rejects the notion of an objective, knowable nature outside society, of the kind promoted by positivist philosophy and much physical geography. It pictures a total reality that is the product of both ecological and social processes. Ecological processes result from structures in the physical and biological worlds (ecological relations) that allow a realist concept of nature (Dickens, 1996). This suggests that nature is the permanent ground of all human activity and environmental change, setting elastic limits on how we live or might try to live. Social processes are a distinct subset of ecological processes since humans have the ability to form social relations that shape their behaviour and affect ecological relations. Habits, customs, laws, language, technology and such institutions as schools are the outcomes of unique articulations of social relations in time and space. They are products of class, gender, political, spatial and other relations that act back on ecological relations ensuring that all places, environments and natures are socially constructed, both in a material and a discursive sense.

While nature in a realist sense sets elastic limits on how people can live in the world, they themselves must decide what forms of ethics, politics and governance should regulate their relations with the rest of human and non-human nature. Environmental ethics and politics emerge once people realise that the world they inhabit is their own construction and responsibility and start turning the actions whereby they constitute nature into the objects of explicit and discursively justified communal choice. Environmental politics then becomes a struggle over social relations and their impact on ecological relations and on our physical, mental and social health. Radical environmental politics seeks to democratise social relations in order that mutually beneficial relations between humans, between humans and other species, and between organisms and their environment, can be sustained. It seeks to change the institutions, beliefs and practices that reproduce unsustainable social relations and to this end seeks to democratise the sites of power that shape all economic production and social reproduction (Hartmann, 1998).

Power, citizenship and global democracy

The global order is constituted by multiple and overlapping dynamic networks of power (see Box 10.3). These networks contain seven sites of power that shape people's capacities and life chances, the kinds of technology and discourse that mediate their relations with one another and the rest of nature, their rights and duties, and hence their status as citizens. The seven sites of power (and the aspects of people's lives that they condition) are:

- the body (physical and psychological well being);
- social welfare (opportunities to become an active member of the community);
- culture (cultural identity);
- civil society (opportunities to join civic associations);
- the economy (capacity to influence the economic agenda);

Box 10.3 Power and authority

What is power? At one level, the concept of power is very simple: it refers to the capacity of social agents, agencies and institutions to maintain or transform their environment, social or physical; and it concerns the resources which underpin this capacity and the forces that shape and influence its exercise. Accordingly, power is a phenomenon found in and between all groups, institutions and societies, cutting across public and private life. It is expressed in all the relations, institutions and structures that are implicated in the production and reproduction of the life of societies and communities. Power creates and conditions all aspects of our lives and it is at the core of the development of collective problems and the modes of their resolution. . . .

But the power of an agent or agency or institution, wherever it is located, never exists in isolation. Power is always exercised, and political outcomes are always determined, in the context of the relative capabilities of parties. Power has to be understood as a relational phenomenon.

Source: Held (1995, p. 170).

In politics and law, authority is now commonly understood as the right to perform some action, including the right to make laws and all lesser rights involved in ruling; it should be distinguished from POWER understood as the ability to compel obedience. This conception of authority has long been the subject of long and ceaseless dispute. . . .

Source: Miller et al. (1991, p. 28).

- coercive relations and organised violence (ability to act without fear of physical force and violence); and
- regulatory and legal relations (ability to participate in political debate and electoral politics).

In the modern period citizenship, or the framework of complex interlocking relations which exist between rights and duties in any legal and moral system, has expanded to embrace civil, political and social citizenship. Citizens have acquired legal, political and welfare rights, along with corresponding duties, and each phase of development has been associated with particular ideas of justice. The primary container of citizenship has been the nation state, but the growth of global networks of power, the urgency of global issues such as climate change, and the emergence of local groups, movements and nationalisms from below, now challenge the power and legitimacy of the nation state and that of the present undemocratic inter-state system. Calls for new systems of global governance and citizenship are intensifying and political theorists such as David Held (Box 10.4), suggest models for our consideration.

In seeking to embed the principle of autonomy or self-determination into all sites of power, at all levels from the local to the global, Held seeks to further extend the depth and breadth of citizenship. He wishes us to have rights and responsibilities across all

Box 10.4 Towards a cosmopolitan world order

- Global governance should be based on **the principle of autonomy**. All the world's people should enjoy equal rights, and accordingly equal obligations, in the specification of the political framework which generates and limits the opportunities available to them. They should be free and equal in the determination of the conditions of their own lives, so long as they do not deploy this framework to negate the rights of others. People should be self-determining and democratic government should be limited government. It should allow 'the people' to determine the conditions of their own existence while limiting 'the people's' power through a regulatory structure that is both constraining and enabling.

- Enactment of the principle of autonomy requires an expanding framework of legal principles, institutions and procedures, to extend and deepen democratic accountability at all levels from the local to the global. These can provide and enforce rights and responsibilities that cut across networks of power and provide the foundation for new forms of **global democracy, governance and citizenship**. Laws would delimit the form and scope of individual and collective action within the organisations and associations of the state, economy and civil society, creating minimum standards of treatment for all, and ensuring the effective co-ordination of social development in the common interest.

- Global democracy could reshape and redistribute political powers. It could **recast territorial boundaries of accountability** so that issues and agents which currently escape the control of nation states could be brought under democratic control. It could **reform regional and global regulatory and functional agencies** to give them a more coherent and powerful role in realising sustainable development. It could also **ensure that key groups, associations and organisations, from within the economy and civil society, become part of the democratic process,** at all levels from the local to the global. Such changes will require an expansion of the influence of regional and international courts to monitor compliance with an expanded framework of legal principles.

- Global democracy could ensure that the **production, distribution and exploitation of resources take place according to principles of social justice and sustainability**. It could **use the principle of non-coercive relations to govern the settlement of disputes,** using force only as a collective option of last resort in the face of clear attacks on cosmopolitan democratic law.

Source: Held (1995)

aspects of our lives (all sites of power) and for these to be guaranteed and made real by governments and other institutions at all levels from the local to the global. Cosmopolitan democracy and citizenship allow effective co-ordination of social development in the common interest and are likely to lead to the protection, conservation and restoration of bio-physical resources and services in the interests of present and future generations. To use one of Held's examples, it would allow factories to be locally monitored and challenged, nationally regulated and supervised, regionally checked for cross-national standards and risks, and globally evaluated in the light of their impacts on health, wealth and economic opportunities for others. In such ways an emerging global democracy would embrace an ecological citizenship that extends rights to future generations and other members of the biotic community and stems from an enlarged concept of justice (Roche, 1992; Smith, 1998). Some suggest that while the European Union is in need of much reform and democratisation, it has the potential to prefigure such a global democracy. Box 10.5 suggests how such issues can be opened up in the classroom.

We return to the role of rationality, education and social learning in fostering global and ecological citizenship after an examination of contemporary social change and the politics of sustainability.

Sustainable development as a new mode of regulation

Geography teachers seeking to foster ecological citizenship in the context of an emerging global democracy should view much current advocacy of sustainable development and education for sustainability with caution. Such advocacy can be explained by reference to capital's attempts to solve a crisis of profitability that emerged at the end of the 'post-war boom'. The shift from organised (Fordist) to disorganised (post-Fordist) regimes of capital accumulation since 1970 has involved new products and production processes enabled by new information, communication and bio-technologies; the privatisation of state-owned industries and utilities; the deregulation of trade, labour and the environment; the intensification of globalisation and related developments in international political institutions; and the restructuring of social welfare, governance and citizenship. Profits have been restored by creating a capitalism with less work and lower corporate taxes in which *the losers have to pay for everything, from the welfare state to a functioning democracy, while the winners post dream profits and steal away from their responsibilities* (Beck, 1999, p. 26). The resulting contradictions are outlined by Andre Gorz (Box 10.6).

Box 10.5 Fashion, power and identity

Year 7 pupils carry out a survey of the clothing preferences of their peers. They learn about the manufacture and advertising of the most desired products and brands (Klein, 2000); the acquisition of power and identity through consumerism; and the nature of social exclusion in consumer societies. They consider whether fair trade, ethical consumerism and charity shops allow young people to make alternative fashion statements that promote sustainable development and what regulations and incentives, in schools and elsewhere, might encourage such alternatives.

Box 10.6 Capitalism's contradictions: Europe

The economy has grown much faster than the population. Yet the EU now has 20 million unemployed, 50 million below the poverty line and five million homeless. What has happened to the extra wealth? In Germany since 1979 corporate profits have risen by 90 per cent and doubled over the past ten years, while revenue from corporate taxes have fallen by a half. It now contributes a mere 13 per cent of total tax revenue down from 25 per cent in 1980 and 35 per cent in 1960. . . . Developments have been similar in other countries. Most transnational corporations, such as Siemens or BMW, no longer pay any taxes at home.

Source: Gorz, quoted in Beck (1999, p. 26)

As we saw in the introduction to this chapter, this shift to disorganised capitalism (Lash and Urry, 1987), or what some have labelled postmodernity (Crook *et al.*, 1992; Jencks, 1996), has intensified problems of environmental degradation and social exclusion and has led to greater advocacy of sustainable development (see Box 10.7). A growing patchwork of international environmental agreements, increased corporate environmentalism, greater public awareness of environmental issues, and the incorporation of sustainable development into more local and national economic policies, all suggest mounting social concern with the nature and balance of production and consumption, and the emergence of sustainable development as a new mode of regulation (Reid, 1995; Gibbs, 1996). As such, it becomes the justification for an ensemble of institutional forms and practices that guide and stabilise the accumulation process and create a temporary resolution of its crisis tendencies. As a means of institutionalising struggles between competing interests (capitalists, workers' and citizens' movements and the state), sustainable development takes a variety of forms from the 'real' regulations of laws and concrete structures through to more tangible elements such as values and norms of behaviour.

In Britain the new mode of regulation has to establish itself as an integral part of the Blair government's 'third way'. Jacobs (1999) urges the government to rise to the challenges of globalisation, individualism and social exclusion by adopting policies of environmental modernisation that cover economic and industrial policy, health, food, risk management, the quality of urban life, and 'environmental inclusion'.

Criticism of the government in such policy areas as transport suggests that as an emerging mode of regulation (see Box 10.8), sustainable development is contested with different interests arguing for weaker or stronger versions of sustainability. Weak sustainability involves a form of techno-managerialism whereby capital seeks to ensure a continued supply of the conditions of production (natural resources and services, human health and welfare, urban and rural space) on its own terms and the state seeks to maintain the support of the majority of voters. It gives higher priority to environmental concerns in economic policy, employs largely technological and market mechanisms to raise the environmental efficiency of production and consumption, but assumes a high degree of substitutability between human and natural capital. So long as a constant quantity of capital is conveyed from one generation to the next, the conditions

---

Box 10.7 Sustainable development

There are many definitions of sustainable development. Two of the most common are:

Sustainable development is development that meets the needs of the present without compromising the ability of future generations to meet their own needs (Brundtland Report, 1987)

Sustainable development means improving the quality of life whilst living within the carrying capacity of the supporting ecosystems (World Conservation Strategy, 1990)

Agenda 21, agreed at the Earth Summit in 1992, discusses the substance of what sustainable development should mean, the process through which it can be decided on and achieved, and the management tools needed to achieve it.

Substance	*Process*	*Tools*
• Reduce use of resources and production of waste, increase resource efficiency, reuse, recycle • Conserve fragile ecosystems • Social equity (between and within countries and across generations) • Quality of life (broader than standard of living) • Respect for traditional knowledge, ways of life, diversity	• Active planning and management • Consultation, participation, empowerment • Decisions at most local possible level, local government pivotal • Partnerships and collaborations between all sectors	• Education, information, awareness raising • Capacity building, institutional know-how, confidence, experience • Regulations and enforcement • Market management, taxes, levies, subsidies • Public investment

---

of sustainable development are satisfied (e.g. ancient wetland is destroyed in the course of development and substituted by an equivalent area of newly created water space and fringing vegetation). Weak sustainability fails to incorporate a commitment to social inclusion and citizenship through redistribution, democratisation and empowerment, and functions mainly at the ideological level with the media and education used to enlist support. The private sector and the state offer various forms of public consultation and participation to help legitimate the new mode of regulation (e.g. Local Agenda 21) and these can be used to advance stronger alternatives.

Weak sustainability's attempt to internalise nature (to ideologically redefine nature and subsume it within capital as a productive asset henceforth subject to rational management, as in much environmental economics and green consumerism) is compromised by

---

Box 10.8 Mode of regulation

This involves all the mechanisms which adjust the contradictory and conflictual behaviour of individuals to the collective principles of the regime of accumulation. At the basic level, these means of adjustment are simply the extent to which entrepreneurs and workers are in the habit of conforming, or are willing to conform, to these principles, because they recognise them (even reluctantly) as valid or logical. At another level, institutionalised forms are more important – the rules of the market, social welfare provision, money, financial networks. These institutional forms can be state determined (laws, executive acts, public finances), private (collective agreements) or semi-public (a social security system).

Source: Lipietz (1992, p. 2).

---

the need for capitalists and nation states to compete internationally. It meets opposition from those workers' and citizens' movements that seek stronger forms of sustainability. These start from the premise that society cannot simply let economic activity result in a continued decline in the functions and quality of the environment even though it may be beneficial in other ways. They specify minimum levels of environmental quality to be achieved, reject substitution of human capital or critical natural capital, and require an economy that is constrained within ecological limits. For green socialists (Pepper, 1993) ecological sustainability has to be realised along with economic, social, cultural and personal sustainability and this can only be done in a global democracy where the common interest in strong sustainability is likely to emerge. Gorz (1994) and Lipietz (1992) suggest that Europe should pioneer such democracy by using new technologies to liberate people from work and consumerism so that they have the time for personal and social development, including the restoration and revitalisation of civil society and its associated public spheres.

Public spheres, praxis and ecological democracy

Public spheres are political bodies such as trade unions and environmental groups that do not exist as part of formal political authority but rather in confrontation with that authority. Along with the private sphere of the family and household, they constitute the lifeworld, our everyday taken-for-granted world where much social interaction and reproduction are governed by mutual understanding and democratic discourse. It is the lifeworld that allows our common interests to emerge, sustains our culture, and promotes its progressive rationalisation through a process of social learning or praxis (see Box 10.9) whereby useful knowledge is continually refined by reflecting upon the results of applying academic and lay ideas in action (Dickens, 1996).

Praxis reflects dialectical materialism's insistence that all knowledge should be viewed relationally: as part of a totality that is always in a state of movement or change. There are no universal facts, laws or truths, as positivism suggests, and knowledge and truth are best approached as practical questions with the power and validity of ideas being demonstrated by their utility. Theory is a guide for practice and practice a test of theory.

Box 10.9 Praxis

Only with a liberated mind (of the people), which is free to enquire and then conceive and plan what is to be created, can structural change release the creative potentials of the people. In this sense liberation of the mind is the primary task, both **before** and **after** structural change.

This implies breaking the monopoly of knowledge in the hands of the elites, i.e. giving the people their right to assert their existing knowledge to start with; giving them the opportunity and assistance, if needed, to advance their self-knowledge through self-inquiry as the basis of their action, and to review themselves their experiences from action to further advance their self-knowledge. In this reflection-action-reflection process of the people (people's praxis), professional knowledge can be useful only in dialogue with people's knowledge on an equal footing through which both can be enriched, and not in the arrogance of assumed superior wisdom. [Praxis thus alters] the relations of knowledge, to produce and advance 'organic knowledge' as part of the very evolution of life rather than abstract (synthetic) knowledge . . . to be imposed upon life.

Source: Rahman (1993, pp. 195–6).

People are beings of praxis and it is through 'revolutionary' praxis (critical reflection and action) that they can overcome their alienation from one another and the rest of nature and realise higher states of development (Gadotti, 1996).

In an age of disorganised capitalism it is the NGOs and new social movements that are the main agents of praxis as they defend public spheres of democratic discourse from the instrumental rationality of private corporations and bureaucratic states (Jacobs, 1996). The action of environmental and development NGOs over such issues as world trade seeks to translate sustainability from an ethical and political concept into a set of regulative social principles that find expression in the legal and constitutional realm and become an ecological social contract between the institutions of global governance and global citizens. It prefigures the kind of cosmopolitan democracy that Held describes (Box 10.4) and means that the enactment of sustainability, or the creation of sustainable development as a mode of regulation, is not left to experts. It becomes a social learning process that allows ecologically rational relations between society and the bio-physical world to emerge based on moral as well as scientific considerations (Barry, 1996).

The model of discursive or deliberative democracy favoured by advocates of strong sustainability combines representative and participatory democracy, suggesting that decisions should be taken at the lowest level possible (subsidiarity). Discursive democracy is associated with critical theory (see Box 10.10) and Haberman's theory of communicative action. Dryzek (1996) suggests that in an ecological democracy ideal speech situations (competent individuals reaching consensus through an appraisal of knowledge claims that it is not distorted by power relations) should be open to a range of environmental discourses and to the voices of future generations and the rest of nature. Politicians and citizens should listen to signals from the bio-physical world brought to them by scientists and others, and take account of the scientific, aesthetic, economic,

Box 10.10   Critical theory

Critical theory draws on both Marx and Weber and shifts the focus from labour and the social relations of production to social interaction and the nature of language and morals. The principal claim of Jurgen Habermas, the foremost contemporary critical theorist, is that interaction has become distorted by the rise of positivism and instrumental reason that promotes science as universal and value-free knowledge and so fosters a distorted and incomplete understanding of our relations with one another and the rest of nature. His critical theories seek to reveal this distorted and incomplete rationality and empower people to think and act in genuinely rational and autonomous ways.

Habermas's ideas have been applied to environmental politics (Goldblatt, 1996) and geographical and environmental education (Huckle and Sterling, 1996; Huckle, 1997).

cultural and existence values that people find in nature when making their decisions. This is not to argue for the kind of ecocentrism associated with deep ecology, but for an ecological humanism that allows the continued coevolution of the human and bio-physical worlds (Soper, 1999).

Geography education for sustainability

So, what is to be done? How should these ideas from dialectical materialism, regulation theory and critical theory shape the content and process of school geography in the light of new curriculum guidance both for the subject and for citizenship education?

Firstly, geography teachers convinced of my argument should regard themselves as transformative intellectuals seeking the further democratisation of society alongside progressive elements of civil society. They should engage in forms of professional development that extend their grasp of the kinds of critical social theory outlined in this chapter, its development and application by academic geographers, and the ways in which it might reform the contents of their lessons. They should become familiar with environmental politics (Elliott, 1998; Connelly and Smith, 1999), social theory and the environment (Goldblatt, 1996), alternative models of democracy (Held, 1987), and the ways in which nature is being increasingly capitalised and enframed by new forms of economic production and consumption (Braun and Castree, 1998). They should also develop their abilities to engage students as researchers in praxis or socially critical action research in democratic institutions that have extensive links with the community and the wider world. This means running schools and classrooms in democratic and sustainable ways and applying the extensive range of experiential teaching and learning strategies used by progressive social, development and environmental educators (Huckle and Sterling, 1996). Children and young people have the right to participate in their learning and in the social construction of environments and sustainability, and there is a wealth of advice encouraging teachers to educate them in primary environmental care (Hart, 1997; Adams and Ingham, 1998; Johnson *et al.*, 1998). Local Agenda 21 has revived the theory and practice of community planning and development (Selman, 1996) and

---

Box 10.11   Valuing the environment

We value the environment, both natural and shaped by humanity, as the basis of life and a source of wonder and inspiration.

On the basis of these values, we should:

- accept our responsibility to maintain a sustainable environment for future generations
- understand the place of human beings within nature
- understand our responsibilities for other species
- ensure that development can be justified
- preserve balance and diversity in nature wherever possible
- preserve areas of beauty and interest for future generations
- repair, wherever possible, habitats damaged by human development and other means.

Source: QCA, *National Forum on Values in Education and the Community* (London, 1998).

---

progressive local authorities are involving schools in such new initiatives as visioning conferences and young people's parliaments.

Secondly, geography teachers should recognise the value and limitations of the new guidance contained in 'Curriculum 2000'. This seeks to secure students' *commitment to sustainable development at a personal, local, national and global level* and gives geography a major role in developing citizenship through reflection and action on environmental issues and the *issues and challenges of global interdependence and responsibility*. It is supported by the findings of the national forum on values in education and the community: that schools and teachers can expect the support and encouragement of society if they base their teaching and the school ethos on commonly agreed values. The forum's statement of values relating to the environment (Box 10.11) requires clarification if it is to reflect an ecological humanism, but by embracing responsibility to future generations and other species it points to an appropriate ethical foundation for ecological citizenship.

Citizenship education is to be based on a framework of learning outcomes (key concepts, values and dispositions, skills and aptitudes, and knowledge and understanding) that promotes concern for the environment and common good; encourages reasoned argument and critical problem solving; and requires knowledge and understanding of sustainable development and environmental issues. It is sufficiently open to allow teachers to develop students' political literacy by exploring the nature of power, rights and responsibilities, across all seven sites of power at all levels from the local to the global. At best it allows the kind of global citizenship education proposed by Lynch (1992), and developed in the *What We Consume* module of WWF's *Global Environmental Education Programme* (Huckle, 1988–92), but without more detailed guidance of the kind provided by the Panel on Education for Sustainable Development (Box 10.12), there is a danger that teachers will define citizenship too narrowly and that emerging forms of global governance will receive insufficient attention. Pupils are to be taught about *the world as a global community, the political, economic, environmental and social implications of this, and the role of*

Box 10.12 Education for sustainable development

Some proposed outcomes relating to citizenship and stewardship

By the end of key stage 3 pupils should:

- Acknowledge their personal and collective responsibilities in relation to the social, economic and environmental health of their community and value their participation in activities that enhance its sustainability;
- Know how decisions about social, economic and environmental issues are made, that they impact on each other, and how they can be influenced locally and nationally through direct or indirect participation;
- Know how considerations of sustainable development, stewardship and conservation currently affect environmental planning and management.

By the end of key stage 4 pupils should:

- Understand and value the goal of sustainability and the collective decision making processes required to achieve it;
- Be prepared to work with others in partnership to resolve sustainable development issues;
- Understand how values and beliefs influence behaviour and lifestyles, and how some behaviour and lifestyles are more sustainable than others;
- Understand the rights and responsibilities that are emerging as necessary to achieving a sustainable society, and how they apply to themselves and to other groups in the community and wider society.

Source: *Education for Sustainable Development in the Schools Sector*, Panel for Education for Sustainable Development, (London, 1998).

---

the European Union, the Commonwealth and the United Nations (key stage 3), and about *the wider issues and challenges of global interdependence and responsibility, including sustainable development and Local Agenda 21* (key stage 4) but the effective delivery of such outcomes will require significant investment in professional and curriculum development.

Thirdly, geography teachers should acknowledge that in our disorganised capitalist society the foundations of social structure and agency are shifting from the sphere of production to that of consumption. Identity and politics are increasingly focused on the goods and services people consume, the images and meanings that surround these commodities, and related issues of trust, risk and quality of life. The old politics of distribution, government and political parties has partly given way to the new politics of risk, governance and the public sphere, but the new guidance on citizenship fails to adequately reflect this change (Lent, 1998). The politics of GM foods (see Box 10.13) suggests that style, image and presentation are everywhere and that, for young people particularly, the body is increasingly a statement of power, freedom, lifestyle, pleasure and identity. Disorganised capitalism encourages and requires more fragmented,

---

Box 10.13 Engaging with the GM debate

Inspired by the WWF publication *Internet to Go!* (Webster, 1998), geography and English departments co-operate on a Year 10 study of the role of language and images in the debate over genetically modified crops and food. Students visit the websites of agro-chemical corporations such as Monsanto (www.monsanto.com/), NGOs such as Greenpeace (www.greenpeace.org) and government departments such as the MAFF (www.maff.gov.uk/), as well as more general sties (www.connectoltel.com/gmfood). Lessons explore the ways in which language and images communicate risk, uncertainty and trust, and how politicians seek to manage risk in order to maintain public support.

---

decentred, somatic and reflexive individuals who are able to assess and criticise their own values and behaviour and alter them if necessary. The unified knowable self has ceased to exist and teachers should therefore learn to work with students' diverse identities, desires and pleasures, engaging them in dialogue and activity that draw on their grounded cognitive and aesthetic understandings of nature, environments and sustainability (Hartley, 1997; Parker, 1997).

Such activity is likely to contain significant elements of media and consumer education (Morgan, 1997) and give greater attention to the body as a site where nature is constructed (Payne, 1999). It will convey a questioning and reflexive attitude; enable students to perceive the structural origins of their subjectivities (Castells *et al.* 1999); accommodate diverse voices, from peoples and species variously located within ecological and social relations; and so develop the kind of communicative rationality that allows the democratic assessment of risk at the same time as it fosters ecological democracy, sustainability and the re-enchantment of nature. Elements of such pedagogy can be seen in the work of such organisations as Body Shop, AdBusters and Greenpeace, and in such new educational settings as the Eden Project in Cornwall and the Earth Centre near Doncaster.

Identity and ecological democracy

Furlong and Cartmel (1997) remind us that the young people we teach are confronted by an epistemological fallacy. While class, gender and other social relations continue to shape their life chances and the environments in which they live, these relations tend to become increasingly obscure as lifestyles diversify, collectivist traditions weaken, and individual values intensify. Unaccountable and undemocratic powers continue to deny them more sustainable ways of living, yet they are increasingly encouraged to regard the resulting risks, setbacks and anxieties as individual shortcomings that they must solve on a personal basis rather than through politics. Educational reform that promotes greater competition within and between schools to raise narrowly defined standards of attainment reinforces this fallacy and so compounds problems of establishing identity (Klaassen, 1996). It is to be hoped that the introduction of citizenship education will empower young people to reflect and act on a more realistic view of society and thereby become part of the growing movement for strong sustainability.

FOR FURTHER THINKING

1   (a) What should be your learning goals and objectives when teaching pupils to 'understand sustainable development' (a requirement of the geography national curriculum)?

    (b) How do these goals and objectives translate the contested nature of sustainable development into opportunities for political and citizenship education?

2   Examine your schemes of work on sustainable development. To what extent should they be revised to address national curriculum requirements in citizenship and to allow consideration of ecological citizenship?

3   To what extent does the content and approach of your teaching help pupils confront the 'epistemological fallacy' (p. 158)?

References

Adams, E. and Ingham, S. (1998) *Changing Places, Children's Participation in Environmental Planning*, London: The Children's Society.

Barry, J. (1996) 'Sustainability, political judgement and citizenship: connecting green politics and democracy', in B. Doherty and M. de Geus (eds) *Democracy and Green Political Thought*, London: Routledge.

Beck, U. (1999) 'Beyond the nation state', *New Statesman*, 6 December, 41 pp. 25–7.

Braun, B. and Castree, N. (1998) *Remaking Reality, Nature at the Millennium*, London: Routledge.

Castells, M., Flecha, R., Freire, P., Giroux, H.A., Macedo, D. and Willis, P. (1999) *Critical Education in the New Information Age*, Oxford: Rowman & Littlefield

Connelly, J. and Smith, G. (1999) *Politics and the Environment*, London: Routledge.

Cornforth, M. (1961) *Dialectical Materialism, An Introduction, Volume 1: Materialism and the Dialectical Method*, London: Lawrence & Wishart.

Crook, S., Pakulski, J. and Waters, M. (1992) *Postmodernisation, Change in Advanced Society*, London: Sage.

Dickens, P. (1996) *Reconstructing Nature, Alienation, Emancipation and the Division of Labour*, London: Routledge.

Dryzek, J. (1996) 'Political and ecological communication', in F. Matthews (ed.) *Ecology and Democracy*, London: Frank Cass.

Dryzek, J. (1997) *The Politics of the Earth*, Oxford: OUP.

Elliott, L. (1998) *The Global Politics of the Environment*, London: Macmillan.

Ellwood, W. (ed.) (2000) 'Redesigning the global economy', *New Internationalist*, 320, Jan./Feb.

Furlong, A. and Cartmel, F. (1997) *Young People and Social Change, Individualisation and Risk in Late Modernity*, Buckingham: Open University.

Gadotti, M. (1996) *Pedagogy of Praxis, a Dialectical Philosophy of Education*, New York: SUNY.

Gibbs, D. (1996) 'Integrating sustainable development and economic restructuring; a role for regulation theory?', *Geoforum*, 27/1, pp. 1–10.

Goldblatt, D. (1996) *Social Theory and the Environment*, Cambridge: Polity.

Gorz, A. (1994) *Capitalism, Socialism, Ecology*, London: Verso.

Hart, R.A. (1997) *Children's Participation, the Theory and Practice of Involving Young Citizens in Community Development and Environmental Care*, London: Earthscan.

Hartley, D. (1997) *Re-schooling Society*, London; Falmer.

Hartmann, F. (1998) 'Towards a social ecological politics of sustainability', in R. Keil, D.V.J. Bell, P. Penz and L. Fawcett (eds) *Political Ecology, Global and Local*, London: Routledge.

Harvey, D. (1996) *Justice, Nature and the Geography of Difference*, Oxford: Blackwell.

Held, D. (1987) *Models of Democracy*, Cambridge: Polity.

Held, D. (1995) *Democracy and the Global Order, From the Modern State to Cosmopolitan Governance*, Cambridge: Polity.

Huckle, J. (1988–92) *What We Consume* (a teacher's handbook and nine curriculum units for 14–18 year olds), Richmond: WWF/Richmond Publishing.

Huckle, J. (1997) 'Towards a critical school geography', in D. Tilbuty and M. Williams (eds) *Teaching and Learning Geography*, London: Routledge, pp. 241–52.

Huckle, J. and Sterling, S. (eds) (1996) *Education for Sustainability*, London: Earthscan.

Jacobs, M. (1996) *The Politics of the Real World*, London: Earthscan.

Jacobs, M. (1999) *Environmental Modernisation. The New Labour agenda*, London: Fabian Society.

Jencks, C. (1996) *What is Postmodernism?*, London: Academy Editions.

Johnson, V., Ivan-Smith, E., Gordon, G., Pridmore, P. and Scott, P. (eds) (1998) *Stepping Forward, Children and Young People's Participation in the Development Process*, London: Intermediate Technology.

Klaassen, C. (1996) 'Education and citizenship in a post-welfare state', *Curriculum*, 7/2, pp. 62–73.

Klein, N. (2000) *No Logo*, London: HarperCollins.

Lash, S. and Urry, J. (1987) *The End of Organised Capitalism*, Cambridge: Polity.

Lent, A. (ed.) (1998) *New Political Thought*, London; Lawrence and Wishart.

Lipietz, A. (1992) *Towards a New Economic Order, Postfordism, Ecology and Democracy*, Cambridge: Polity.

Loh, J., Randers, J., MacGillivray, A., Kapos, V., Jenkins, M., Groombridge, B. and Cox, N. (1998) *Living Planet Report*, Gland: WWF.

Lynch, J. (1992) *Education for Citizenship in a Multi-cultural Society*, London: Cassell.

Miller, D., Coleman, J., Connolly, W. and Ryan, A. (eds) (1991) *The Blackwell Encyclopaedia of Political Thought*, Oxford: Blackwell.

Morgan, I. (1997) 'Consumer culture and education for sustainability', in F. Slater, D. Lambert and D. Lines (eds) *Education, Environment and Economy: Reporting Research in a New Academic Grouping*, London: Institute of Education, University of London, pp. 161–72.

Parker, S. (1997) *Reflective Teaching in the Postmodern World*, Buckingham: Open University.

Payne, P. (1999) 'Postmodern challenges and modern horizons: education "for Being for the environment"', *Environmental Education Research*, 5/1, February, pp. 5–34.

Pepper, D. (1993) *Eco-Socialism, from Deep Ecology to Social Justice*, London: Routledge.

QCA (Qualifications and Curriculum Authority) (1999) *Citizenship Education*, London: QCA.

Rahman, A. (1993) *People's Self-Development*, London: Zed Books.

Reid, D. (1995) *Sustainable Development, an Introductory Guide*, London: Earthscan.

Roche, M. (1992) *Rethinking Citizenship. Welfare, Ideology and Change in Modern Society*, Cambridge: Polity.

Selman, P. (1996) *Local Sustainability, Managing and Planning Ecologically Sound Places*, London: Paul Chapman.

Smith, M. J. (1998) *Ecologism, Towards Ecological Citizenship*, Buckingham: Open University.

Soper, K. (1999) 'The politics of nature; reflections on hedonism, progress and ecology', *Capitalism Nature Socialism*, 10/2, pp. 47–70.

UNDP (United Nations Development Programme) (1998) *Human Development Report*, New York.

Webster, K. (1998) *Internet to Go! Effective Environmental Education Using the Power of the Internet*, Godalming, World Wide Fund for Nature.

Chapter 11

Global citizenship

Choices and change

Ros Wade

> Global citizenship is not an interesting supplement to the curriculum but is actually the foundation for national and international development and for peaceful relations.
>
> (Davies, 1999: 3)

Introduction

This chapter explores the concept of the global citizen as a mechanism for change and looks at the potential of geography as a subject to contribute to this. This inevitably means considering what kind of future society and, therefore, what kind of schools we want. It also means reflecting on what teachers and educators can do at the personal and institutional levels to bring about this change, and how this relates to change locally and globally.

The first section looks at key global issues and the need for a new concept of global citizenship which is both empowering and critical. The second section focuses on personal change and implications and opportunities for the geography classroom. Finally, the chapter turns to the potential for institutional change in schools through the notion of global citizenship.

Understanding global change

Change seems to be happening at an ever accelerating pace and as educators not only are we having to grapple with this ourselves, but we also have to help our students to do so. The world of today is very different from that of ten years ago, let alone fifty or a hundred. Since 1990 political, economic and even geographical landscapes have been radically reshaped, with new nation-states emerging and old empires collapsing. Divisions between rich and poor are increasing, both between and within countries, and there is a continuing deterioration of the ecosystems upon which we all depend. One-quarter of the world's population live in absolute poverty, while the impact of the average US citizen on the environment is 250 times greater than that of the average African citizen (Jacobs, 1996). This pressure is clearly unsustainable and, according to the Real World Coalition, a grouping of voluntary organisations and pressure groups, if everyone on the planet were to achieve the levels of consumption of the northern industrialised countries then two extra planet earths would be needed.

Agenda 21, the set of commitments made at the UN Earth Summit of 1992, represented an acknowledgement by all the countries of the world that poverty and environmental degradation are inextricably linked and that sustainable development for all is not achievable without the eradication of poverty. A world where large numbers of people lack the basic needs for living is, by definition, a very polarised world that cannot guarantee a foundation for global peace and security. In order to change this, it is clear that a vision of citizenship is needed which transcends national boundaries, which enables us all to become, in effect, global citizens with 'a commitment to sustainable development at personal, local, national and global levels' (DfEE/QCA, 1999a: 11).

Agenda 21 acknowledged many of the new challenges which were facing the world, and 178 countries committed themselves to take action for sustainability, yet today many of these pledges are still unfulfilled. Instead of action that promotes sustainable development, globalisation became the *leitmotif* of the latter part of the twentieth century and ideological choice seems to have been limited to free market capitalism and representative democracies of varying efficacities. Global institutions (like the IMF and World Trade Organisation) wield immense influence over all our lives, and have grown in prominence and influence and 'without any complaint and discussion in parliaments, without any decision in governments and without any change in the law' (Beck, 1999). At the meeting of the World Trade Organisation in Seattle, in December 1999, more than 50,000 demonstrators from many different countries and organisations underlined the frustration and anger felt at this global disenfranchisement.

A MORI poll (Jan.–Feb. 1998) of 11–16-year-olds shows that 70 per cent of young people want to know more about the world and global issues like these, but 54 per cent felt powerless to change anything. The British Election Study reports that 25 per cent of the 18–24 age group said they would not vote in the 1992 general election, a figure rising to 32 per cent in 1997. This is the highest abstention rate among all age groups (QCA, 1998: 15), and the government's Citizenship initiative is largely founded on concerns about this decreasing participation in the political process by the young. Yet, if the traditional political process is seen to be increasingly irrelevant to this cohort, then this disengagement is not really surprising.

On its own, of course, education for global citizenship cannot solve all the complex problems of the world, but it could and should help to provide the basis for young people to make informed decisions and to participate in action for change.

What are the challenges for the twenty-first century?

The Delphi project (an international research project on global citizenship involving people in the USA, Europe, Japan and Thailand) identified the following key trends facing us in the next twenty-five years:

- The economic gap between countries and between people in countries will widen significantly
- Information technologies will dramatically reduce the privacy of individuals
- The inequalities between those who have access to information technologies and those who do not will increase dramatically

- Conflicts of interest between developing and developed countries will increase due to environmental deterioration
- The cost of obtaining adequate water will rise dramatically due to population growth and environmental deterioration
- Deforestation will dramatically affect diversity of life, air, soil and water quality
- In developing countries, population growth will result in a dramatic increase in the percentage of people, especially children, living in poverty

(Cogan and Derricott, 1998: 77)

These issues concern and involve us all in debates about what kind of future we really want. The trends are predicated on the assumption that there will be no real change in the present world order, that we are helpless in the face of invisible forces. This is a recipe for despair that we cannot afford to accede to. Despite the immense challenges facing us today, we should also acknowledge and celebrate the considerable progress that has been made globally in the last fifty years. According to the *UN Human Development Report* of 1997, world mortality rates for children have been cut by half, life expectancy has increased from 31 to 62 years, and the number of people with access to safe water has doubled (UNDP, 1997).

The conclusion of the 1997 *UN Human Development Report* was that the elimination of poverty is both affordable and achievable. What has been lacking is the political will and, according to Clare Short, 'if people in this country and elsewhere believe that the elimination of poverty is achievable and not a hopeless enterprise they would demand action and generate the political will' (quoted in Oxfam, 1997: 5).

Because of disillusionment with the traditional political process we sometimes seem to forget that personal choice and change can influence political agendas, as witnessed, for example, by the public outcry against GM foods. Many young people may choose not to vote but this does not mean that they do not care or that they will not take action. However, without an understanding of the wider political and social context, and without a belief that individual action **can** make a difference, then the potential for effective action will be limited. Geography as a subject is better placed than any to provide the context and to support pupils' understandings, and therefore geographers have a particular and very valuable contribution to make.

This assertion is underlined by research carried out by the NFER (National Foundation for Educational Research) in 1995 on environmental awareness and action. Regarding individual subjects, 'the role of the geography department seemed key, with any constraints there having a significant effect on overall levels of student awareness, attitudes and feelings of power within the environment'. In addition, the research concluded that 'those young people who had both factual awareness and conceptual understanding were more predisposed to action' (Morris and Schagen, 1995: 24).

In order to address the issues and challenges of the twenty-first century many would argue that the concept of *national* citizenship alone is not sufficient. It is, in any case, a problematic notion in the UK, made up of four different nations and a huge diversity of cultures. For Lynch (1992) and others, this situation offers the opportunity to abandon a citizenship limited to national boundaries and develop a more global model for a sustainable and equitable world. Lynch describes three levels of citizenship:

1   The local community, including familial, cultural and social groupings, defined by
     language, religion and ethnicity but not necessarily geographical location.
2   National citizenship, determined by birth or choice but which may not be restricted
     to one nation.
3   International citizenship, drawing on interdependencies between members of the
     world community, regardless of the other two levels.

Geography has the potential to make a significant contribution to the third category
in particular, as the geography Programmes of Study for the first time require teachers
to 'explore the idea of global citizenship'. Geographers are well placed to develop this,
by enabling pupils to 'learn about geographical patterns and processes and how political,
economic, social and environmental factors affect contemporary geographical issues.
They also learn how places and environments are interdependent' (National Curriculum
Geography Programmes of Study, 1999, Key Stage 3). This is also supported by
the introductory rationale to the POS, which talks of the importance of geography in
inspiring pupils to 'think about their own place in the world, their values and their rights
and responsibilities to other people and the environment' (DfEE/QCA 1999b: 154).

At a time when geography as a subject is perceived as under threat, this is an opportunity that we cannot afford to ignore. Indeed this is an important time for geography to
demonstrate its relevance and importance within the new orders, and in particular within
the realm of citizenship.

What do we mean by global citizenship?

To ensure breadth of study across the key stages, the Geography National Curriculum
at KS3 requires teachers to develop 'an awareness of global citizenship through understanding of how places are interdependent in the global community'. The Curriculum
documents define global citizenship as 'what it means to be a citizen in the local
community and of the UK, Europe and the wider world'. This rather limited definition
begs more questions than it answers, but it does provide an opportunity to explore and
develop the concept ourselves. Given that the whole notion of citizenship in schools is
relatively new in the UK, this is clearly essential.

The National Curriculum handbook (DfEE/QCA 1999b: 11) states that

> the school curriculum should pass on enduring values, develop pupils' integrity
> and autonomy and help them to be responsible and caring citizens capable of
> contributing to the development of a just society . . . [it] . . . should develop their
> awareness and understanding of, and respect for, the environments in which they
> live and secure their commitment to sustainable development at a personal, local,
> national and global level.

In 1997 Oxfam's development education team, in consultation with a wide number
of educationists, outlined key elements of knowledge and understanding, skills, and
values and attitudes which could make up a 'curriculum for global citizenship'. It stressed
that awareness raising alone is not enough to develop global citizens. By definition, the
notion of citizenship also implies action.

Oxfam (1997) defined a global citizen as someone who:

- is aware of the wider world and has a sense of his or her own role as a world citizen;
- respects and values diversity;
- has an understanding of how the world works, economically, politically, socially, culturally, technologically and environmentally;
- is outraged by social injustice;
- participates in and contributes to the community at a range of levels from the local to the global;
- is willing to act to make the world a more equitable and sustainable place;
- takes responsibility for his or her actions.

A curriculum framework was then developed across all the key stages, with examples from a range of subject areas. This framework is already being used by a number of schools as a basis for teachers to interpret this concept within their own practice. The key elements of the framework are identified below.

Knowledge and understanding

- Social justice and equity;
- peace and conflict;
- diversity;
- sustainable development;
- globalisation.

Skills

- Critical thinking;
- ability to argue effectively;
- co-operation and conflict resolution;
- ability to challenge injustice and inequalities;
- respect for people and things.

Values and attitudes

- Value and respect for diversity;
- empathy;
- sense of identity and self-esteem;
- belief that people can make a difference;
- commitment to social justice and equity;
- concern for the environment and commitment to sustainable development.

While skills and knowledge elements are of course very important, the Oxfam framework argues that values and attitudes of global citizenship are **essential** if society is to become more equitable and sustainable. The teaching of values has, of course, always been a notoriously difficult area for teachers. But whether implicitly or explicitly, this is what we are doing all the time, by the way we relate to our subject, to students and to other colleagues. By understanding our own values and perceptions, and those that inform the subject matter, can help teachers better able to support students' learning.

Hopefully, we should all be able to subscribe to these universal values of global citizenship but, clearly, we may also interpret them in quite different ways. For this reason, the **process** of reaching common understandings must be considered to be all-important, for teachers as well as students. In understanding what we mean by these common values we are, in effect, trying to understand what kind of society we really want. There are bound to be some different perspectives and this can be helpful and enriching in a complex multi-dimensional society. But sometimes it may be useful to rely on the benchmark of essential human rights, however problematic a concept this can sometimes be. For example, we can ask ourselves the question, does the present world trading system ensure essential human rights for all? If it does not, then it is failing to fulfil the universal values of global citizenship. Of course, other examples may not be so clear-cut, especially when we start to examine the finer details of world trade. There may be conflicts of interest, particularly in relation to short-term and long-term interests. A few years ago the BBC's *Modern Times* made a programme about the cultivation of mange-tout peas in Zimbabwe. This crop, which is easy to grow in the UK and which is not eaten in Africa, was then flown thousands of miles so that it could be on our supermarket shelves all the year round. From an environmental perspective it is clear that the crop is harmful and certainly teachers who watched the film at a Geographical Association conference felt that consumers should boycott it. But from the point of view of the local people, although the pay was meagre it was the only work that was on offer. So, from a human rights perspective, the response is different – and not simple or straightforward. Political literacy is thus essential if both teachers and students are to have an awareness of the complexities of issues and the complex results of our actions.

> When we try to be neutral, like Pilate, we support the dominant ideology. Not being neutral, education must be either liberating or domesticating. Thus we have the right to recognise ourselves as politicians. It does not mean that we have the right to impose on students our political choice. Students have the right to know what our political dream is. They are then free to accept it, reject it or modify it. Our task is not to impose our dreams on them but to challenge them to have their own ideals, to define their choices, not just to uncritically assume them.
>
> (Freire, 1985.)

FOR FURTHER THINKING

1 Can you subscribe to the values of global citizenship as identified by Oxfam on p. 165? (Most of them are enshrined in world religions and ethics and even international law.)
2 Do you want to add anything to the list?
3 How do you interpret them in practice?
4 How explicit are you about the values that underpin your teaching?
5 Do you feel confident that you are expressing these values through your teaching?

Look at the teacher brainstorm below on the theme of refugees which relates to the values of diversity and commitment to social justice and equity. It focuses on action at the personal, classroom and school levels. Could you use this framework for other themes?

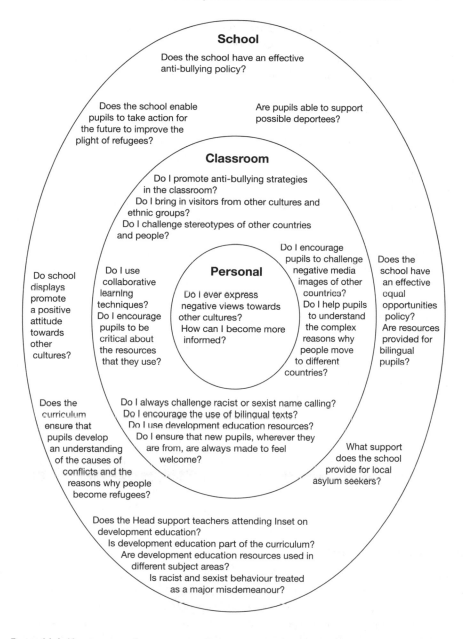

School

Does the school have an effective anti-bullying policy?

Does the school enable pupils to take action for the future to improve the plight of refugees?

Are pupils able to support possible deportees?

Classroom

Do I promote anti-bullying strategies in the classroom?
Do I bring in visitors from other cultures and ethnic groups?
Do I challenge stereotypes of other countries and people?

Personal

Do I ever express negative views towards other cultures?
How can I become more informed?

Do I encourage pupils to challenge negative media images of other countries?
Do I help pupils to understand the complex reasons why people move to different countries?

Do school displays promote a positive attitude towards other cultures?

Do I use collaborative learning techniques?
Do I encourage pupils to be critical about the resources that they use?

Does the school have an effective equal opportunities policy?
Are resources provided for bilingual pupils?

Does the curriculum ensure that pupils develop an understanding of the causes of conflicts and the reasons why people become refugees?

Do I always challenge racist or sexist name calling?
Do I encourage the use of bilingual texts?
Do I use development education resources?
Do I ensure that new pupils, wherever they are from, are always made to feel welcome?

What support does the school provide for local asylum seekers?

Does the Head support teachers attending Inset on development education?
Is development education part of the curriculum?
Are development education resources used in different subject areas?
Is racist and sexist behaviour treated as a major misdemeanour?

Figure 11.1 Key issues: refugees

Source: Sally Inman and Ros Wade, *Development Education within Initial Teacher Training: Sharing a Better Future* (Oxford: Oxfam, 1997), p. 7. Reproduced with permission from Oxfam Publishing, 274 Banbury Road, Oxford, OX2 7DZ.

Global citizenship in the geography classroom

According to David Hicks (Hicks and Holden, 1995: 112):

> Whilst some pupils feel that they can act on a personal level to help create a better future, many do not. They feel that school has given them an inadequate education in this area. While they often hope for a more just and sustainable future, school provides little opportunity for discussion on such issues.

The geography classroom is one place where there are many such opportunities if we choose to exercise them. *Final Frontier*, a geography teaching pack produced by Leeds Development Education Centre, enables students to deconstruct the tourist trade, using a case study of Kenya. A role play involves them in trying to estimate how much of the £1,000 price of a safari holiday should go to the Travel agent, the Hotel, the safari company, the Kenyan government, and the Maasai. At the end of this exercise, students are generally outraged to find out that the Maasai receive absolutely nothing although their lands are being used for tourism, and in fact are being degraded into the bargain (Leeds DEC, 1996).

The danger for the teacher here is to leave students feeling they are powerless and can do nothing to express their concerns. But if time is allowed for discussion on possible actions, then possibilities emerge. They may wish to contact Tourism Concern, for example, and find out about their initiatives to develop more ethical and sensitive approaches to tourism. They may want to carry out a survey of local travel agencies and find out which are able to give information about the impact of tourism on local communities, or whether they have any ethical guidelines or standards for selling holidays. Students themselves could develop their own codes for sensitive tourism, both within the UK and overseas, and try to apply them to their own lives.

This type of lesson would address many aspects of the Citizenship programmes of study, such as (Skills 2a and b):

> use imagination to consider the experience of others and be able to reflect on, express and explain viewpoints contrary to their own; to exhibit skills of negotiation and accommodation and be able to reflect on the process of participating in school and community-based activities.
>
> (DfEE/QCA, 1999a: 29)

Skills for global citizenship

The skills which students are able to develop at school depend to a great extent on the methodology used by teachers in the classroom that sets the framework to enable them to participate in the learning process. Pedagogical processes common in the geography classroom, of enquiry-based or experiential learning, have a contribution to make to the promotion of citizenship skills. These can be further developed through cross-curricular work with other subject areas on particular themes. Working for their Certificate of Achievement in 1999, Year 9 students at Greenshaw High School in Sutton used their geography and tutorial time for a project on fair trade. A local resident came in to talk

---

Box 11.1 Role play

Role plays like this can be very engaging and involving but sometimes on their own they can lead to simplistic interpretations of complex issues.
   Some suggestions to avoid oversimplification of issues:

- develop the context (make use of the whole teaching pack, not just the role play);
- give plenty of preparation time and debriefing time;
- encourage the pupils to be critical and to assess the unashamedly anti-poverty 'agenda' behind the activities. Ask them to assess whether the role play brought out the complexities of the situation. How would they change it to enable it to do so?

---

about growing up on a sugar plantation in Guyana and students then went on to do their own research on coffee, sugar and banana production which they used to compile a report on world trade. Using simulations and role play, such as the Coffee Chain Game (Oxfam 1995), the learners were introduced to some of the mechanisms of international trade (see Box 11.1). They learned how countries like Tanzania were having to produce more and more cotton for less and less return as commodity prices slumped, and they learned how international debt was eating away most of these foreign earnings. In so doing they began to gain an understanding of the inequities of world trade and of the reasons why some countries are caught in a poverty trap and unable to break free. They intend to go on to do a survey of local shops to see how much Fair Trade produce is stocked. They would also like to encourage the school (and the staffroom in particular) to make more use of fairly traded goods where possible.

As we all know, learning does not take place in subject boxes and to become rounded citizens, capable of making decisions about complex issues, we need to be able to draw on all available sources, from all relevant disciplines. In today's fast changing society we need to be flexible and lateral thinkers and this requires 'an approach to education which is socially critical, open to new and radical insights, prepared to leave outmoded practice behind and to pioneer new ways of being and learning' (Hicks 1999).

Current outmoded practice could include what Paulo Freire called the 'banking' system of education, where knowledge is deposited into pupils ostensibly to increase their 'value' in the market place. This view of education accepts the status quo and sees society solely as individuals competing with each other for the best jobs. The present preoccupation with literacy and numeracy targets can be constructed to reflect this perspective. But the 'banking' system also perpetuates the present world order which, as we have seen, is unsustainable. Education can never be neutral. It

> either functions as an instrument which is used to facilitate the integration of the younger generation into the logic of the present system and bring about conformity to it, or it becomes 'the practice of freedom', the means by which men and women deal critically and creatively with reality and discover how to participate in the transformation of their world.

(Shaull, 1972)

Geography as a subject has often been seen as 'political'. In Chapter 2 above Professor Marsden describes its early associations with promoting a vision of the British Empire on which the sun never set. In China during the Cultural Revolution, geography was labelled a bourgeois discipline because it encouraged travelling and sightseeing. As a result, it was completely removed from the middle school and university curricula and geography teachers were either dismissed, forced to teach other subjects or sent to the countryside for re-education (Yat-ming, 1991: 34). In more recent times, Tory ministers personally interfered in the English, geography and history National Curriculum documents. Thus it is, perhaps, particularly important for geographers to regularly question their practice and to ensure that a wide range of views and perspectives are available so that students learn to question and think critically about key global issues.

At Central Park East Secondary School (CPESS) in New York, the main concern is that pupils learn to use their minds well, become passionate about their work, feel cared for and learn to care for others. In order to fulfil this, **in every class and in every subject**, pupils learn to ask and to answer these questions:

1   From whose viewpoint are we seeing, reading or hearing? From what angle or perspective?
2   How do we know what we know? What is the evidence and how reliable is it?
3   How are things, events or people connected to each other? What is the cause and what is the effect? How do they fit together?
4   What if? Could things be otherwise? What are the alternatives? Supposing . . .
5   So what? What does it matter? What does it all mean? Who cares?

(Lieberman, 1999: 42)

In a school that promotes global citizenship we might want to add a final question:

6   What can we do about it? Individually or with others? How do we change things?

FOR FURTHER THINKING

To what extent are current curricula appropriate for the twenty-first century?

Critics complain that, even after the NC Review, we are still basing our school curriculum on a late Victorian model. The new learning society and the *knowledge economy* require flexible thinkers with a variety of transferable skills, the most important of which is, perhaps, the ability to know how to learn.

1   Does this mean a different conceptualisation of the meaning of teacher? Perhaps as more of an enabler than an expert in a particular field?
2   What could this mean for geographers in particular?
3   What are the opportunities and threats for geographers within this model?

Teachers as global citizens

Secondary geography teachers are perhaps uniquely placed in their potential to grasp key global issues and to have an overview of the solutions and changes required to tackle them. But in order to do this we need to take our own responsibility as global citizens seriously; this means accepting that we are all learners as well as teachers.

Teachers with personal experience of the developing world are even 'more likely to have the notion of global citizenship at the heart of their teaching' (Walkington, 1999: 21). This research related to primary geography teachers teaching about a distant locality, but it does not seem unreasonable to generalise from it. We are all touched by our own individual experiences and changed by them. Helen Walkington found that

> teachers lacking direct experience of the developing world focused upon knowledge and information-based aims and practices. With increasing confidence this progressed into a values focus, based around consideration of images of the locality in a cultural context. Finally, teachers with experience of the developing world used development education methods to provide experiences for learners in order to develop critical thinking skills and a sense of global citizenship.
>
> (Walkington, 1999: 23)

Although this research concentrated on teachers with VSO or school-linking experience in the developing world, it should also highlight for us the importance of valuing widening participation in the teaching force by, for example, black teachers in the UK as well as teachers with direct personal experience of developing countries.

But, given that we will not all have access to these personal experiences of migration or travel, what other strategies can we employ to prepare ourselves and our pupils for global citizenship (see Box 11.2)? The most effective geography teaching involves reaching out to students, to their concerns and interests, but it also involves engaging them in issues that are going to be relevant to them in the future. Many of these issues are daunting to adults as well as young people; some of them are controversial. How do we as teachers prepare ourselves to address the problem of global warming, for example? Do we know enough about the causes and consequences? Have we reflected on our own lifestyles and considered what action we could take in our own lives to cut down on energy use?

In our all too busy lives, do we allow ourselves time for reflection, for self-development? A project on sustainable development with trainee geography teachers at Goldsmiths College in 1995 (Inman and Wade, 1997) clearly highlighted the need for time to **think and reflect**. Despite their geography or social science degrees, the student teachers all found the concept of sustainability extremely difficult to grasp at first. This was not surprising as it affected their view of the world and they needed time to reflect, to discuss, to rethink, in order to develop their own perspective of the term. Like the notion of global citizenship, it is an emerging concept which carries with it both an opportunity and a responsibility for us all to contribute to its development.

Box 11.2 A challenge for all

- How can we widen participation in the geography teaching force?
- How can we encourage interest from black and ethnic minority students?

Some questions:

- Do you ensure that you use a variety of texts to reflect different viewpoints of countries studied?
- Do you encourage students to critique geography textbooks (e.g. for racist imagery and neocolonial attitudes)?
- Do you try to ensure that, if you are studying a particular country, you invite visitors who can give a personal perspective?
- Do you ensure that positive examples of achievement by people in so-called 'developing countries' are included in your teaching?
- Do you enable students to critique the western model of development?
- Do you encourage students to critique the use of language such as 'Third World' or 'developing' country? These phrases used uncritically can imply a sense of inferiority or worse. They can make black and ethnic-minority students feel uncomfortable and turn them off the subject completely.

FOR FURTHER THINKING

How do you see your teaching role?

1   How would you prioritise these roles?

- pastoral
- subject specialist
- whole school
- cross-curricular
- community links
- other

2   Where would you place yourself on this continuum?

Role as a teacher ◄──────────► *Role as a learner*

3   Are you happy with the balance between subject specialist and your pastoral role, for example?
4   How will this influence your role in teaching global citizenship?

Policies are most effective when they resonate with what people feel to be important and what is consistent with their experience, in short when they become meaningful. Global citizenship has to be seen as choice rather than prescription. Behaviour and action that are rooted not in personal conviction but in pretence or fear will eventually prove to be unsustainable. This is demonstrated clearly in the fall of authoritarian regimes with the terrible consequences inherent in the vacuum of values that they leave behind. As Richmond and Morgan outlined in 1977 in a major survey of Year 11 understanding and beliefs about the environment: 'If attitudes of young people are to be translated into responsible social behaviour it would appear that these attitudes should be deeply rooted and based upon knowledge, experience and conviction, rather than superficially learned or instilled by indoctrination' (Richmond and Morgan, 1977).

The Citizenship Orders offer us a real opportunity to become engaged in debates about meanings. When schools start to develop their citizenship policies, geographers should have much to contribute in terms of knowledge, skills and methodologies which could be shared with other staff members. This is also a chance to involve the wider community in debates about citizenship and to establish links with voluntary groups and organisations.

In many ways this is, perhaps, not surprising since to change both ideas and attitudes is not a simple process. Vygotsky suggested that the basis of all learning is 'internal conversations' in which we constantly shift between 'two planes of learning' (which he called 'intermental' and 'intramental') and between two planes of enactment (individual and collective). Through continuous progression around these cycles we acquire knowledge and skills and we adapt and creatively remake such learning for ourselves, our own purposes and circumstances (Daniels, 1993). A major constraint to personal change is, therefore, as much as anything, habit and custom.

Paulo Freire believed that only what he called 'transformative' education could result in both personal and social change (Freire, 1985b). He described four basic reactions to key issues of social change: *conforming, reforming, deforming* and *transforming*. Conforming implies acceptance of the status quo, an inability to question or take action. Reforming implies an individualistic approach which believes that a person can succeed if he or she plays the game, works hard, achieves success. Deforming implies an angry, destructive approach based on the belief that change is only possible if we first destroy the present system. Transforming, on the other hand, implies both personal and social change, with the personal and social in a dialectical relationship with each other. It is an active, learner-centred approach, focusing on issues and concerns, which seeks to develop the skills and confidence to take action.

Paulo Freire was working with community educators in the field of adult literacy for poor and disenfranchised peasants in Brazil. Teachers working in the much more regulated school sector in Britain have not often been in the habit of seeing themselves as transformative educators and this concept offers quite a challenge. But teachers have to be creative and have shown themselves to be adept at interpreting and mediating National Curriculum orders over quite a long period (Bowe *et al.*, 1992). The Citizenship Orders offer real encouragement to teachers who wish to develop a more transformative approach.

However, since the introduction and subsequent reviews of the National Curriculum, the trend towards the commodification of education has developed almost in parallel, with no softening of this approach under New Labour. Many would argue that this has led us to a situation of increasingly unequal educational provision, imposing constraints on the concept of transformative education or education for global citizenship, as described in this chapter. In addition, there is a danger that we may reach a situation where 'Education here becomes a product like bread or cars and the only culture worth talking about is "enterprise culture" and the flexible skills, knowledge, dispositions, and values needed for economic competition' (Apple, 1996: 20). However, while this may be the way that some policy makers now talk about education, at the same time there are strong contradictions in the government's actions. Support for development education, for example, has greatly increased since New Labour came to power. The QCA, DfEE and DfID (Department for International Development) are working with the Development Education Association to bring out guidance on teaching global perspectives in the National Curriculum. These, of necessity, include a focus on social justice and equity and teachers can and should take heart from these initiatives and build on them, as Apple exhorts, to 'name the world differently' (Apple, 1996: 21).

Schools for global citizenship?

The final report of the government's Advisory Group on Citizenship and the teaching of democracy in schools stressed the need for a whole school, cross-curricular approach:

> Schools need to consider how far their ethos, organisation and daily practices are consistent with the aim and purposes of citizenship education . . . schools should make every effort to engage pupils in discussion and consultation about all aspects of school life on which pupils might reasonably be expected to have a view.
>
> (Quoted in Gold, 1998: 17)

The ethos and practice of the school community are even more important in developing global citizenship, as 'the values and attitudes of young people will shape the kind of future world in which we will live' (Oxfam, 1997: 13).

This is not an easy task when most secondary schools are hierarchical and bureaucratic, and provide few opportunities for teachers, never mind students, to contribute to their organisation or curriculum. Yet if citizenship education is to become a reality, this will have to change.

> If schools are experienced, not as places of shared meaning and purpose, but as fragmentary and divided, we should not be surprised that the society emerging from them also reflects divisive values. This vicious circle is hard to break and requires that citizenship education nurtures the capacity for active, critical, practical engagement and a sense of belonging by young people. Education that does not do this risks taking us down the road of an indoctrinated, compliant and unthinking citizenry, perhaps also cynical and alienated.
>
> (Maiteny and Wade, 1999: 42)

Despite the confusion felt by many teachers as a result of seemingly contradictory educational initiatives by the government and the pressures of a crowded curriculum, there are examples of schools that are taking this seriously. The Small School in Devon, with headteacher Caroline Walker, is trying to develop a holistic approach to education which involves the whole school community. This school can be described as a community, because students have responsibility for cleaning up, for growing food, for helping to prepare meals. The school sees itself as functioning within a local and global community. For example, it has contributed to a successful campaign to keep open the local village shop and, thinking globally, has also used this opportunity to involve people in debate and discussion about fair trade issues. In a small school of around 400 students it is obviously easier to develop a consensus and community spirit, but this does not mean that it is impossible in a larger school. Constraints should not be underestimated and these include difficulties of communications across large departments or faculties; the complicated micro-politics, conflicts of status and interest between different departments in large secondary schools. Nonetheless, there are lessons to be learned from the Devon Small School experience and, in resolving these issues, we are mirroring the political processes with which we have to engage as global citizens.

The challenge for secondary schools is to encourage purposeful participation and to develop a sense of the school as a community within a wider community. Schools do not exist in isolation. They are communities within wider communities, local, national and global. Geographers should know this better than anyone and so are more ready to take the concept of global citizenship on board. Communities are very complex and we all belong to a complicated network of different groups, which relate to these levels in a variety of ways. Students could at the same time identify themselves as part of a youth group, an internet group, a sports club, a fan club, a family network, a friendship group and at any one time any of these could be most important. Other students may feel socially excluded from many of these groups; they may belong to groups of the socially excluded who truant or get involved in petty crime or they may become very solitary.

However, there is a great deal of evidence to show that, given support, young people respond very well to being given responsibility and authority. Wath School in South Yorkshire responded to the problem of bullying by setting up a Bully Court for Year 7. Two children from each tutor group are chosen as members of the court and everyone takes turns to attend hearings so that they can gain some experience. A teacher or sixth former sees the person who has been bullied straight away and offers help if necessary. The court talks to both the bully and the victim and makes a decision about what is to be done. There are no fixed punishments but these could include a detention or, for more serious cases, a letter home. Teachers only act as advisers and help to carry out decisions made, but this system has been so successful that it has been extended to Years 8 and 9.

This example forms part of an exciting teaching pack for personal and social education called *Developing Rights*, which shows how it is possible to combine personal, local and global concepts of citizenship. The Unit on Bullying begins with a role play about street children in Brazil and looks at how the national Movement of Street Children supported children in claiming their rights. Although adults set up the movement, in 1989, the children organised a demonstration and took their concerns to the Brazilian parliament. This eventually resulted in a change in the law that gave street children protection against violence and other injustices. Following on from the role play on Brazil, students go on to relate the experience of the street children to their own experiences of the misuse of power, and focus on issues of bullying and how to deal with it. The particular strength of this pack is that it does not leave students feeling powerless; it encourages young people to consider how they can contribute to action for change and offers examples of how injustices have been tackled. At the same time, it also enables students to engage with complex issues and to look at and experience some of the frustration that is a requisite component of change. In our society of instant gratification, patience and tenacity are virtues that are not always sufficiently valued.

As yet, there is no ideal model of a school for global citizenship, just as there is no model for an ideal school, but that does not prevent us from considering what might be some key components. If we are unable to imagine such a school, then we are never going to be able to achieve it, just as if we are unable to imagine a better society then we are never able to achieve it. Futures educators like David Hicks have long been researching people's hopes and dreams for a better future. He describes the work of Elise Boulding, who has run many futures workshops in different parts of the world with social activists, businesses and religious and other organisations, and points out the striking similarities between people's preferred futures. Most people hope for:

- a lack of divisions based on age, race or gender
- a non hierarchical world with no one 'in charge'
- a strong sense of place and community
- low profile and widely shared technology particularly relating to communications and transport
- people acting out of a more peaceable 'new consciousness'
- education taking place 'on the job'

(Hicks, 1999: 13)

If these aims and aspirations are shared by so many people, then surely it should not be beyond the bounds of human skills and imagination to achieve them. Schools and teachers alone cannot create this new world vision, but they can certainly contribute.

FOR FURTHER THINKING

How can we be agents for change at an institutional level?

The answer to this will obviously depend on how you see your role as a teacher and your position within the school.

A headteacher is obviously in a much more powerful position to initiate change than a classroom teacher. But we can all exert influence by, for example:

- building allies among like-minded colleagues;
- understanding the micro-politics of our school and how decisions are made (in the staff meeting, by the school management team, in the pub!);
- finding a powerful champion;
- building on strengths and current good practice;
- using key opportunities, such as a review of the school development plan, development of the citizenship curriculum;

- developing partnerships with appropriate community groups;
- involving students in discussions about school organisation and practice;
- becoming involved with the governing body.

Elements of a school for global citizenship

John Cogan, in a pathfinder book *Citizenship for the 21st Century* (which was based on the research of the Delphi project), talks of the need to organise 'the school itself in such a way that it becomes a model of multidimensional citizenship, i.e., that its whole atmosphere and functioning model equitable policies and practices, environmental stewardship, ethical issues of informational technologies and global awareness' (Cogan and Derricott, 1999: 173). Based on the research of the Delphi project, and on the Oxfam *Curriculum for Global Citizenship*, the following might provide possible elements of a school for global citizenship:

- open, fair and enabling leadership;
- sense of inclusion, participation and responsibility by teachers and pupils;
- commitment to environmental protection and awareness;
- links with the local community;
- awareness of the wider world and global issues;
- respect for and celebration of diversity;
- commitment to social justice and equity;
- a welcoming, safe, nurturing environment;
- capacity to take part in public life from local to global levels.

What might this look like in practice?

To misquote Tolstoy, 'all happy schools are alike, but unhappy schools are unhappy in their own way'. We would all probably know a functioning, effective school for global citizenship when we see it but how do we achieve it? So much relates to school ethos, which is not easily measured by school league tables or OfSTED reports. Some useful work has, however, been done in this area by schools' self-evaluation. Lesley Saunders, head of the School Improvement Centre at the National Foundation for Educational Research (NFER), criticises the current DfEE schools' self-evaluation model because 'it fails to do full justice to principles of ethics, affect, non-rationality and democracy' (Saunders, 1998: 7). By this she means that the DfEE model is too 'instrumentalist, action-oriented, rationalistic and managerial'. She feels that its main intent is to measure intellectual, academic and technical achievement, whereas schooling is centrally also concerned with other activities, such as 'the development of insight and empathy; the encouragement of creativity and imagination; critical reflection about social and personal values' (Saunders, 1998: 8). A research project on school self-evaluation in seven different European countries produced a set of guiding principles for school self-evaluation which seeks to include some of these components and which relates much more closely to the concept of global citizenship. For example, it states that school self-evaluation should 'involve values and ethical questions as well as techniques' (Saunders, 1998: 6).

Developing this into measurable indicators is not, of course, a simple process. A school which promotes global citizenship might, however, include some of the following aspects.

Democratic participation and inclusion

- Commitment to and practice of values of global citizenship by a majority of staff;
- real participation by staff and pupils in school organisation and curriculum;
- an effective school council;
- an open, effective and inclusive governing body;
- effective equal opportunities and anti-racist policies and practice;
- cross-subject teacher groups or faculties;
- a teaching staff from diverse cultural and social backgrounds;
- parental and community involvement;
- an effective and affirming PSE curriculum which promotes peaceful conflict resolution;
- school displays that celebrate diversity and positive attitudes to all cultures;
- co-ordinators for citizenship and environmental education.

A curriculum with global and critical dimensions

- A curriculum which encourages critical thinking and challenges negative stereotypes and attitudes;
- a strong geography department with expertise in teaching key global environmental and development issues;
- an assembly programme which includes global citizenship themes;
- regular cross-curricular activities and events on themes of global importance.

Capacity to take action in school and public domains

- Positive environmental policies and practice, e.g. involvement in Local Agenda 21, an effective reuse and recycling scheme;
- regular visitors from diverse religious and cultural backgrounds;
- links with local voluntary organisations, such as Development Education Centres, Amnesty or Friends of the Earth;
- commitment to buying fairly traded products where possible;
- commitment to ethical investment for school banking and finances;
- involvement in local community issues and projects by staff and pupils;
- a commitment to global citizenship in the school development plan.

We should not underestimate some of the constraints on achieving these aims. These include lack of time, pressures from OfSTED, constraints of exam syllabuses, lack of LEA or government support in resources or training. Schools under special measures or under pressure from league tables may find it hard to think beyond the day-to-day grind of survival. Yet constraints can sometimes be turned into opportunities. For example, establishing strong links with local communities can lead to an active school support base and a reservoir of talent and skills to be drawn on. Here we can perhaps learn from research on effective schools in the poorest countries of the world. In Tanzania, for example, where teachers are often expected to teach classes of sixty or more pupils with few books and resources, community support has often proved able to make the difference between the success and failure of a school. In Peru an innovative project working with whole communities in the Amazon has transformed schooling into a relevant cultural and environmental experience for all, and has enabled communities to voice their hopes and aspirations for the future.

When the Citizenship requirements become statutory in 2002, all schools will, in any case, be required to address some of these issues. Rather than wait to be told how to do this, we have an opportunity to contribute to policy and practice.

Advocates for global citizenship?

As educators and teachers, we are in positions of power. We can choose to use this to become advocates for change or we can choose not to. We are also members of wider civil society and as such, many of us may be involved with community groups and initiatives, voluntary organisations and campaigns. The World Wide Fund for Nature has a network of teacher representatives who take on roles within their school of highlighting key issues and sharing information. They also encourage their schools to become involved in curriculum projects and to develop 'greener' policies. Teachers who are interested in development education have forged links with local Development Education Centres and invited speakers from a range of different backgrounds. They have publicised campaigns by Oxfam and other agencies, such as the campaign against Third World debt, Jubilee 2000, and have encouraged pupils who wished to set up school support groups.

Despite the strong influence of TV on young people's lives today, the NFER survey, perhaps surprisingly, found that this was more as a source of information than a spur to action. The major finding that emerged strongly in fieldwork interviews was that 'it is the beliefs and practices of environmentally motivated teachers which are the most significant elements in prompting young people to undertake environmental action' (Morris and Schagen, 1995: 20).

Conclusion

The Citizenship Orders provide an ideal opportunity for schools in the UK to take up these challenges. Schools could become, in effect, a focus for local debates about new meanings of citizenship in our complex, multicultural society. These could help to inform Local Agenda 21 discussions about preferred futures, which in turn could involve pupils in contributing to local projects and initiatives. The Global Footprint project in Tower Hamlets is one example of this, where schools are developing literacy and numeracy skills through an examination of the impact of their schools, environmentally, socially and economically, on both the local and global neighbourhoods. Through this project, schools hope to contribute to a reduction of their negative impact, for example by cutting down energy use and by trying to ensure that, as consumers, they buy from companies that have good employment conditions. Obviously this will involve students and teachers in some very complex issues and in making difficult decisions but it could also help to set a standard for starting to measure what we mean by global citizenship. Supported by Local Agenda 21 officers, the project has now received backing from DfID and from the EU and is expanding to involve a number of Development Education Centres in different parts of the country.

Unless we all start to tackle the difficult issues today we risk losing the possibility of realising our vision of tomorrow. We cannot wait for governments, we cannot wait for policy makers. We need to influence the processes of change, to know that we have a part to play, no matter how small. But first we need to reflect on our present vision of the world and think about what we would like our future vision to be. What kind of world do we want in this new century for our students and following generations? How can we engage students and colleagues in these discussions? As Patricia Williams succinctly put it, in the Reith lecture of 1997, 'I do believe that to a very great extent we dream our worlds into being: an optimistic course might be charted if only we could **imagine** it' (Williams, 1997; my emphasis).

References

Apple, M.W. (1996) *Cultural Politics and Education*, Buckingham, Open University Press.

Beck, U. (1999) *What Is Globalisation?*, London, Polity Press.

Bigger, S. and Brown, E. (eds) (1999) *Spiritual, Moral, Social and Cultural Education: exploring values in the curriculum*, London, David Fulton.

Bowe, R., Ball, S. and Gold, A. (1992), London, Routledge.

Cogan, J. and Derricott, R. (1998) *Citizenship for the 21st Century: an international perspective on education*, London, Kogan Page.

Daniels, H. (ed.) (1993) *Charting the Agenda: educational activity after Vygotsky*, London, Routledge.

DfEE/QCA (1999a) 'Secretary of State's Proposals: the review of the national curriculum in England'.

DfEE/QCA (1999b) *The National Curriculum: handbook for secondary teachers in England*, London.

Freire, P. (1985a) 'Reading the World and Reading the Word: an interview with Paulo Freire', *Language Arts* 62: 1.

Freire, P. (1985b) *The Politics of Education: culture, power and liberation*, London, Macmillan.

Gold, K. (1998) *Times Educational Supplement*, 17 July.

Hicks, D. (1999) 'Praxis of the Heart: reflections on education for the new century', paper for the Raja Roy Singh Lecture at the Fifth UNESCO–ASCEID International Conference, Bangkok, 13 December.

Hicks, D. and Holden, C. (1995) *Visions of the Future: why we need to teach for tomorrow*, Stoke on Trent, Trentham.

Inman, S. and Wade, R. (eds) (1997) *Shaping a Better Future: development education within initial teacher training*, Oxford, Oxfam.

Jacobs for the Real World Coalition (1996) *The Politics of the Real World*, London, Earthscan.

Leeds OEC (1996) *Final Frontier*, Leeds: Leeds Development Education Centre.

Lynch, J. (1992) *Education for Citizenship in a Multicultural Society*, London , Cassell.

Morris, M. and Schagen, I. (1995) *Green Attitudes or Learned Responses?*, London, NFER.

Oxfam (1997) *A Curriculum for Global Citizenship*, Oxford, Oxfam.

Oxfam (1998) *Developing Rights: teaching rights and responsibilities for ages 11 to 14*, Oxford, Oxfam.

QCA (1998) Final report of the Advisory Group on Citizenship: education for citizenship and the teaching of democracy in schools', London QCA.

Richmond, J.M. and Morgan, R.F. (1977) *A National Survey of the Environmental Attitudes of Fifth Year Pupils in England*, Columbus, Ohio, The Ohio State Information Centre.

Saunders, L. (1998) 'Who or What Is School Self Evaluation for?', NFER (unpublished paper presented at the European Conference on Educational Research, University of Ljubljana, 1998).

Schaull in Freire, P. (1972) *Pedagogy of the Oppressed*, London, Penguin.

Walkington, H. (1999) 'Global Citizenship Education in the Primary School: an experience from geography', *Development Education Association Journal* 6.1, October.

Williams, P. (1997) Reith Lecture, Radio 4.

Yat-ming, Julian Leung (1991) 'Modernising the Geography Curriculum in Post 1976 China', from Lewin, K.M. and Stuart, J.S. (eds) *Educational Innovation in Developing Countries*, London, Macmillan.

UNDP (1997) *UN Human Development Report*, New York: UN.

Chapter 12

Citizenship in geography classrooms

Questions of pedagogy

Mary Biddulph

Introduction

This chapter considers how the teaching of geography can contribute to citizenship education. The discussion that follows will consider the potential of different models of teaching in geography and their relative contribution to the pedagogical processes associated with learning 'citizenship'. What is suggested here is that there are more, and less, appropriate pedagogies for citizenship education and that elements of these can inform and contribute to geography teaching. However, underpinning this is the assumption that consideration of pedagogic practices must be related to clear and appropriate curriculum goals for both geography and citizenship education, as failure here would result in a curriculum experience for pupils that lacked focus, direction and purpose. This chapter also discusses the characteristics of the 'democratic' classroom environment where teaching geography and citizenship can take place and the potential of geography resources for developing the skills necessary to citizenship learning.

Defining pedagogy

Pedagogy has been variously defined as 'the science of teaching' , 'the art of teaching' and the 'craft of teaching'. However, Watkins and Mortimore (1999: 3) define pedagogy in a more 'inclusive' way as: 'any conscious activity by one person designed to enhance the learning in another'.

Embedded in this definition are a series of assumptions about the nature of pedagogy and the implication that 'conscious activity' requires thought, understanding and an intellectual investment, as well as practical application and action, on the part of the teacher. Working from this definition, it is more possible to appreciate the complex nature of teaching and to consider those factors which impinge upon pedagogy such as teaching style, the location of teaching (the context) and what teachers actually consider 'teaching' to mean. This definition also expands the meaning of pedagogy from what these authors describe (ibid., 2) as the 'limited term of didactics' (i.e. considering solely the role and activities of the teacher), to take account of the relationship between teaching and learning. The logical consequence of such a definition is that geography teachers need first and foremost to engage in discourse about the pedagogical processes associated with good geographical learning, which can at the same time serve to enhance pupils' potential and confidence to become active and empowered global citizens. In other

Table 12.1 Ways of thinking about teaching and learning

Teachers' conception of teaching	Teachers' conception of learning
Imparting information	Getting more knowledge
Transmitting knowledge	Memorising and reproducing
Facilitating understanding	Acquiring and applying procedures
Changing students' conceptions	Making sense of meaning
Supporting student learning	Personal change

words, geography teachers need to consider what they understand *teaching* to mean within the context of *learning* geography, prior to engagement with the challenges and opportunities of the citizenship curriculum.

Table 12.1 suggests some possible conceptions of teaching and learning. The categories are not mutually exclusive and it is recognition of the overlap between 'teaching' and 'learning' which exposes the complexity of the task which teachers face. What we have is a generalised classification of possible teaching approaches from which it is possible to consider different types of learning.

Shulman (1999) has been prominent in describing the 'knowledge base' from which teachers need to draw. Alongside 'content knowledge' (in this case a sound knowledge and understanding of geography and an ability to practise geographical skills proficiently), he has identified:

- general pedagogical knowledge, with special reference to those broad principles and strategies of classroom management and organisation which transcend subject matter, and

- pedagogical content knowledge, that special amalgam of content and pedagogy that is uniquely the province of teachers, their own special form of professional understanding

(Shulman 1999: 64)

It is the 'pedagogical content knowledge' which may provide the challenge with regard to the relationship between teaching geography and teaching citizenship. A key question follows from this realisation: do geography teachers have the necessary pedagogical content knowledge to inform decisions they need to make in relation to teaching citizenship skills and concepts within the context of geography? For simplicity's sake I am assuming that elements of the *content* of geography lessons are appropriate to fulfil such a goal; other chapters in this book take a more critical view of geography and the geography curriculum, and its capacity to serve the needs of citizenship education.

Pedagogy and citizenship

Rowe (1997) identifies three domains within which citizenship learning can take place, the cognitive, the affective and the active/experiential. Within these domains he locates eight different models of learning which have implications for pedagogy. Although elements of these models relate to learning *outside* the school setting, such learning needs to be taken into account when planning teaching *within* school. The models are not mutually exclusive and they can impact upon each other in many different ways. For example, for certain individuals and communities the parental model and the religious model will have particularly strong influence where the adherence of parents to certain religious beliefs influences their interpretation of citizenship. Likewise the constitutional knowledge model could serve to inform the school ethos model or the community action model.

This multiplicity of models, Rowe argues, is a response to the nature of citizenship education within democratic societies where, paradoxically:

> the very existence of value pluralism in society has tended to prevent liberal democracies from developing . . . mature [i.e. pluralist] programmes of civics education because of fear that such arrangements would be used by one group to indoctrinate the young in partisan values.
>
> (ibid., 194)

In other words, poorly developed curricula have resulted from fears of indoctrination, which in turn have led to unplanned, unconscious citizenship learning where young people acquire an understanding of what it means to be a citizen through limited and perhaps uncritical sources. Also, there is too frequently a knowledge deficit and, put this way, there can be little doubt as to the efficacy of introducing a curriculum for citizenship. But what Rowe's analysis provides is a view of the complexities facing teachers implementing such a curriculum, especially through the subject disciplines. It is a helpful articulation of forms of citizenship learning. What would also be helpful is a framework for thinking about teaching, and it is this to which we turn.

How can geography teachers think about pedagogy in geography? What is required is a framework to structure thinking about teaching. Here I use Roberts's (1996) proposal based upon a model from a TVEI evaluation report conducted by the University of Leeds. The model provides a framework for teaching *styles* in geography and it also provides a context within which geography teachers can consider their approach to citizenship education. The three different styles are classified as 'closed', 'framed' and 'negotiated' although in reality these overlap. The contribution of each style to citizenship education is now summarised.

The 'closed' category

In the 'closed' category the teacher adopts a very dominant role. It can argued that if this approach to teaching becomes habitual the pupils are not afforded the opportunities necessary to develop their understanding of citizenship skills and concepts. Teaching is 'content-driven' and the knowledge base narrowly interpreted to mean a form of civics teaching based around national legal and political systems, which Davies (1999) argues can in turn feed individual notions of nationalism, not all of which may be healthy. In some contexts such an approach is justifiable: for example, for pupils who feel socially excluded an increased knowledge and understanding of the legal and political processes which influence British society could provide them with a knowledge base from which to question, challenge and change those processes. However, a knowledge base alone is not enough and it is likely that the majority of pupils will not *feel* empowered or valued as a consequence of such teaching approaches and in turn will not develop essential citizenship skills. Using such a model it is difficult to see the role of geography within citizenship education, and the contribution each can make to the other. Any overlap would be relatively superficial and restricted to:

- locational frameworks;
- atlas skills;
- general knowledge; and
- aspects of 'cultural literacy' (see Dowgill and Lambert 1992).

Other issues such as regional and global inequalities, the interdependence of trade and economic systems and the geography of controversial issues such as health and welfare could be subsumed under regional geography frameworks.

The 'framed' category

Within this category pupils become more involved in their own learning and are given more responsibility to explore issues for themselves. It is in a 'framed' classroom that some, though not all, of the skills and content associated with a broader definition of citizenship can be developed. These practical skills include open-ended discussion, problem solving and enquiry, and require teachers to provide structures within which pupils can explore issues using a range of evidence and consider such evidence critically. The development of a practical skills base is important, as are the acquisition and practice of intellectual skills such as those identified by Leat (1998), for example analysis, synthesis and criticality, among others. These, coupled with appropriate knowledge and understanding, can make a significant contribution to pupils' understanding of citizenship in a geographical context.

The knowledge base is more 'open' and is therefore able to deal directly with contested concepts and controversial issues through pedagogic strategies such as debate, role play, problem solving and decision making. Such strategies are open to the pupils' prior knowledge and understanding – through, for example, devices such as brainstorming, mind movies and so on. The approach can therefore open up the understanding of topical issues such as global inequalities, sustainable development, the place of the individual within local, national and global contexts, consideration of economic processes at a range of scales and an understanding of decision making. At all stages of the learning pupils are expected to develop their enquiry and decision-making skills, such as:

- critical thinking
- the ability to argue effectively
- the ability to challenge injustices and inequalities
- respect for people and things
- co-operation and conflict resolution

(Oxfam 1997: 17)

The 'negotiated' category

The third teaching style is the 'negotiated' category. The emphasis here is on a process of teaching where pupils are given the opportunity to exercise a considerable degree of autonomy over *how* they learn and significantly *what* they learn. A negotiated style of teaching requires great confidence and authority on the part of the teacher and a clear place within a scheme of work that would identify a range of styles, relating different 'approaches' to different educational 'purposes'.

In comparison with the other two categories the negotiated category enables teachers to provide pupils with opportunities to *experience* many of the processes advocated by citizenship education; they become participants in their own learning and as such have to take responsibility for the learning outcomes – whatever they may be. The potential outcome of this kind of pedagogy is that the pupil's voice is heard and *valued*. Pupils are genuine participants in their own learning and thus this category enables learning in geography to mirror learning through citizenship education.

Teaching citizenship – an appropriate classroom environment

Some of the ideas advocated in the previous section are based upon the assumption that the environment for learning is conducive to active and experiential approaches. Despite the centralist tendencies of the 1990s geography teachers still have considerable autonomy over what to teach as well as how they choose to teach it, and certainly the revised 'Curriculum 2000' (DfEE 1997) encourages this, being more explicitly a frame-work for planning rather than purporting to be a 'curriculum' in itself.

What teachers have obvious control over is the 'environment' of their individual classrooms – the atmosphere, the appearance, the sense of belonging, the acceptance of difference, trust, the valuing of the individual. All of these factors and other less tangible aspects of the classroom environment need to be planned and monitored if successful learning is to take place. Indeed, Barnes (1999) maintains that teachers can *learn* 'positive teaching' techniques that can encourage in pupils the dispositions and skills for 'positive learning' that almost certainly are conducive to promoting positive attitudes to considering intricate matters of citizenship. But what of citizenship and *democracy* education? Are there special demands that these make on the classroom environment? Steiner advocates a positive response:

> Democracy is best learned in a democratic setting where participation is encour-aged, where views can be expressed openly and discussed, where there is freedom of expression for pupils and teachers and where there is fairness and justice. An appropriate climate is, therefore, an essential complement to learning.
>
> (Quoted in Fisher 1998: 77)

The democratic classroom is a place where pupils are safe to learn, and it is within this relative safety that they can then explore their own value system and those of others, engage with complex issues and begin to live with uncertainty. It is one in which participants expect to work fairly frequently within an open, negotiated frame.

A teacher who organises a democratic (or negotiated) classroom is still the 'subject expert', for expert knowledge is required to ensure the quality of the subject learning. For example, knowledge guides the formulation of good questions; it helps the teacher see how to make 'the penny drop' with an individual or group. In other words, the teacher's role goes beyond that of 'subject exposition'. The teacher is also a mediator and facilitator; that is, teachers guide and challenge pupils' perceptions and understandings in a continuous cycle of reflection and action. The teacher still needs to provide appropriate interventions and guide actions, but essentially the focus is on pupils learning rather than teachers 'teaching'.

The real and perceived difficulties inherent in operating a negotiated, democratic classroom are potentially off-putting. This is because the fulfilment of a democratic classroom is not only to do with the teacher–pupil relationships, but also to do with overt procedural matters including those operating on a whole school level. How well, for example, do pupils understand procedural roles and decision-making structures within the school? These can be taught via the use of individual and group investigations, both in the field and in the classroom, and through strategies such as role play and simulations. However, if two of the three strands of 'citizenship' learning identified in the final report, namely 'political literacy and moral and social responsibility' (QCA 1998, 8) are to be addressed, then pupils must be required to question, communicate and evaluate difficult and complex issues which involve power relationships and the distribution of responsibilities as well as rights and so on.

Teaching citizenship: handling complexity

It is in 'real-world' circumstances such as those alluded to above that pupils are afforded the opportunity to consider complexity. One special aspect of the geography classroom, with its concern with people–environment relationships (involving social, economic, political, cultural and various physical processes), is that it is the place where pupils are introduced to wider real-world issues – what Barnett (in Lambert 1999) refers to as a 'supercomplex' world. Lambert describes the nature of supercomplexity within the context of secondary geography education. Writing about the ethics of environmental education, he argues that it is *morally careless* for teachers to teach complex geographical issues as if there were 'clear cut' answers (on the one hand) or, on the other, 'no right answers' (which can imply to pupils that 'anything goes' and encourage a 'who cares?' approach to serious matters): 'If students were never to experience uncertainties or handle the ambiguities which are part and parcel of searching for a good personal response to supercomplex environmental issues, then their education would fail to contribute effectively to their moral development' (ibid., 14).

The search for a 'personal response' is fundamental to citizenship education, and helping pupils learn how to cope with and respond to the uncertainties which they will inevitably encounter in their daily lives would seem to be of paramount importance in the teaching process.

However, to re-emphasise a crucial point, not *any* kind of geography classroom can 'teach for uncertainty' effectively or (using Lambert's phrase) in a 'morally careful' way. Lambert himself has identified the importance of the open, negotiated classroom in this respect, by characterising (after Jones 1987) morally careful education as 'education for conversation'. This identifies communication skills as critical in promoting in pupils the capacity to make worthwhile attachments and meaningful distinctions – through 'conversation'. He writes:

> the scholarship of communication . . . consists of intellectual processes harnessed to seek understanding: one improves understanding through communication and one needs to make oneself understood by communication. Good communication facilitates deliberation and reflexive insight, though not necessarily agreement or compromise. Effective communication is the goal of good conversation – with other people, but also with data, information technology and images – and good conversation is a method available to us to expose falseness and inaccuracy.
>
> (Lambert 1997, 3)

If learning through geographical investigation can be equated with educating for conversation, bouncing ideas and information about the exciting but confusing (and sometimes frightening) world out there to and fro between teachers and pupils, then it begins to provide an appropriate pedagogy for promoting the development of active, concerned future citizens.

The analysis, in this and the previous section, of the classroom environment shows that citizenship education can be either limited or enhanced by pedagogic conventions. The decisions teachers make with regard to 'what to teach', 'how to teach it' and 'the environment in which to teach it' will all serve to influence pupils' experiences of learning about citizenship as a concept and of developing the skills and values necessary to be an active and participatory citizen.

Promoting empathy and feeling and the teaching of citizenship through geography

Central to the use of 'conversation' as a means of extending pupils' understanding of citizenship are specific teaching approaches where communication (by teacher and pupils) is essential and where 'participation' is an expectation. Simulations such as games or the use of teaching methods drawn from drama, such as role play, are directly referred to in the final report as being appropriate approaches to developing citizenship education, and both can contribute significantly to the teaching and learning of geography. In its simplest form, a simulation could be defined as an activity (simple or complex in structure) which requires pupils to empathise – 'put themselves in somebody else's shoes' (Walford 1996: 139) – in other words, to draw on their geographical knowledge and understanding and to use their imagination in order to begin to appreciate the lives, dilemmas, decisions and emotions experienced by other people in other places. The term 'simulation' is an umbrella term under which many active approaches to teaching can reside and which can include games, various forms of drama, computer simulations and others. What such teaching approaches have in common is that:

> They can improve pupils' understanding of geographical processes and provide intellectual stimulation through a variety of more demanding skills such as analysing, synthesising and evaluating, which may need to be used in the process of making decisions or solving problems. They also provide further opportunities for

purposeful classroom discussion, negotiation and other collaborative activities that help develop pupils' social, co-operative and communication skills.

(Lambert and Balderstone 2000: 272)

Hence, teaching methodologies such as simulations can succeed in enabling pupils to learn about and appreciate the complex nature of such processes as decision making and can thus serve to enhance their sense of what it means to 'participate'. For example, a simulation activity about world trade (see Box 12.1 for the key ideas) provides pupils with the opportunity to build on prior knowledge and to engage with complex ideas. Pupils play a game using a series of chance cards which refer directly to real events, real places and real consequences, all of which relate to international trade. In playing the game pupils work together, co-operating in small groups, negotiate with each other and have to make decisions; all skills associated with global citizenship. The teachers' role in such an activity is complex. They are required to: have a clear goal which relates to wider curriculum structures; be familiar with the process, organisation and management of the game; know and understand the underlying political, economic and 'geographical' concepts; support and encourage pupils as individuals and in groups; monitor progress of learning and of the game itself; know when to and when not to intervene in pupils' discussions/arguments; and finally, be skilled at managing the debriefing process after the game. Such teaching skills do not lie within the pedagogy of the 'closed' category identified earlier, but within the 'negotiated' or 'open' category.

All of these key ideas relate to aspects of the revised National Curriculum for geography (DfEE/QCA 1999), in particular themes such as 'environmental issues', 'development' and 'resource issues' (ibid., 25).

Within the context of citizenship and geography dramatic approaches such as role play can help to ensure that, what Hornbrook (1989: 79) describes as the 'detached knowledge' of the curriculum, such as 'know about local government, the services it offers and opportunities to contribute at a local level' or 'know about the aims and ideas of political parties and pressure groups' (ibid., 50), can be made to *feel* more real to pupils as they arc afforded opportunities to explore their personal values. Such approaches,

---

Box 12.1   Key ideas associated with a simulation activity about world trade

- The relationship between national governments, trans-national corporations and the global economy
- The highly competitive nature of the global market and the instability of commodity prices
- Dramatic events such as natural disasters and war can disrupt an economy
- Development and short term economic gains
- Inequality in the global economy
- The interdependent nature of the global economy
- The relationship between economic policies and environmental sustainability

Source: Blythe and Richards (1997: 66).

in other words, take us beyond limited and limiting 'civics' lessons. The process of values exploration can provide teachers and pupils with the understanding necessary to question and challenge values – both their own and those of others.

What 'dramatic' approaches to teaching in geography can do is provide teachers with structures for teaching which in turn enable pupils to live through the less tangible aspects of geographical issues and to develop their empathy with others in a unique way. For pupils to want to participate in issues which affect their lives and to feel motivated to act for change, it is necessary to involve their emotions – to ensure that they 'feel' as well as know and understand (see Slater 1994). Slater is not alone in contemplating how 'feelings' are sometimes worryingly absent from geography lessons. Dramatic approaches can help rectify this:

> When in role or watching the drama you may become emotionally involved. In other words, you care about the characters and the situations. Sometimes when people watch a play they laugh, they cry or worry about the characters. This is the aesthetic, the emotional living out of the drama . . . the process involves the emotions.
>
> (McGuire 1998: 5)

McGuire (ibid) identifies a range of teaching methods which can significantly enhance many aspects of geographical and citizenship learning (see Boxes 12.2–4 for some practical examples). These approaches enable students to 'make lateral moves outside their established framework of thought so as to generate fresh insights and perspectives' (Macleod, 1992). The generation of these fresh insights and perspectives then allows pupils to re-examine their own values and beliefs and to relocate their understanding in different contexts.

What is perhaps very important to take account of here is that although such approaches to teaching can seem challenging they provide an enjoyable and motivating way to learn: there is a need to build in appropriate opportunities for pupils to enjoy what they are doing. This is not to trivialise the challenge of teaching aspects of both citizenship and geography, but the sense of personal achievement that can emerge from enjoyable active participation in lessons must be greater than routinely working through a double-page spread of a geography textbook.

Box 12.2 A values continuum

Values and attitudes can be explored in a practical and active way via a values continuum. Students can be asked to position themselves (literally) along a 'strongly agree – strongly disagree' continuum in relation to issues such as 'I agree that individuals have the right to roam wherever they choose in the countryside' or 'I agree that the debt of Third World countries should be cancelled'. As well as considering their own values position, students are then invited by the teacher to justify their position to themselves and others in the group. To do this they have to draw on reasoned and informed argument and have to listen to and appreciate the ideas expressed by others. The role of the teacher is to establish the structure, to ask the open-ended questions and to provide the students with the opportunity to probe each other's thinking.

Box 12.3 The teacher 'in role'

Students are given the opportunity to 'interview' a local 'expert' on issues, for example, relating to a local national park. The teacher supports the student in asking searching and detailed geographical questions of the 'expert', and therefore the teacher – in role – needs a very secure knowledge base from which to draw. The opportunity to ask questions is essential in geography as it is the basis on which geographical enquiry is founded. Such a technique can work at all levels of the curriculum and can also provide a vehicle for participation.

Box 12.4 Freeze frame

Students can participate in a series of 'freeze frame' activities where they are asked to create a 'still image' of different interest groups, for example within a national park. Creative use can be made of whatever props are available as the students set out to identify with different interest groups such as the local water company, walkers, visitors from a local city, cyclists, farmers and a local quarrying company. Via the freeze frame the students, now in role, have their thoughts tracked by the teacher. This is *not* an opportunity for the students to develop an argument in support of their own point of view but rather an exercise in empathy. The students' views can be elicited in the brainstorming process that precedes this exercise. But it is an opportunity for the students to express what might be going on in the mind of an individual caught up in the scenario which they have created. As a means of developing empathy this process can be powerful learning for the students as they have to articulate inner thoughts and feelings.

FOR FURTHER THINKING

It is difficult to establish and maintain links with other curriculum areas, but such links can be fruitful in recharging enthusiasm for different approaches to teaching. Drama departments and modern foreign languages (MFL) departments have distinct approaches that can support learning in geography and contribute to citizenship education. Research undertaken at the School of Education, University of Nottingham (Coyle 1996), demonstrates that teaching geography through the medium of a modern foreign language enhances pupils' MFL development without having a detrimental effect on learning in geography. The combination of the two can serve to tie together the relevance of both subjects within the context of a real 'place'.

Resources for teaching geography and citizenship

It has always been essential for geography teachers to view the potential of teaching resources critically to ensure:

- the relevance of resources to teaching and learning objectives;
- the appropriateness of resources in relation to geographical content to be taught and learnt;
- the appropriateness of resources to the teaching context, such as the age and ability of individuals and groups;
- the accuracy of certain kinds of resources such as maps, data tables and statistical information.

Bias and any inaccuracies (be they visual, numerical or textual) are considered via appropriate learning objectives.

There is a wealth of geography education literature in journals such as *Teaching Geography* to support teachers' understanding of the advantages and pitfalls associated with the use of certain resources, as well as the existence of a range of frameworks to support:

- Teachers' evaluation of resources such as textbooks (Butt and Lambert 1997; Rawling and Westaway 1998; Winter 1997);
- The critical analysis of television programmes (Durbin 1995);
- Consideration of the internet (Donert 1997; Durbin 1995).

The final report of the Advisory Group (QCA 1998) advocates the use of a wide range of resources with which to teach citizenship, including the use of politically biased material from, for example, political parties. Also, organisations such as Oxfam, World Wildlife Fund (WWF) and development education centres all develop and publish teaching and learning material which can be used across both geography and citizenship. However, Winter (1997: 181) argues, in relation to certain resources, namely textbooks, that: 'geography teachers need to both review text books critically in order to reject those which show evidence of ethnocentric bias and to select and develop materials which address such issues'.

While she states that it is impossible for any resource to be 'value free', as there are both implicit and explicit values underpinning the writing and selection of particular resources, it is perhaps unhelpful to urge 'rejection' of those that show 'evidence of bias'. After all, even the interpretation teachers put on the resources will be influenced by the personal as well as professional values of individual teachers. She goes on to argue that it is the responsibility of the teacher to use resources and teaching approaches through which geographical knowledge can be restructured, and issues such as bias, cultural values and misleading stereotypes can be interrogated and challenged.

The work of the GeoVisions Group on the interpretation of 'text' and 'alternative readings' of different texts in geography (Bermingham *et al.* 1999) presents a challenging set of alternative ways of using text and images to support the development of pupils' criticality. They suggest that texts (including visual 'texts' such as photographs) can be used by pupils not to present information, but to generate questions. These questions, the group suggests, could include:

- Where are we?
- Why are these places like this?
- Why these views?
- What feelings does the photographer create in the observer?
- What messages are given?
- Do the photographs tell the whole story about the place?

(ibid., 160)

Molyneaux and Tolley (1987) proposed that questions should be asked about visual images and that pupils need to consider how they 'read' and question images to identify the nature of bias within them. As a process, such detailed analysis could be time consuming, but enabling pupils to read and reread pictures and to develop their ability to question what they see is an essential aspect of geography, since the representation of people, places, events and issues is so often visual. Also:

> if geography teachers wish to contribute more substantially to the general education of their pupils they should seek to promote in them the capacity to read visual materials critically in contexts other than the geography classroom . . . if this is to be achieved, children will need to become accustomed to using a range of visual materials in their geography lessons and learn how to go about the task of analysing them critically from a non-specialist as well as a geographical point of view.
>
> (Molyneaux and Tolley 1987: 52)

What Molyneaux and Tolley, and now the GeoVisions Group, are saying is that pupils need to be taught the skills necessary to 'handle' the range of information they are confronted by, not just in school but in other areas of their lives. Such 'handling' does not involve the uncritical acceptance of the ideas and images of others, but rather the critical appraisal of representation from any source – textbooks, television, newspapers/ magazines, CD-Roms and the internet. The implications for geography teachers is that they need to develop lesson structures built around the 'negotiated' and 'open' models for teaching *and* models for learning that will enable pupils to question the source, nature, purpose and intentions of different types of geographical information.

Conclusions

The new proposals for the curriculum 2000 are explicit about the place of citizenship in the geography curriculum, and the draft teaching schemes developed by QCA (1999b) identify where and how citizenship can be taught in six of the twenty-four units. The Geographical Association (GA), in its position statement for geography (1999), also supports the contribution of geography:

> geography makes both a distinctive and wider contribution to the curriculum, and . . . geography is an essential component in preparing young people for life in the

twenty-first century. Indeed, as the pace of change quickens, communication gets faster, and challenges to the environment multiply, a knowledge and understanding of geography is more vital than ever.

The GA is anxious to support teachers of geography in taking up citizenship and other aspects of what it has called the 'new agenda' (Grimwade 2000), principally personal, social and health education plus education for sustainability. Though this clearly results partly from its desire to serve its members' interests, the GA also has a long-standing instinct for survival. It is not too fanciful to suggest that the new agenda could seriously marginalise geography subject specialists in school – unless, that is, geography teachers can demonstrate through their successful classroom actions that the discipline and its associated pedagogies can serve wider educational goals. What this chapter has argued is that geographers merely laying claim to certain content areas ('we've always done that in geography') will not determine success. The pedagogy of geography is as important an issue as content and requires equivalent hard-headed and critical reflection.

Such statements may give an impetus to geography teachers to take up the challenge of teaching aspects of citizenship, and the very existence of the proposals from the advisory group and the way they are framed could be used as an opportunity to reinvigorate geography teaching at all levels. However, such a renaissance will not take place unless geography teachers show that they *believe* that the subject has a viable and unique contribution to make to pupils' learning. They need to be able to say what this is. Using geography effectively as a medium of citizenship education requires more than good intentions. It requires a critical understanding of the relationship between the content and pedagogies of both geography and citizenship education so that informed decisions about 'what to teach?' and 'how to teach?' can be made.

FOR FURTHER THINKING

1   Discuss the idea of 'education for citizenship'. In terms of geography lessons contributing to citizenship education, to what extent is it a useful metaphor for an appropriate pedagogy?
2   Examine your schemes of work. To what extent are they explicit about pedagogy in relation to specific learning outcomes?
3   In what way do you (or not!) run a democratic classroom?

References

Barnes, R. (1999) *Positive Teaching, Positive Learning*, London: Routledge.
Bermingham, S., Slater, F. and Yangopoulos, S. (1999) Multiple texts, alternative texts, multiple readings, alternative readings, in *Teaching Geography*, 24, 4, pp. 160–4.
Blythe, C. and Richards, D. (1997) Uneven playing fields – a simulation activity, in *Xchanging the World*, Reading: Reading International Solidarity Centre.
Butt, G. and Lambert, D. (1997) Geography assessment and key stage 3 assessment, in *Teaching Geography* 22, 3, pp. 146–7.

Coyle, D. (1996) Language medium teaching in Britain, in Fruhauf, G., Coyle, D. and Christ, I. (eds) *Teaching Content in a Foreign Language – Practice and Perspectives in European Bilingual Education*, Onderwijs: Stichting Europees Platform voor het Nederlandse.

Davies, L. (1999) Citizenship education in a global context, in *The Development Education Journal*, 6, 1, pp. 1–3.

DfEE (1997) *Excellence in Schools*, London: DfEE.

DfEE/QCA (1999) *The National Curriculum: Handbook for Secondary Teachers in England*, London.

Donert, K. (1997) *A Geographer's Guide to the Internet*, Sheffield: The Geographical Association.

Dowgill, P. and Lambert, D. (1992) Cultural literacy and school geography, in *Geography*, 77, 2), pp. 143–52.

Durbin, C. (1995) Using televisual resources in geography, in *Teaching Geography*, 20, 3, pp. 118–21.

Durbin, C. and Saunders, R. (1996) Geographers on the Internet, in *Teaching Geography*, 21, 6, pp. 15–19.

Fisher, T. (1998) *Becoming a Teacher of Geography*, Cambridge: Chris Kington Publishing.

Fry, P. (1987) Dealing with political bias through geography education. Unpublished MA dissertation, University of London, Institute of Education.

Geographical Association (1999) Geography in the curriculum: a position statement from the GA, in *Teaching Geography*, 24, 2, pp. 57–9.

Grimwade, K. (ed.) (2000) *Geography and the New Agenda*, Sheffield: GA.

Hornbrook, D. (1989) *Education and Dramatic Art*, Oxford: Basil Blackwell.

Jones, M. (1987) Prejudice, in Haydon, G. (ed.) *Education for a Pluralist Society*. Bedford Way paper No. 30, London: University of London, Institute of Education, pp. 39–57.

Lambert, D. (1997) Geography education and citizenship: identity and intercultural communication, in Slater, F. and Bale, J. (eds) *Reporting Research in Education – Monograph No. 5*, London: Institute of Education.

Lambert, D. (1999) Geography and moral education in a supercomplex world: the significance of values education and some remaining dilemmas, in *Ethics, Place and Environment*, 2, 1, pp. 5–18.

Lambert, D. and Balderstone, D. (2000) *Learning to Teach Geography in the Secondary School: a Companion to School Experience*, London/New York: Routledge/Falmer.

Leat, D. (1998) *Thinking through Geography*, Cambridge: Chris Kington Publishing.

Mccleod, H. (1992) *Teaching for Ecologically Sustainable Development*, Queensland: Department of Education.

McGuire, B. (1998) *Students Handbook for Drama*, Cambridge: Pearson Publishing.

Molyneaux, F. and Tolley, H. (1987) *Teaching Geography: a Teaching Skills Workbook*, London: Macmillan Education.

Oxfam (1997) *A Curriculum for Global Citizenship*, Oxford: Oxfam.

QCA (1998) *Education for Citizenship and the Teaching of Democracy in Schools: Final Report of the Advisory Group on Citizenship*, London: QCA.

QCA (1999a) *Geography. The National Curriculum for England: Key Stages 1–3*, London: HMSO.

QCA (1999b) *Key Stage 3 Scheme of Work: Geography. Teachers' Guide. Consultation Draft*. September 1999, London.

Rawling, E. and Westaway, J. (1998) Analysis of key stage 3 geography text books, in *Teaching Geography*, 22, 3, pp. 36–8.

Roberts, M.(1996) Teaching styles and strategies, in Kent, A., Lambert, D., Naish, M. and Slater, F. *Geography in Education: Viewpoints on Teaching and Learning*, Cambridge: Cambridge University Press.

Rowe, D. (1997) Value pluralism, democracy and education for citizenship, in Leicester, M., Mogdil, C. and Mogdil, S. (eds) *Education, Culture and Values. Volume VI: Politics, Education and Citizenship*, London: Falmer.

Shulman, L. (1999) Knowledge and teaching: foundations of the new reform, in Leach, J. and Moon, B. (eds) *Learners and Pedagogy*, London: Open University.

Slater, F. (1994) Education through geography: knowledge, values, understanding and culture, in *Geography*, 79, 2, pp. 147–63.

Walford, R. (1996) The simplicity of simulation, in Bailey, P. and Fox, P. (eds) *Geography Teachers' Handbook*, Sheffield: Geographical Association, pp. 139–49.

Watkins, C. and Mortimore, P. (1999) in Mortimore, P. (ed.) *Understanding Pedagogy and its Impact on Learning*, London: Paul Chapman Publishing Ltd.

Winter, C. (1997) Ethnocentric bias in geography text books, in Tilbury, D. and Williams, M. (eds) *Teaching and Learning Geography*, London: Routledge.

Part III

Conclusion

Chapter 13

Conclusion

Citizens in a risky world

David Lambert and Paul Machon

Introduction

This book has been a challenging one to put together. Many of the contributors have told us how difficult they found their chapter to write. This concluding chapter seeks to explore why this might be so and to pin down why the discussion of citizenship through geography education has proved to be so difficult to capture in print.

The difficulty is, we believe, highly significant but not entirely unexpected. It has, perhaps, two main roots. The first concerns the potential and limits of geography as a subject component of the curriculum which, we must remember, not all and a declining number of older pupils study. The emphasis here is on the subject's place in the curriculum and not on any intrinsic weakness of the discipline at large, as the many contributions here so richly illustrate. Secondly, there are the terms in which citizenship is being defined or configured in the curriculum – and that is as a subject defined by its outcomes. Taking this approach, we argue, downvalues citizenship's more significant importance as a personal, reflective and liberating process.

There is a third consideration to add to these analyses, occasionally hinted at in a number of chapters in this book. This is the wider educational context in which geography teachers undertake their job. If schools are to teach, according to law, a 'balanced and broadly based curriculum which a) promotes the spiritual, moral, cultural, mental and physical development of pupils at the school and of society; and b) prepares such pupils for the opportunities, responsibilities and experiences of adult life' (HMSO 1988), then geography teachers clearly need to be aware of the 'wider educational context' and their capacity to contribute to such a mission. But what do these fine words mean in practice, particularly to the geography specialist classroom teacher? Just taking the latter part of this quotation from the 1988 Education Act, which in itself provides a succinct statement on the purpose of citizenship education, in what ways can geography lessons contribute to a pupil's preparation for adult life? This final chapter addresses this fundamental question with a discussion that links geography, citizenship and moral education contextualised in a changing world, one that exhibits environmental, economic, political, social and cultural instabilities.

Facing facts: the residuals of a geography education

Answers to questions concerning how well geography 'prepares pupils . . . for adult life' are both easy *and* hard to provide, depending on one's starting point. From the *subject* perspective, the Geographical Association (GA) has produced a useful and highly successful publication (Grimwade 2000), available to teachers well in advance of the start of the new national curriculum arrangements in September 2000. This outlines geography's position in relation to the whole of the so-called 'new agenda' (of which citizenship is a part). But apart from pointing out some of the 'evidence of declining political engagement, particularly amongst the young' (ibid., p. 12) which is deployed to justify the introduction of citizenship as a statutory component of the secondary curriculum from 2002, it provides little discussion of the means, or of *pedagogy* or of the concept's contested nature. What we emphasise here is the need for a serious analysis of pupil needs both at the level of their lived experience and, at a greater scale, in terms of their understanding and engagement with a 'supercomplex' world (see Lambert 1999) and rapid social change. The geographer John Adams provides one illustration of what we mean here in his book *Risk*:

> Everyday around the world, billions of . . . decisions get made. The consequences in most cases appear to be highly localised, but perhaps they are not. Chaos theorists have introduced us to a new form of insect life called the Beijing butterfly – which flaps its wings in Beijing and sets in motion a train of events that culminates two weeks later in a hurricane in New York. Extreme sensitivity to subtle differences in initial conditions, the chaos theorists tell us, makes the behaviour of complex natural systems inherently unpredictable. Prediction becomes even more difficult when people are introduced to such systems – because people respond to predictions, thereby altering the predicted outcome. Rarely are risk decisions made with information that can be reduced to quantifiable probabilities; yet decisions, somehow, get made.
>
> (Adams 1995, pp. 3–4)

In what ways does what goes on in geography classrooms prepare young people to operate in conditions of such complexity – that is, to make risk decisions (also see Beck 1992) for themselves and take into consideration the impact of these decisions on others? Making claims for geography's utility as a subject remains simple – we can teach form (e.g. the location and structure of Beijing and New York), and even processes, (the way hurricanes work and the impact they can have) – but this utility is partial and so too are any claims that the discipline enfranchises in the longer term. It is far more difficult to help young people to make connections between such understandings and their own political and economic contexts, so that they can become reflecting and autonomous decision makers.

Justifying geography's role and purpose must therefore not just be confined to its content. Such an approach runs the danger that geography's educational capacity is reduced to that of a provider of general knowledge. The *residuals* of a geography education, by which we mean what resides in the person long after he or she has finished being a school student, are thin indeed if we only measure them in terms of acquired information (some of which in any case has a very short shelf-life). We can claim that geography can do this or that, but the acid test of the subject's impact is to ask the consumers (see Dowgill 1998). Doing this provides some evidence that students do not perceive the purpose of geography in quite the way that their teachers or the syllabus designers intended. If we take the post-1988 14–16 curriculum as a whole, where geography still plays a prominent part, there is broad acknowledgement that it has failed to engage a significant proportion of young people. This is partly because they failed to connect with the specified content, but partly because the pedagogy of delivery was inappropriate to their needs (see Elliott 2000). But never mind the disaffected minority! Do pupils at large see the relevance of geography lessons to their lives, both now and in the future? Can they spot how the discipline helps them understand how the big, booming world works? Does the subject help them feel confident handling the struggles and dilemmas they will encounter when they finish school? And, in relation to Adams's injunction about decision making, do pupils learn about the complexity and uncertainty that takes place beyond the oversimplified, stylised and even stereotypical situations or locales that are the feature of some popular secondary textbooks and mechanistic modelling.

The big messages emanating from this book (and the preceding paragraph) could be construed as casting doubts on geography's state of preparedness to make a convincing contribution to citizenship education. As we noted in our Introduction, some chapters are hesitant in tone, while others are more openly critical of the subject, at least as it is most often configured in schools. Others are indirectly critical of teachers who appear to have little time or incentive to grapple seriously with the issue that the Teacher Training Agency (TTA) refers to as subject knowledge. School geography that is locked into circa 1950s 'capes and bays' (uncommon), or *circa* 1970s 'location and links' narratives (more common), may well have difficulty engaging pupils when it comes to thinking about the spatiality of global economic or environmental issues. Geography classes may seem to pupils to be divorced, or at least semi-detached, from their own personal interaction with the digital, fast-moving and changing world with its surfeit of signs and signals. Geography teachers who do not read in, and beyond, the popular school subject realm of their discipline may be in a weakening position when it comes to developing schemes of work that capture a changing world and their changing understanding of it – even though their knowledge of existing syllabuses may be confident and secure.

However, all this is to miss a still deeper message. As John Morgan recently pointed out, following Goodson's (1992) work on the school curriculum, subjects are not timeless 'givens' but are socially constructed. From this assertion he identifies important implications for the debate about the role of geography in educating for citizenship:

It suggests that rather than look to a body of disciplinary knowledge and then seek to draw out relevant themes and perspectives that can contribute to a blueprint for citizenship, we should seek to understand how existing forms of school geography already reflect the identities, values and interests of the groups that have constructed the subject in particular ways. Understanding how school geography has been socially constructed may allow us to evaluate and reconstruct the subject to include other 'geographical imaginations' that have so far been excluded.

(Morgan 2000, pp. 66–7)

To this we add the urgent need for teachers actively to engage with the discourse that makes and remakes what we do. Teachers are often seen as purveyors of knowledge. Critically, we also see them as makers of meaning.

Both sentiments remind us of the significance of identifying *purpose* in teaching. We think it is important for geography teachers to realise their own goals and motives that arise from their own geographical imaginations. The broad message that we would prefer readers to take from this book is, therefore, *not* a negative one although there are some concerns that result from a critique of maintaining the *status quo* for its own sake, as well as calls for geography in schools to embrace change and to adopt critical positions. Critique as a process should, however, not be confused with negativity. After all, *deconstruction* (arising from critique) always presages positive activity because it invites a period of *reconstruction* based upon fresh thought, analysis and design. The recent call for citizenship education in England and Wales provides the forum and the stimulus to interrogate the geography curriculum in a way that was lacking during the last decade or so of the last century (see Morgan 2000; also Daugherty and Jones 1999). But the twinned intellectual activities of critique and design in relation to the geography curriculum *are* difficult, and we think this book is a testament to that. What has made them more difficult is the need to undertake such thinking in relation to citizenship specified as a *subject* that, as we have suggested, is a confusing configuration. And finally, to state it again, the difficulties are compounded by the inescapable need to address 'the inner being of pupils and their personal and social development in a rapidly changing and increasingly complex world' (Elliott 2000, p. 248). That is, there is a need to connect with pupils through exciting and inviting pedagogies. This book has endeavoured to incorporate discussion within these themes.

We believe there is a wonderful opportunity for geography teachers, at least at KS3 (11–14 years), to rise to the challenges identified throughout the book. These challenges follow the substantial change of heart represented by the current national curriculum reforms that, if teachers (and textbook writers) are ready to grasp it, removes much of the pressure to deliver a specified content syllabus. There are similar opportunities in the post-14 and post-16 settings. But geography is an optional course of study at these levels. This means that the threats to geography's existence are much greater in the post-14 curricula. Geography at the time of writing is still popular at GCSE, and post-16, but unless it can reach out and convincingly embrace aspects of the content and pedagogy of citizenship education, then it may not always remain so. Is it feasible that a subject called citizenship could work against GCSE geography?

What this book has discussed are some key issues that we believe geographers should seek to embrace. But the book has shown that significant change and development are needed for this to occur. This development particularly extends to those tired and cynical protestations heard from some quarters that, as far as citizenship is concerned, geographers have 'always done it', for we would argue if they have then it was only partial or, worse, subconscious and acquiescent. The following section briefly looks at the implications of this change.

Geography and educated citizens

If this book has been challenging to put together, then it is worth recording that the brief we set ourselves and the authors was a demanding one, covering a wide field. We have assembled chapters that *contextualise* citizenship in geography education historically, internationally and through processes of values education that have long been advocated for use in geography classrooms (Chapters 2–5). A sequence of five chapters (Chapters 6–10) *explored* the capacity of geography as a school subject to help pupils' encounters with environmental debates, with questions of identity and community, with 'otherness' and exclusion. These chapters have together produced an extensive list of concepts that geography can introduce and clarify for young people, including political structures, democracy, culture, racism and the contingent nature of nations, their boundaries and much more. In short, these chapters have discussed place and space in pursuit of understanding society and environment. We believe discussions of this nature are not only desirable but essential for teachers to have, given that they are producing educated citizens. The authors of a further two chapters (Chapters 11–12) take the discussion *right back into school*, reviewing appropriate classroom pedagogies for citizenship education and discussing issues arising from the tensions that inevitably arise when change is advocated or imposed.

Although written in the wake of the revised curriculum framework for geography and the 2002 proposals for citizenship education, these contributions have not been bounded by them, and the authors have been encouraged to provide fresh and vigorous disciplinary perspectives. We believe, taken together, the chapters show a healthy ambition for what geography may achieve – but not a single vision of the form and contents that geography should take. It would be astonishing if they did, and a serious weakness in our view, for we do not see the discipline in the closely bounded way that would be required for one view to prevail. We emphasise again that geography needs to 'take on' citizenship but that this should not be seen as a threat forcing practitioners behind the defensive walls of perceived disciplinary boundaries. On the contrary, to retreat into some universe of disciplinary purity would spell disaster for the discipline, particularly at secondary-school level.

Citizenship should be grasped as an opportunity – but this can only be achieved convincingly if geography teachers are prepared to move beyond the present boundaries of their disciplinary citadel into other disciplines like history, politics, economics and sociology, as well as those disciplines dealing with the physical world. Disciplinary boundaries are only a taxonomic convenience, socially and culturally defined and not fundamental categories in the real world. Geography has always been good in creative dialogue with other disciplines in pursuit of those insights that help account for aspects of place, space and nature that will inform the development of informed and skilled citizens. It is interesting, but perhaps not surprising in this context, that the Geographical Association's (GA's) most recent citizenship guidance states that in taking up the new agenda '[t]here is also a danger that geography's subject integrity will be compromised by contributing to too many other subjects and/or aspects. This is not a new problem . . . but one to be guarded against' (Grimwade 2000, p. 8). We disagree and suggest that the problem here results from thinking about subjects in a way that emphasises their differences, while underplaying their similarities of purpose. Policing a discipline's boundaries results in static and impermeable boundaries between disciplines, and geography, of all subjects, is ill-advised to do this. Let us explain ourselves more fully.

Geography's scope is so vast that geographers have often experienced a certain discomfort defining their subject terrain, often resorting to unhelpful portmanteau statements of geography's ontological project such as 'making sense of the world' or (more desperately) 'geography is what geographers do'. Geographers are often nervous about being accused of being generalists, or merely descriptive, 'Jacks (and Jills) of all trades'. And yet advocacy of a single coherent vision of geography, and its place in the whole curriculum, is precisely what lay behind the national curriculum specification. The outcome of this was that a particular and rather abstract sub-discipline called 'school geography' was created, dedicated to teaching about the world – or rather, selected aspects of a world categorised and divided into distorted groups of nations, all of which have somehow become set in stone. It is striking just how quickly this school geography has lost touch, both with the discipline at large and again with the lived experience of its students. Nevertheless, school geography did acquire the mantle of the official 'given'. As this status solidified teachers forwent much of their role in choosing what (and how) to teach according to their local circumstances and needs. Consequently there was very little incentive to engage with the wider discipline or with local issues in the low-risk/high-accountability climate of the 1990s.

As we have noted this may change, for example with the introduction of the revised Curriculum 2000 for post-16 students. There is every possibility that geography teachers can reinvent themselves as curriculum developers, looking within and beyond the subject for inspiration and material. The interesting question that follows, however, is: what should guide this process? Arguably, the original national curriculum for younger students in geography became so prescriptive because the politicians controlling the process had lost confidence (for whatever reason) in teachers making curriculum choices (see, for example, Lambert 1994; Rawling 1993, 1996). But the state has now stepped back, returning to teachers some opportunity for school-based curriculum development. This reminds us that curriculum development is a process shot through with ethical questions: essentially, on what grounds can it be said that teaching this, or in that way, is 'right'? The new national framework for geography returns this question to teachers, and the only way to handle it ethically is on the basis of reflective thought about the goals of geography education. In short, what is our purpose? If curriculum goals can convincingly encompass aspects of citizenship education, and we believe they can, then we have a sound basis for developing the curriculum.

Finally, we acknowledge the ambiguous and conflicting messages that emanate from the centre on curriculum matters. For example, the Standards Minister Estelle Morris is reported to be 'no longer interested in philosophical debates about the purpose of education' (Wallace 2000, p. 15). This lack of interest is presumably built on the assertion that education's aims and objectives have now been agreed and the educational compass set: the only challenge left is for teachers to work out how to deliver that consensus efficiently – a dangerous and short-term stance to take.

Citizenship and moral education

The closure of vexed and awkward debates of a reflective sort by government may offer some account of why the Advisory Group finally offered citizenship as a subject with specific outcomes; better that than a wholesale rejection of the project. After all, what better way to promote citizenship education than to package and label it – even examine it – ready for delivery? However, although there are clear benefits to be derived from making citizenship more legible, there are serious drawbacks too, for we believe that there are fundamental flaws in closing down the philosophical debate.

On the benefits side of the balance sheet it is possible to list the core knowledge and understandings that are central to learning citizenship, elements that we would argue are often badly or incompletely taught in schools in England and Wales. These elements include key concepts such as democracy, the state, inclusive and exclusive citizenship and identity. The list also includes institutional knowledge, as well as complex political and legal processes and structures, and this book has demonstrated how geography lessons can reveal and employ such material. But we would be the first to acknowledge that merely showing that geography *can be* a vehicle for developing knowledge and understanding of this kind certainly does not guarantee that it *will be* such a vehicle, and although many elements identified here are capable of being included in English and history as well as geography lessons, others may still have to be covered as a separate subject.

A problem with such a picture, however, is that it contains what Elliott (2000) calls a 'design fault'. This is because knowledge and understanding of the kind mentioned above only consitute a starting point for any serious attempt at citizenship education. Identifying such learning outcomes may be relatively straightforward, but is a far cry from achieving the real goal, that of developing young people's capacities to become active, responsible, informed and critical citizens. It is this realisation that allows several writers in this book to appear to be comfortable, as we are, with linking citizenship education with moral education (see also Lambert and Balderstone 2000, Chapter 7). Active and responsible citizenship can be encouraged by developing students' moral *agency* within existing socio-political structures; that is, developing their capacity for moral reasoning, making distinctions of merit and forming healthy allegiances and attachments (after Wilson 1992). Note that this does not mean teaching morality in a prescriptive way. Instead, it means providing opportunities for students to discuss conflicts, issues and dilemmas which arise across the full range of temporal and spatial scales: in their day-to-day lives, in their locality, in the national and international news and in major events. Just as the formal teaching of moral education does not take place in a vacuum, but in various social, political, economic and environmental contexts, the same is true for citizenship education. In Elliott's own words, the flaw in the citizenship-as-subject formulation is as follows:

> The frameworks proposed for both PSHE and Citizenship Education are somewhat lacking in clarity. This is because they use outcomes-based frameworks to articulate aims, which cannot be articulated independently of the learning processes involved in realizing them. Specific knowledge objectives tend to get mixed up with aims that imply certain teaching and learning processes. Elements in these frameworks appear

to be inconsistent with the claim that teachers are entirely free to decide on their own approaches. For example, the aim of *learning to discuss and debate topical issues and events* says a great deal about the learning processes involved. The pursuit of this aim would involve a significant pedagogical shift for many teachers from an instructionally based classroom to a discussion based one. As an aim it is very different in kind [from] a specification of content objectives.

(Elliott 2000, pp. 252–3)

The pedagogical shift referred to above is discussed more fully by Mary Biddulph in Chapter 12. The point we wish to emphasise here is that making the shift is more likely to be achieved successfully by geography teachers in geography classrooms than by geography teachers (or any other specialists) in citizenship lessons dealing with partially digested or inappropriately 'framed' material in the form of a pack or textbook. Looking at the question this way, we argue that much of the process side of citizenship and moral education should happen in specialist geography (and other subject discipline) classrooms, at the same time as conceding that there are likely to be informational aspects of civics education that may need to be covered in their own distinctive lessons.

Geography, citizenship and a risky world

Citizenship and moral education are linked. Both are synonymous with geography education although we are cautious in this claim, because the links between these educations are not all that easy to make in practice. However, as we and several other authors in this volume have implied, attempting to do so at least provides an opportunity to reflect creatively on the spirit and purpose of geography in the school curriculum, an opportunity for curriculum renewal (e.g. Fien 1999).

In his observations on the National Curriculum 2000 revisions, Elliott (2000) describes the profound social, economic and cultural challenges facing education. Among these are the growing complexity of people's lives and relationships, and their need to cope with enormously difficult and unscripted day-to-day decision making. The context of this, as we noted earlier, is an increasing awareness on the part of citizens that they live in a 'risk society' where the consequences of technological change have ambiguous and uncertain outcomes for human well-being. The significance of this issue is well illustrated by research conducted since 1990 under the Economic and Social Research Council (ESRC) Global Environmental Change Programme (2000), which has contributed to a greater public understanding of environmental processes. However, they also point out that:

> The public has a wide range of views and understandings about the environment. People's knowledge is experience-led and is embedded in their social and political relationships. Relying solely on formal scientific knowledge to make decisions is short sighted. . . . The general public everywhere is divorced from decision-making processes [and] trust is fragile.
>
> (ESRC Global Environmental Change Programme 2000, p. 5)

This statement provides a glimpse of the difficult nature of environmental knowledge making in the contemporary world – and of course that includes knowledge making by teachers working with school students. What are geography teachers to make of this, charged as they often are with contributing to a citizenship that also incorporates sustainability education? It seems that even if answers and solutions to difficult environmental questions were available to teachers to impart to students, they wouldn't be believed anyway.

David Harvey, in his book *Spaces of Hope* (2000), discusses the profound difficulties with much of the current environmental discourse. He usefully reminds us that '[c]oncern for our environment is concern for ourselves' (ibid, p. 224), and argues for 'respectful negotiation' with all who possess knowledge on the web of life – including those who use (in his view) a dangerous and 'alarmist rhetoric of crisis and imminent catastrophe' (ibid., pp. 223, 216). He suggests that:

> 'where and who we learn it from and how we learn it' overrides the contemporary postmodern fascination with 'where we see it from' as the basis for intellectual engagements. Knowledges are and can be constituted in a variety of ways and how they are constructed plays a crucial role in our ability to interpret and understand our way of being in the world.
>
> (ibid.: p. 225)

This, to us, is a useful distinction to make. For one thing, it neatly reminds us of the reason to take care about the origin of knowledge otherwise taken for granted in geography classrooms – which is the main reason why we have often used the device of 'boxes' in this book to highlight or to pin down important ideas or theories, e.g. of Social Darwinism (p. 127) or the Chicago School (p. 101). It also returns us to confront, once again, the positioning of geography, or any other discipline that may be deemed worthwhile and relevant enough for young people to have to study for a number of years.

Perhaps a primary purpose of school geography is to stimulate and inspire some kind of participation and engagement with knowledge about societies and environments, as if they really mattered. This would require students to converse, or 'respectfully negotiate', with geography. Good geography textbooks and good teachers therefore have a role almost akin to seduction, pulling students into appropriate mental efforts, which from time to time will be tough. Geography's success will depend on how successfully it speaks to young people and can entice them into a struggle with ideas, with argument, with uncertainty.

A key aspect of what geography offers that is of special importance to such 'conversations' is its concern with human–environmental interrelationships (in which cultural, economic, social and political processes intermesh with physical environmental processes), and the commitment to pursue such concerns in 'real spaces'. Interest in the human occupation of place and space has led Harvey and others (see for example Marston 2000) to an understanding of the significance of scale understood as a social construction. Though we cannot open up this matter fully as we conclude this book, it is clear that 'scale matters': not least, we would urge that the current fixation on so-called 'globalisation' and the related dazzle of global effects needs careful reconsideration. While there are clearly physical and economic processes that do operate globally, there are also social processes that operate to establish local truths within the wider risk society. These also need to be understood, and so we return again to Elliott:

The challenge the 'risk society' presents for teachers is to 'develop both an appreciative and critical stance towards scientific knowledge' through inducting pupils into social processes within their own localities and communities aimed at establishing 'local knowledge' about the impact of technology on their own and others' well being.

(Elliott 2000, p. 254)

Readers who have already delved into the contents of this book will recognise that this kind of discussion takes us back to Bill Marsden's review of the purposes of geography education in relation to citizenship. Education for good causes, he shows (Marsden 1989), has its limits. It is perhaps this realisation more than any other that has led us to make the explicit links described earlier (p. 205) between geography education, citizenship and moral education, and the links between citizenship education and ethics. It is noteworthy that there is also a surge of renewed interest in 'moral terrains' in academic geography (Smith 2000; Proctor and Smith 1999). We expect and would encourage geography teachers to draw from this, and not just rely on 'delivering' that sub-set of the discipline that we have referred to as 'school geography'. Such geography we have characterised as static, backward-looking, with only tenuous links with the contemporary discipline and possessing only limited powers of explanation (and seduction) to engage future citizens with the 'big questions'. It is big questions that can drive important conversations in geography and it is participating in these that contributes to young people growing as citizens.

Conclusion

Emphatically, geography does have the capacity to ask the big questions because of its concern to avoid closing explanation down, and by its ability to stretch across the boundaries of contained knowledge. It is interested in the physical *and* the human world, it is both an art, a humanity *and* a science, and it studies people as individuals, in societies *and* globally. Here is a subject that potentially has the means to help pupils understand their world holistically (or ecologically). There are, of course, blindspots and weaknesses, dangers and pitfalls, all of which reduce this capacity, as contributors to this book have not hesitated to point out. But the book as a whole demonstrates the potential of geography education and provides enormous stimulus for teachers, as the makers of meaning – and the curriculum vehicles for the exploration of meaning with students – to clarify or reposition what they do. The environmental educator, David Orr, has reminded us that the designers of Auschwitz were widely considered to be the best-educated people on Earth, but 'their education did not serve as an adequate barrier to barbarity' (Orr 1999, p. 166). He therefore concludes that 'it is not education, but education of a certain kind, that will save us' (ibid). This is a bold, even a melodramatic, statement. But we hope that this book, suitably quarried, will provide a means of saying what kind of geography education will contribute effectively to the promotion of good citizenship – which may in turn contribute to our survival.

References

Adams, J. (1995) *Risk*, London: University College Press.

Beck, U. (1992) *Risk Society: Towards a New Modernity*, London: Sage.

Daugherty, R. and Jones, S. (1999) 'Community, culture and identity: geography, the National Curriculum and Wales', *The Curriculum Journal*, 10, 3, pp. 443–61.

Dowgill, P. (1998) 'Pupils' conceptions of learning geography under the National Curriculum', unpublished Ph.D. thesis, Institute of Education, University of London.

Elliott, J. (2000) 'Revising the national curriculum: a comment on the Secretary of State's proposals', *Journal of Education Policy*, 15, 2, pp. 247–55.

ESRC Global Environmental Change Programme (2000) *Risky Choices, Soft Disasters: Environmental Decision Making under Uncertainty*, Brighton, University of Sussex.

Fien, J. (1999) 'Towards a map of commitment: a socially critical approach to geographical education', *International Research in Geographical and Environmental Education*, 8, 2.

Goodson, I. (1992) On curriculum form: notes toward a theory of curriculum, *Sociology of Education*, 65, 1, pp. 66–75.

Grimwade, K. (2000) *Geography and the New Agenda*, Sheffield: The Geographical Association.

Harvey, D. (2000) *Spaces of Hope*, Edinburgh: Edinburgh University Press.

HMSO (1988) *The Education Reform Act*, London: Her Majesty's Stationery Office.

Lambert, D. (1994) 'The National Curriculum: what shall we do with it?', *Geography*, 79, 1, pp. 65–76.

Lambert, D. (1999) 'Geography and moral education in a supercomplex world: the significance of values education and some remaining dilemmas', *Ethics, Place and Environment*, 2, 1 pp. 5–18.

Lambert, D. and Balderstone, D. (2000) *Learning to Teach Geography in the Secondary School*, London: RoutledgeFalmer.

Marsden, W. (1989) '"All in a good cause": geography, history and the politicisation of the curriculum in nineteenth and twentieth century England', *Journal of Curriculum Studies*, 21, 6, pp. 509–26.

Marston, S. (2000) 'The social construction of scale', *Progress in Human Geography*, 24, 2, pp. 219–42.

Morgan, J. (2000) 'To which space do I belong? Imagining citizenship in one curriculum subject', *The Curriculum Journal*, 11, 1, pp. 55–68.

Orr, D. (1999) 'Education for globalisation', *The Ecologist*, 29, 3, pp. 166–8.

Proctor, J. and Smith, D.M. (1999) *Geography and Ethics: Journeys in a Moral Terrain*, London: Routledge.

Rawling, E. (1993) 'School geography: towards 2000', *Geography*, 78, 2, pp. 110–16.

Rawling E (1996) 'The impact of the National Curriculum on school-based curriculum development in secondary geography', in Kent, A., Lambert, D., Naish, M. and Slater, F., *Geography in Education: Viewpoints on Teaching and Learning*, Cambridge: CUP.

Smith, D.M. (2000) *Moral Geographies: Ethics in a World of Difference*, Edunburgh: Edinburgh University Press.

Wallace, W. (2000) 'The standards bearer', *Times Educational Supplement*, 19 May 2000, pp. 13–15.

Wilson, J. (1992) 'Moral education, values education and prejudice reduction', in Lynch, J., Modgil, C. and Modgil, S. (eds) *Cultural Diversity and the Schools; Volume 2: Prejudice, Polemic or Progress?*, London: Falmer.

Index